The Poetry of Emily Dickinson

READERS' GUIDES TO ESSENTIAL CRITICISM

CONSULTANT EDITOR: NICOLAS TREDELL

Published

Thomas P. Adler	Tennessee Williams: *A Streetcar Named Desire/Cat on a Hot Tin Roof*
Pascale Aebischer	Jacobean Drama
Lucie Armitt	George Eliot: *Adam Bede/The Mill on the Floss/Middlemarch*
Dana E. Aspinall	William Shakespeare: *As You Like It*
Simon Avery	Thomas Hardy: *The Mayor of Casterbridge/Jude the Obscure*
Paul Baines	Daniel Defoe: *Robinson Crusoe/Moll Flanders*
Brian Baker	Science Fiction
Annika Bautz	Jane Austen: *Sense and Sensibility/Pride and Prejudice/Emma*
Matthew Beedham	The Novels of Kazuo Ishiguro
Nick Bentley	Contemporary British Fiction
Richard Beynon	D. H. Lawrence: *The Rainbow/Women in Love*
Scott Boltwood	Brian Friel
Peter Boxall	Samuel Beckett: *Waiting for Godot/Endgame*
Claire Brennan	The Poetry of Sylvia Plath
Susan Bruce	Shakespeare: *King Lear*
Sandie Byrne	Jane Austen: *Mansfield Park*
Sandie Byrne	The Poetry of Ted Hughes
Alison Chapman	Elizabeth Gaskell: *Mary Barton/North and South*
Peter Childs	The Fiction of Ian McEwan
Christine Clegg	Vladimir Nabokov: *Lolita*
Jay Corwin	Corwin: *Gabriel García Márquez*
John Coyle	James Joyce: *Ulysses/A Portrait of the Artist as a Young Man*
Martin Coyle	Shakespeare: *Richard II*
Jessica Cox	Victorian Sensation Fiction
Sarah Davison	Modernist Literatures
Sarah Dewar-Watson	Tragedy

Justin D. Edwards	Postcolonial Literature
Robert C. Evans	Philip Larkin
Michael Faherty	The Poetry of W. B. Yeats
Sarah Gamble	The Fiction of Angela Carter
Jodi-Anne George	*Beowulf*
Jodi-Anne George	Chaucer: The General Prologue to *The Canterbury Tales*
Jane Goldman	Virginia Woolf: *To the Lighthouse/The Waves*
Huw Griffiths	Shakespeare: *Hamlet*
Vanessa Guignery	The Fiction of Julian Barnes
Louisa Hadley	The Fiction of A. S. Byatt
Sarah Haggarty and Jon Mee	William Blake: *Songs of Innocence and Experience*
Geoffrey Harvey	Thomas Hardy: *Tess of the d'Urbervilles*
Paul Hendon	The Poetry of W. H. Auden
Terry Hodgson	The Plays of Tom Stoppard for Stage, Radio, TV and Film
William Hughes	Bram Stoker: *Dracula*
Stuart Hutchinson	Mark Twain: *Tom Sawyer/Huckleberry Finn*
Stuart Hutchinson	Edith Wharton: *The House of Mirth/The Custom of the Country*
Betty Jay	E. M. Forster: *A Passage to India*
Aaron Kelly	Twentieth-Century Irish Literature
Elmer Kennedy-Andrews	Nathaniel Hawthorne: *The Scarlet Letter*
Elmer Kennedy-Andrews	The Poetry of Seamus Heaney
Daniel Lea	George Orwell: *Animal Farm/Nineteen Eighty-Four*
Jinqi Ling	Asian American Literature
Rachel Lister	Alice Walker: *The Color Purple*
Sara Lodge	Charlotte Brontë: *Jane Eyre*
Philippa Lyon	Twentieth-Century War Poetry
Merja Makinen	The Novels of Jeanette Winterson
Stephen Marino	Arthur Miller: *Death of a Salesman/The Crucible*
Britta Martens	The Poetry of Robert Browning
Matt McGuire	Contemporary Scottish Literature
Timothy Milnes	Wordsworth: *The Prelude*
Victoria N. Morgan	The Poetry of Emily Dickinson
Jago Morrison	The Fiction of Chinua Achebe

Merritt Moseley	The Fiction of Pat Barker
Pat Pinsent	Children's Literature
Carl Plasa	Toni Morrison: *Beloved*
Carl Plasa	Jean Rhys: *Wide Sargasso Sea*
Nicholas Potter	Shakespeare: *Antony and Cleopatra*
Nicholas Potter	Shakespeare: *Othello*
Nicholas Potter	Shakespeare's Late Plays: *Pericles/Cymbeline/The Winter's Tale/The Tempest*
Steven Price	The Plays, Screenplays and Films of David Mamet
Julia Round, Rikke Platz Cortsen and Maaheen Ahmed	Comics and Graphic Novels
Berthold Schoene-Harwood	Mary Shelley: *Frankenstein*
Nicholas Seager	The Rise of the Novel
Nick Selby	T. S. Eliot: *The Waste Land*
Nick Selby	Herman Melville: *Moby Dick*
Nick Selby	The Poetry of Walt Whitman
David Smale	Salman Rushdie: *Midnight's Children/The Satanic Verses*
Enit Steiner	Jane Austen: *Northanger Abbey/Persuasion*
Patsy Stoneman	Emily Brontë: *Wuthering Heights*
Susie Thomas	Hanif Kureishi
Fiona Tolan	The Fiction of Margaret Atwood
Nicolas Tredell	Joseph Conrad: *Heart of Darkness*
Nicolas Tredell	Charles Dickens: *Great Expectations*
Nicolas Tredell	William Faulkner: *The Sound and the Fury/As I Lay Dying*
Nicolas Tredell	F. Scott Fitzgerald: *The Great Gatsby*
Nicolas Tredell	Shakespeare: *A Midsummer Night's Dream*
Nicolas Tredell	Shakespeare: *Macbeth*
Nicolas Tredell	Shakespeare: The Tragedies
Nicolas Tredell	The Fiction of Martin Amis
David Wheatley	Contemporary British Poetry
Michael Whitworth	Virginia Woolf: *Mrs Dalloway*
Martin Willis	Literature and Science
Matthew Woodcock	Shakespeare: *Henry V*
Gillian Woods	Shakespeare: *Romeo and Juliet*
Angela Wright	Gothic Fiction
Andrew Wyllie and Catherine Rees	The Plays of Harold Pinter

The Poetry of Emily Dickinson

Victoria N. Morgan

BLOOMSBURY ACADEMIC
LONDON • NEW YORK • OXFORD • NEW DELHI • SYDNEY

BLOOMSBURY ACADEMIC
Bloomsbury Publishing Plc
50 Bedford Square, London, WC1B 3DP, UK
1385 Broadway, New York, NY 10018, USA
29 Earlsfort Terrace, Dublin 2, Ireland

BLOOMSBURY, BLOOMSBURY ACADEMIC and the Diana logo
are trademarks of Bloomsbury Publishing Plc

First published in Great Britain 2023
This paperback edition published 2025

Copyright © Victoria N. Morgan, 2023

Victoria N. Morgan has asserted her right under the Copyright, Designs and
Patents Act, 1988, to be identified as Author of this work.

For legal purposes the Acknowledgements on p. x constitute
an extension of this copyright page.

Cover design: Rebecca Heselton
Cover image: Emily Dickinson c. 1846 copyright Lebrecht Authors/ Bridgeman Images

All rights reserved. No part of this publication may be reproduced or
transmitted in any form or by any means, electronic or mechanical, including
photocopying, recording, or any information storage or retrieval system,
without prior permission in writing from the publishers.

Bloomsbury Publishing Plc does not have any control over, or responsibility for,
any third-party websites referred to or in this book. All internet addresses given
in this book were correct at the time of going to press. The author and publisher
regret any inconvenience caused if addresses have changed or sites have ceased to exist,
but can accept no responsibility for any such changes.

A catalogue record for this book is available from the British Library.

A catalog record for this book is available from the Library of Congress.

ISBN:	HB:	978-1-3503-8011-0
	PB:	978-1-3503-8007-3
	ePDF:	978-1-3503-8010-3
	eBook:	978-1-3503-8009-7

Typeset by Integra Software Services Pvt. Ltd.

To find out more about our authors and books visit www.bloomsbury.com
and sign up for our newsletters.

*For my three children – Hartley, Elliott and Allegra,
and my husband William, with love*

Contents

Acknowledgements		x
Introduction		1
1	Biographies and publication	11
	1.1 Biographers	11
	1.2 Dickinson as poet: Self-publication and early publication	24
2	Style and meaning	35
	2.1 Early criticism	39
	2.2 Later revaluations	45
3	The female tradition, gender and sexuality	65
	3.1 The female tradition	68
	3.2 Writing the body	73
	3.3 Queering Dickinson	82
4	History, Civil War and race	97
	4.1 Historicizing Dickinson	98
	4.2 The US Civil War	108
	4.3 Dickinson, ethnicity and race	116
5	Religion and hymn culture	127
	5.1 Rejecting orthodoxy	131
	5.2 Religion and aesthetics	134
	5.3 Dickinson and hymnody	140
6	Performance and reception	155
	6.1 Performance in Dickinson's poetry	157
	6.2 Dickinson and popular culture	160
	6.3 Digital Dickinson and international reception	172
Conclusion		185
Bibliography		192
Index		210

Acknowledgements

I would like to thank Nicolas Tredell, Ben Doyle and the staff at Bloomsbury for their assistance during the writing of this book. I would also like to acknowledge the students I have taught over the years, at the University of Liverpool, Liverpool Hope University and the University of East Anglia, whose enthusiastic discussion and questioning about Dickinson in many ways led to this book. On a personal note, thanks are due to my family, without whose love and support it could not have been completed, and to whom this book is dedicated. All poems cited in this book are reprinted by permission of the publishers and Trustees of Amherst College from *The Poems of Emily Dickinson: Variorum Edition*, edited by Ralph W. Franklin, 3 vols., Cambridge, MA: The Belknap Press of Harvard University Press, Copyright © 1998, by the President and Fellows of Harvard College. Copyright © 1951, 1955, 1979, 1983 by the President and Fellows of Harvard College.

Introduction

This guide aims to assist readers of Emily Dickinson's poetry by taking them through the various stages, approaches and modes of criticism, identifying both the essential critical texts and the key debates within them. The texts chosen for discussion include those canonical readings that have shaped the area of Dickinson studies throughout the twentieth- and twenty-first centuries in order to provide a lens through which to view current and emergent critical trends. For example, early-nineteenth-century reviews of Dickinson and twentieth-century discussions of Dickinson's poetic style are useful when considering the issues faced by twenty-first-century translators of Dickinson into languages other than English. Twentieth-century debates about gender and the body are informative when considering contemporary LGBTQ+ readings of Dickinson. The current critical move to 'decentre' Dickinson can be seen through the matrix of twentieth-century feminist readings of Dickinson and the language of exceptionalism, and by examining how she was 'centred' in the first place, and how relatively recently that happened. Looking at the various ways earlier critics sought to describe Dickinson's engagements with race, the language of abolition and Civil War contexts are useful for foregrounding our understanding of Dickinson and race in the twenty-first century. The critical drive to historicize Dickinson can be seen, in part, as a reaction to the earlier psychological and biographical readings of her work. A polarized view of Dickinson's religious sensibilities has been replaced overall by a more flexible and broader approach such as critical readings of religious aesthetics and the exploration of hymn culture. Similarly, twentieth-century critical interventions on the role of performance in Dickinson shed light on debates about Dickinson's engagements with nineteenth-century popular culture as well as those on the performance of Dickinson within our own popular culture and forms of media. When re-reading key critical texts over the decades there are many crosscurrents, and it is useful to highlight these. Certain critical texts will therefore re-appear in chapters throughout the guide where there is a particular pertinence to the themes and issues being discussed. Where less well-known texts have been included, they have been chosen for the way in which they have shaped areas in the field and pointed towards a new direction. All the latest research on Dickinson cannot be covered in a book such as this, which aims to be selective in its approach to represent essential criticism on Dickinson from the past several decades. Newer, and less well-known, critical texts are important because they represent emergent strands of research which are yet to take up their place within the Dickinson critical canon. This guide describes some of these strands but does not aim to represent new directions *in toto* as a collection of essays might do, but, rather, it intends to highlight examples of some of the new directions as well as foreground them with a history of the essential criticism on Dickinson.[1] The book will serve any reader of Dickinson as a user-friendly reference tool for negotiating the sometimes dauntingly vast, historical body of criticism written on the poems since their publication to date by suggesting key starting points and underlining critical highlights. It will provide the student and reader of Dickinson with a sense of where these selected critical texts can be placed in relation to one another, and it will also provide an understanding of some of the major moments within the history of Dickinson's reception from late-nineteenth-century reviews up to some of the important critical interventions of the twenty-first century.

Dickinson's work demands much of the reader, and as a result we return to it repeatedly to appreciate its expansiveness and the potential it has for critical interpretation. We inherit the poems freely in their materiality: Harvard's open online access to the manuscripts since 2013 means that we can view them from every angle with, and finally without, editorial restrictions. With the decades of criticism of her work we also encounter the attitudes of a particular age or its cultural persuasion, as well as the ways her poetry was materially presented to the reader, including editorial decisions and the technologies of publishing processes. Similarly, any guide to essential criticism must entail editorial choices, and this book is no exception. The key texts and debates identified cannot encompass the entire canon of critical work done on the poet but must reflect what is culturally significant and essential to an understanding of that critical tradition, and of Dickinson's work, at this moment in time.

The cultural significance of Dickinson's poetry, then, is a marker which has shape-shifted over the decades of criticism since her first poems were published. Chapter 1 looks at the history of Dickinson biography, and this is also something which, to a lesser extent, reflects the cultural attitudes of the decades they were written in. It also traces the various representations of the life of Dickinson through the wealth or dearth of research and information available to the biographer at the time of writing. The issue of Dickinson's relation to publication and the extent of control she had over her poems and the representation of herself as poet are discussed in critical works such as *Emily Dickinson's Fascicles: Method and Meaning* (1994) by Dorothy Huff Oberhaus as well as Cristanne Miller's introduction to her recently annotated volume of Dickinson's poetry, *Emily Dickinson's Poems: As She Preserved Them* (2016).

Chapter 2 outlines the earliest critical themes her poems generated, primarily, with the publication of Mabel Loomis Todd's first collection of her poems, *Poems of Emily Dickinson*, edited with Thomas Wentworth Higginson in 1890. These nineteenth-century and early-twentieth-century reviews focus on formal concerns of the style, themes, rhythm, metre and punctuation of the poems and how they measure up to contemporary poets as well as the canonical and typically male ones. The preoccupation with the formal and perceived 'correctness' of Dickinson's poetry, grammatical and otherwise, in the early reception of her work reflects the extent to which women poets had to be approved or disapproved of on formal grounds because the subject matter of female experience was in itself alien, especially to predominantly male reviewers. It also shows how early critics of Dickinson's work were thoroughly unprepared for her radical and inventive modes of expression.

Critics' preoccupation with the mechanics of Dickinson's verse, and how it invariably fell short of that evident in canonical Romantic or Victorian poetry, gave way to thematic concerns in the first half of the twentieth century which later became energetically politicized. The twentieth century saw many important critical interventions. The rise of feminist discourse and the politics of gender gave way to an extremely prolific period for Dickinson studies. There are therefore points at which Chapter 2 will cross-reference texts, such as when analysing elements of Dickinson's 'style' where it looks at how feminist critics such as Cristanne Miller and Shira Wolosky carefully identified Dickinson's inventive way of using language and shed new light on her use of formal components such as rhythm and metre. These arguments are also referred to in Chapter 5 in relation to Dickinson and hymn culture. The chapter considers how, perhaps inspired by the early damning reviews of the formal aspects of Dickinson's poetry, Miller (1987) and Wolosky (1988) demonstrate Dickinson's work as breaking the hitherto agreed set of rules governing poetic construction to forge a unique mode of expression.

Crucial strands of feminist enquiry, such as the representation of gender, sexuality, and the importance of recognizing female tradition, and their manifestation in twentieth-century responses to Dickinson's work, are explored in Chapter 3. One important strand in feminist criticism of Dickinson which concerns itself with gender is that which utilizes psychoanalysis and readings of the poems through this system of gendered subject formation. This chapter examines the explosion of feminist and psychoanalytical perspectives which dominated twentieth-century critical writing on Dickinson. Critics who use psychoanalytic theory, the body and psychoanalytic concepts of binary opposition and 'difference' as a focus for critical debate, such as Paula Bennett's *Emily Dickinson: Woman Poet* (1990) and Sabine Sielke's *Fashioning the Female Subject: The Intertextual Networking of Dickinson, Moore and Rich* (1997), will be analysed. The influence of these critical texts can be seen in the work of later scholars such as Helen Shoobridge's '"Reverence for Each Other Being the Sweet Aim": Dickinson Face to Face with the Masculine' (2000). These works will be examined to show how critics read Dickinson's poetry as a radical articulation of the subversive feminine body.

The impact of queer theory in Dickinson studies can be seen in the critical interest in the poet as voicing LGBTQ+ identities; homoerotic, lesbian, gay, bisexual, trans, queer and gender non-binary identities, and in the numerous ways that Dickinson destabilizes the gendered body. The second section in this chapter provides an analysis of the critical 'queering' of Dickinson and looks back at texts such as Mary E. Galvin's *Queer Poetics: Five Modernist Women Writers* (1999) which employs queer theory and locates Dickinson within a tradition of women writers by focusing on her 'trickster' lesbian identity. It also explores critical texts which focus upon reading lesbian identity through Dickinson's letters and biography, such as Lena Koski's exploration of sexual metaphors and lesbian expression in 'Sexual Metaphors in Emily Dickinson's Letters to Susan Gilbert' (1996). Joy Ladin's work (2013; 2010) offers a trans perspective on Dickinson, one which positions her within a canon of writers that make visible the instability of American public discourse. For Ladin, Dickinson's reclamation of 'I' and her poetic renegotiation of identity beyond gender binaries make her an empowering ally for social justice. The third section of this chapter summarizes the arguments of critical texts which explore Dickinson as being part of a literary tradition; first, in her reading of and responses to a masculine tradition, such as Benjamin Lease's *Emily Dickinson's Reading of Men and Books* (1990) and then in her proximity to other women poets, both contemporary and more recent. Texts such as Margaret Homans's *Women Writers and Poetic Identity: Dorothy Wordsworth, Emily Bronte and Emily Dickinson* (1980), Cheryl Walker's *The Nightingale's Burden: Women Poets and American Culture before 1900* (1982),

Sharon Leder and Andrea Abbott's *The Language of Exclusion: The Poetry of Emily Dickinson and Christina Rossetti* (1987) and Elizabeth Petrino's *Emily Dickinson and Her Contemporaries: Women's Verse in America 1820–1855* (1998) helped to establish Dickinson within a tradition of nineteenth-century women poets. Wendy Martin's *An American Triptych: Anne Bradstreet, Emily Dickinson and Adrienne Rich* (1984) offers a trans-historical reading of Dickinson and female literary tradition. The second wave of texts which examine Dickinson alongside other female writers, thus underscoring a continuum of the female literary tradition, such as Vivian R. Pollak's *Our Emily Dickinsons: American Women Poets and the Intimacies of Difference* (2017), will be discussed.

Chapter 4 examines the twentieth-century turn to historicist interpretations of Dickinson's work, along with critical engagement with the issue of race and ethnicity. Essays which are concerned with the issues surrounding the act of placing Dickinson within a specific historical context are examined, such as Jane Donahue Eberwein's 'Dickinson's Local, Global and Cosmic Perspectives' (1998). Politically inflected historical readings such as Betsy Erkkila's 'Emily Dickinson and Class' (1992) are examined with reference to the historical approach of Jay Leyda's groundbreaking book *The Years and Hours of Emily Dickinson* (1960), which is also discussed in Chapter 1. The collection of critical debates in Pollak's edited volume, *A Historical Guide to Emily Dickinson* (2004), is examined as important twenty-first-century directions on Dickinson and history. Judith Farr's work on Dickinson and her engagement with specific aspects of nineteenth-century culture such as the visual arts (1992) and her interest in the cultivation of plants – *The Gardens of Emily Dickinson* (2004) – are also summarized in relation to placing her work within a particular historical context. Texts which focus on the way Dickinson's work sounds and the different forms she used to achieve aural effects, such as Cristanne Miller's *Reading in Time: Emily Dickinson in the Nineteenth Century* (2012), will be discussed as criticism which situates Dickinson within the context of her nineteenth-century textual borrowings and influences, such as the popular ballad stanza. The extensive range of books, chapters and articles which are concerned, with varying critical perspectives, with the Civil War in Dickinson's work and its related topics such as slavery and abolition, death and exile will be examined closely. Among the key texts covered are Shira Wolosky's *Emily Dickinson: A Voice of War* (1984), Karen Sanchez-Eppler's *Touching Liberty: Abolition, Feminism and the Politics of the Body* (1993), and essays such as Leigh-Anne Urbanowicz Marcellin's 'Emily Dickinson's Civil War Poetry' (1996). This chapter concludes with a consideration of critical treatments of issues of race and ethnicity in Dickinson's work. Although still a much understudied area within the field, this chapter considers how race has been explored more directly by critics such as Paula Bennett, in her essay '"The Negro Never Knew": Emily Dickinson and Racial Typology in the Nineteenth Century' (2002), and by Vivian Pollak, in the essay 'Dickinson and the Poetics of Whiteness' (2000). As we are well into the new millennium, new ways of viewing Dickinson are being voiced, from a variety of racial, ethnic and intersectional perspectives. A consideration of twenty-first-century criticism which places such perspectives and concerns at the centre of their studies on Dickinson will be provided, including Aífe Murray's '*Maid as Muse: How Servants Changed Emily Dickinson's Life and Language*' (2009), Erica Fretwell's essay 'Dickinson in Domingo' (2013) and her chapter on Dickinson and the racialization of aesthetics in *Sensory Experiments: Psychophysics, Race, and the Aesthetics of Feeling* (2020), as well as Hiroko Uno's essay 'Emily Dickinson's Encounter with the East: Chinese Museum in Boston' (2008) and Li-Hsin Hsu's essay 'Emily Dickinson's Asian Consumption' (2013).

Chapter 5 focuses on the topic of religion and of the role of hymn culture in Dickinson's work. The much-debated topic of Dickinson's relation to the religious culture of her day is something which has gathered momentum in critical force from the twentieth century to the present and has often presented a polarized view of the poet's religious sensibilities. Essays which portray Dickinson as ultimately antagonistic to the religious drive of the second Great Awakening such as Alfred Habegger's 'Evangelicalism and Its Discontents: Hannah Porter versus Emily Dickinson' (1997) are examined in this chapter alongside critical texts which view her engagement with religion as productive, such as Martha Winburn England and John Sparrow's *Hymns Unbidden: Donne, Herbert, Blake, Emily Dickinson and the Hymnographers* (1966). This is followed by discussion of criticism which examines religious imagery as an aesthetic in Dickinson's poetry, such as Linda Freedman's *Emily Dickinson and the Religious Imagination* (2011). The body of criticism dealing with Dickinson's relation to religion through her engagement with hymns will be summarized. Essays such as Shira Wolosky's 'Rhetoric or Not: Hymnal Tropes in Emily Dickinson and Isaac Watts' (1988) and Christine Ross's 'Uncommon Measures: Emily Dickinson's Subversive Prosody' (2001) will be explained. Victoria N. Morgan's book *Emily Dickinson and Hymn Culture: Tradition and Experience* (2010) examines the relevance of an entire hymn culture to Dickinson's work and views Dickinson's engagement with orthodox religion as a creative process which culminates in a re-envisioned theological perspective. This work crucially identifies 'hymn culture' as encompassing the writing, editing and singing of hymns which serve to describe and shape theology. Morgan shows how this definition is central to a deeper understanding of Dickinson's engagement with hymns. Further, Morgan uncovers and explores the matrilineal roots of Dickinson's relation to hymn culture. Finally, an important collection of essays which appeared in the journal *Religion and Literature* (2016) and appeared as a special forum on the subject of Dickinson and religion with contributions by eminent Dickinson scholars is examined at the end of this chapter to summarize recent key debates in this wide-reaching area within Dickinson studies.

The final chapter in the guide, Chapter 6, discusses the role of performance and popular culture within Dickinson studies. It is concerned with performance as a topic in Dickinson's work and within current critical debates upon her work, but also as an important aspect of Dickinson's place within popular culture and the role of today's media within it. Noble (2021) sees the popularity of Dickinson in recent times as being partly the result of 'the rise of networked selves, and changes in how we access and interpret Dickinson's work'.[2] This chapter will look at the work of critics, and the role of scholars, critic-curators, directors, writers and artists who are engaged in producing our access to Dickinson in the twenty-first century. As an introduction to the area of performance and its elements within Dickinson's work, influential twentieth-century critical texts such as Sandra M. Gilbert and Susan Gubar's *The Madwoman in the Attic: The Woman Writer and the Nineteenth-Century Literary Imagination* (1979) and Camille Paglia's *Sexual Personae: Art and Decadence from Nerfertiti to Emily Dickinson* (1990) which each have chapters analysing the performances and various personae in Dickinson's work will be summarized. Essays which are concerned with Dickinson's engagement with the nineteenth-century American popular culture of her day, such as David S. Reynolds' 'Emily Dickinson and Popular Culture' (2002) and Sandra Runzo's *'Theatricals of Day': Emily Dickinson and Nineteenth-Century American Popular Culture* (2019), will be explored. Work which has been inspired by the recent digitization of Dickinson's music binder, such as George Boziwick, *Emily Dickinson's Music Book: The Musical Life of an American Poet* (2022), will be discussed with reference to Dickinson's notion of performance and interest in music. This is followed by consideration of Jonnie Guerra's essay 'Dickinson Adaptations in the Arts and the Theater' (1998) which analyses the performance of Dickinson, the role of media and her place within contemporary popular culture. Critics who provide a critique of the desire to own, inhabit and perform various Dickinsons will be discussed. Artistic interpretations of Dickinson's life and work within contemporary popular culture will then be surveyed, including musical settings, an artistic installation and museum exhibition, as well as televisual and filmic interpretations and fictionalized accounts in novels such as *The Lovers of Amherst* (2015) by William Nicholson which merge details of Dickinson's life with the lives of contemporary fictional characters. Essays which explore the impact of latest developments in technology, such as the digitization of Dickinson archive material, will be explained. The critical impact of the public access release of the Emily Dickinson Archive (EDA) in 2013 as well as other online resources will be explored. The international reception of Dickinson will be considered in the final section of Chapter 6, including a brief overview of the history of international reception as well as the relationship between translation and reception. The perception of Dickinson within Latino/a and Chicano perspectives is explored in texts which touch on this, such as *The Routledge Companion to Latino/a Literature* (2012) edited by Suzanne Bost and Frances R. Aparicio, and *Latina and Latino Voices in Literature: Lives and Works* by Frances Ann Day (2003). The editors' introduction to the 2020 special edition of *The Emily Dickinson Journal*, 'International Dickinson: Scholarship in English Translation', is cited as a new direction in forging a dialogue between Dickinson scholars of different languages and cultures. Several essential international voices will be highlighted, thus illustrating a potential and burgeoning area within Dickinson studies. The Conclusion to the guide will summarize the areas within Dickinson studies which are gathering critical momentum, and it will outline the current and future scope for Dickinson studies.

    A note on the Dickinson poems and editions referred to in this guide. For students and scholars wishing to delve deeper into Dickinson's work, Franklin's *Manuscript Books* made the variants of her poems more readily accessible by presenting facsimile copies of Dickinson's manuscripts complete with editorial markings. The online presence of Dickinson's work to be found at the Emily Dickinson Archive (EDA) (edickinson.org) and the Dickinson Electronic Archives (DEA) (emilydickinson.org) has made accessing Dickinson's texts much easier and has radically changed the landscape of Dickinson studies. The availability of composite and extraneous material and the ability to access her work in all its forms and variants mean that the way we view what constitutes as a poem has also altered. Cristanne Miller's edition of her work *Emily Dickinson's Poems: As She Preserved Them* (2016) has become an invaluable resource for students and scholars interested in Dickinson's writing and her 'self-publishing' processes as it makes a clear distinction between the poems she copied out by hand on to folded sheets and the ones in rougher form which she did not retain. It also provides the reader with an opportunity to consult the order of presentation and the alternate words and phrases Dickinson chose to use on the copies of poems that she retained. This guide is intended as a companion to the poems and should ideally be read alongside a copy of the poems themselves. Multiple variants of the poems in their various forms are all available to view online. Most of the criticism examined in this guide cites either R. W. Franklin's edition, *The Poems of Emily Dickinson: Variorum Edition* (1998), or Thomas H. Johnson's edition, *The Complete Poems of Emily Dickinson* (1955), with the former providing a source for the majority of citations. For the sake of ease, this guide will cite all poem numbers from Franklin's *Variorum Edition* (1998). Poem numbers will be preceded by 'Fr' with their corresponding numbering as they appear in this edition. However, as Miller's (2016) edition importantly provides Dickinson's own ordering and alternate word choices, the guide will also supply the reader with the page reference for each poem as they appear in Miller's edition for the purposes of cross-referencing and for the reader to gain a greater understanding of Dickinson's creative process. Readers will see poems cited from Franklin's edition throughout and then be able to consult Miller's edition with greater ease. Miller does not assign numbers to Dickinson's poems; they are referenced by the page number(s) that the poems appear on in her edition. Each page number will be preceded by 'M' to indicate where each poem can be found in this edition. Where Johnson's edition is referred to specifically, this will be indicated by the poem number as it appears in his edition, preceded by 'THJ'.[3]

Notes

1 Recent collections such as *The New Emily Dickinson Studies*, ed. by Michelle Kohler (Cambridge: Cambridge University Press, 2019) and *The Oxford Handbook of Emily Dickinson*, ed. by Cristanne Miller and Karen Sanchez-Eppler (Oxford: Oxford University Press, 2022), represent very succinctly some of the new directions in Dickinson studies for the twenty-first century. For example, the former volume offers readings of Dickinson's poetry through new as well as newly revisited key critical perspectives such as historical poetics, ecocriticism, animal studies, sound studies, new materialism, posthumanism, object-oriented feminism, disability studies, queer theory, race studies, race and contemporary poetics, digital humanities and globalism.
2 Marianne Noble, 'Emily Dickinson in the Twenty-First Century' *American Literature*, 93.2 (2021), 283–305.

3   All of the poems quoted in this guide refer to *The Poems of Emily Dickinson: Variorum Edition*, ed. by R. W Franklin (Cambridge, MA: The Belknap Press of Harvard University Press, 1998). All poem numbers from this edition are preceded by 'Fr'. Also provided as a reference aid, the page numbering from *Emily Dickinson's Poems: As She Preserved Them*, ed. by Cristanne Miller (Cambridge, MA: Harvard University Press, 2016), is given, preceded by 'M'. *The Poems of Emily Dickinson*, 3 vols, ed. by Thomas H. Johnson (Cambridge, MA: Harvard University Press, 1955). Poems from this edition will be indicated by a poem number preceded by the initials 'THJ'.

1

Biographies and publication

1.1 Biographers	11
1.2 Dickinson as poet: Self-publication and early publication	24

1.1 Biographers

Biographers occupy a privileged position in which to shape the view of their subject for generations of readers to come. This chapter will establish the core biographical and critical-biographical texts to read in the first instance to introduce readers to aspects of her life and the various ways biographers have approached them. In the second instance this introduction to Dickinson biographies will serve to contextualize criticism on the key areas of Dickinson's sense of herself as a poet, the issue of her self-publication and the early publication of her work which followed. The chapter does not provide an exhaustive list of biographies (further reading is, however, provided in the bibliography) but will rather provide the general reader, as well as the more advanced reader, with biographical starting points from both past and more recent biographical texts.

The biographical history of Dickinson is lengthy and holds within it a tension which is perhaps evident in the genre itself – that of the individual, critical urge of the biographer and the need to present something new and exciting to the market of literary biographies, together with the simultaneous desire to offer rigorously researched and above all factual evidence to support the life represented. Dickinson is an especially beguiling subject to track down because of the tendency to become absorbed, as most biographers will, with the elusive 'life' of the subject together with their own opinions and, quite frankly, flights of fancy. As will be discussed in a later chapter, Dickinson's life has been the inspiration of many fictional treatments and responses. The proximity of a fictional account to a biographical one can also sometimes be too close for comfort. Jerome Charyn's novel *The Secret Life of Emily Dickinson* (2010) produced, in his own words, the desire to write a biography because 'I knew less and less the more I learned about her'.[1] The biography he produced – *A Loaded Gun: Emily Dickinson for the 21st Century* (2016) – which draws from research undertaken for the novel – was very well received by critics. It is perhaps the best example of a biographical work which has benefitted from having been written after a novel about the same subject, where the fictional impulses have already been largely spent.

The history of Dickinson biography should begin with the early biographical sketches of the poet conveyed by the people who knew her. Such sketches are to be found in Susan Huntington Gilbert Dickinson's obituary of her, and in T. W. Higginson's recollections of their meeting and of their correspondence, together with information provided by Mabel Loomis Todd, which appear in the earliest editions of her poems and letters. Perhaps the most important of these is the obituary. Notices of Dickinson's death appeared in the *Springfield Daily Republican* (17 May 1886) and the *Northampton Daily Herald* (17 May 1886). Susan Dickinson's obituary of the poet was published three days after her death in the *Springfield Daily Republican* (18 May 1886).[2] The handwritten drafts of the obituary and transcriptions as well as the printed newspaper copy are available to view online at the Dickinson Electronic Archives (DEA) (emilydickinson.org). The obituary text has been reproduced in Jay Leyda's *The Years and Hours of Emily Dickinson* (1960) and discussed notably by Martha Nell Smith in *Rowing in Eden: Rereading Emily Dickinson* (1992).[3] The obituary is an extremely important biographical sketch of the poet (some would argue the most important) because it comes from the person with whom Dickinson was most engaged intellectually, poetically, emotionally, and many would argue, sexually. Numerous critics, and most notably Smith, agree that it is Susan who knew Dickinson's life and work best. Susan is keen to stress Dickinson's generosity and her engagement with the community in the obituary and tells of the many gifts of food and flowers she sent out to 'many homes among the classes', stating how this was representative of her 'unselfish devotion'. Undoubtedly Susan's obituary anticipates the somewhat negative view of Dickinson which held for decades after her death, that of the reclusive invalid, ultimately untouched by those beyond her own doorstep. To counter this view, which no doubt began towards the end of her lifetime and was then proliferated by critics and publishers years later, we hear from Susan that Dickinson's acts of kindness and consideration for the sick crossed social class boundaries as well as the physical boundaries of the house she resided in. Susan is also at pains to stress the fact that Dickinson was 'not disappointed with the world, not an invalid till within the past two years', and when she did reduce personal contact it was to warm her 'sensitive nature' by the fire of her own 'large wealth of individual resources'.[4] What is more, Susan refers to a line in Robert Browning's poem 'Rabbi Ben Ezra' to describe Dickinson's physical disposition ('the "mesh of her soul" as Browning calls the body, was too rare'). In this, Susan provides an elevated, emphatically literary and specifically poetic obituary fitting for her talented beloved Emily. There can be no doubt that Susan wanted to both highlight Dickinson's poetic genius and explain her seclusion in later life as having nothing whatsoever to do with a negative attitude towards the society she lived in. As she explains that Dickinson's life at home was more compatible with her work and her 'rare' disposition, she writes, 'All that is too sacred for words' – meaning that it cannot be faithfully recounted or should not be explained. What is interesting is that she crosses out part of this sentence ('is too sacred for words') and replaces it with 'All that, must be inviolate'. 'Inviolate' is emphatic. It warns future editors, reviewers, critics, publishers and of course biographers to leave well alone. We must not violate or damage Dickinson's literary reputation or her personal legacy by merely speculating about the nature of her seclusion and the conditions which enabled her to produce her work. What is important for Susan to convey is the generosity of her friend, her love of the world and those in it, and the truly original and great work she produced.

It was perhaps inevitable, though, that the earliest biographical sketches of Dickinson's life would be inflected with bias. Martha Dickinson Bianchi's edited volume *The Life and Letters of Emily Dickinson* (1924) includes one of the earliest biographical pieces on the poet to be published.[5] Bianchi, the poet's niece, was keen to represent the view of Emily which her mother, Susan Huntington Gilbert Dickinson, had related to her, as well as her own personal recollections. The need to publish Dickinson's work and to organize it was also fuelled by the continuation of the 'feud' which existed between the two sides of the family. Mabel Loomis Todd was the mistress of Susan's husband Austin Dickinson, Emily's brother. She recognized Dickinson's greatness and wanted to edit her work and present it to the public in the form of a publication. Susan's objective was to protect her friend's legacy from misrepresentation and Mabel Loomis Todd's desire was to take control of Dickinson's work. This tension, and 'feud', is something which Lyndall Gordon writes about so eloquently in her biography, *Lives like Loaded Guns* (2010). Martha Dickinson Bianchi followed this first volume of the poet's life and letters with *Emily Dickinson Face to Face; Unpublished Letters with*

Notes and Reminiscences (1932). The latter volume, in particular, is charming and irresistible because of its provenance, with 'reminiscences' coming to the reader directly from one who knew Dickinson 'face to face'. Details of the timbre of Dickinson's voice, her way of dressing and her character quirks each come through clearly, as well as the effect that the poet exercised over those around her. We are told how the 'hired' people in the Dickinson household each gave their allegiance to Emily.[6] Inevitably such reminiscences offer only snapshots of the Dickinson family in a series of fragmented moments, and in this way even those details can be somewhat unreliable in their representation of a life lived. Millicent Todd Bingham tells us in *Emily Dickinson's Home: Letters of Edward Dickinson and His Family* (1955) that her mother, Mabel Loomis Todd, who is often considered the first serious editor and compiler of Dickinson's letters and poems, disliked Bianchi's initial volume as she felt that it misrepresented the poet's character.[7] However, this was perhaps Mabel's final move to undermine the attempts of her rivals and to stake her claim as the first editorial authority of the Dickinson legacy. As Martha Ackmann rightly observes of Todd's editorial prefaces to the first editions of Dickinson's poems and letters, it is 'Todd's emphasis on the poet's seclusion, and what she views as Dickinson's fragile nature' in which we can see the beginnings of the damaging 'myth' which plagued Dickinson biographies and criticism for decades.[8] Bianchi's biographical sketches have been criticized for their lack of focus on the poetry and for their romantic portrayal of a woman who 'flitted' when she moved. Conversely, it could be argued that Bianchi's intimate descriptions of daily life with her Aunt Emily provide us with just enough detail to silence conjecture and the poems are virtually left alone to speak for themselves. Since then, many full-scale biographies have been written, ranging from those written in the 1930s which are regarded as fusing, somewhat unreliably, the poet and the 'myth' of the reclusive woman in white, to the mid-twentieth-century attempts to recover factual evidence of Dickinson's daily life, to more recent work which seeks to dispel the myths whilst at the same time constructing other rigid views of the poet's life. This chapter will summarize highlights from key biographical works on Dickinson in a roughly chronological order, and discuss others along the way, beginning with Jay Leyda's *The Years and Hours of Emily Dickinson*, 2 vols (1960) and Richard B. Sewall's *The Life of Emily Dickinson*, 2 vols (1974), respectively, then Roger Lundin's *Emily Dickinson and the Art of Belief* (1998) and Alfred Habegger's *My Wars Are Laid Away in Books: The Life of Emily Dickinson* (2001) which both signal a shift in biography of the poet which had tended to shy away from ideologically weighted argument, and, more recently, Lyndall Gordon's *Lives like Loaded Guns: Emily Dickinson and Her Family's Feuds* (2010), which opens up the dramatic landscape of the Dickinson household to the more generally interested reader.

Firstly, however, it will be helpful to mention Martha Ackmann's essay 'Biographical Studies of Dickinson' (1998), which discusses some of the issues within the area and history of the Dickinson biography. Ackmann usefully summarizes the turn in late-twentieth-century biographies of Dickinson to rescue her from the view that she was not culturally engaged. She also recommends a cautionary approach for biographers who would read her work through the lens of events in Dickinson's life or aspects of personality, which Ackmann sees as a reductive approach. She reflects upon the difficulty of biographizing a subject who maintained that her life was remarkably simple, and on the plethora of romantic and misleading portraits which have emerged despite this. She discusses early forms of biography from those who had met her, namely Susan Dickinson's obituary of the poet and T. W. Higginson's correspondence with her. She usefully summarizes the biographical turn in the 1930s for compilers of Dickinson's life to describe her cultural influences. Tracing key biographies of the poet through the decades of the twentieth century, Ackmann suggests that twentieth-century biographers had slowed down in their search for new biographical material, privileging interpretation of previous findings since Sewall's landmark biography. She cites examples such as Cynthia Griffin Wolff's *Emily Dickinson* (1986) with an interpretation of what she sees as a struggle against gender expectations and religious attitudes. This leads her on to discuss feminist interpretations of Dickinson's life, such as Adrienne Rich's essay '"Vesuvius at Home": The Power of Emily Dickinson' (1976), and the ways in which feminist scholarship has affected biographical studies. She underlines how feminist readings of Dickinson's life have made Dickinson's relationships with women and female culture centrally important to understanding her poetry. However, Ackmann underscores the need for the historical discovery and factual work of Sewall and Leyda to be continued in biographical work on the poet. In relation to these two points, she discusses her own fascinating material discoveries relating to Dickinson's mother's education. She describes finding papers relating to the beginnings of Monson Academy and evidence of Emily Norcross Dickinson's enrolment and subsequent ten-year attendance there. She uses the material evidence she finds to support a new view of Dickinson's mother as extremely well educated and intelligent as opposed to the existing view of her as being not particularly interested in learning and also somewhat unintelligent (this is something the poet herself had suggested).[9] It is this example of Ackmann's own research which conveys how new material discoveries can affect the construction of a biographical narrative. She asserts the importance of feminist scholarship as shaping the biographical enquiries in future scholarship and insists biographers must represent Dickinson in her 'entirety', not just as a poet. The issue of what holds importance in biography remains central to the examination of biographical texts in this chapter.

With Ackmann's concern about a reductive approach to biographical writings in mind (that is, viewing the work of a subject as a direct response to a chain of biographical events) it is also useful to briefly consider the mode of the 'biographical critic' in Vivian Pollak's *Dickinson: The Anxiety of Gender* (1984). Pollak organizes her text in two parts in which the first 'The Life' is used to contextualize the second 'The Poems'. What is useful in this book is the way in which Pollak is up-front about the process of writing a critical text which is inevitably shaped by biographical information. For her own purposes she is not concerned with slavishly discerning a development in Dickinson's body of poems and does not believe that tracing each poem to a specific date is a priority. The book takes it as a given that Dickinson's relationship to the world was produced by her experience of the society she lived in, and Pollak therefore sees Dickinson's work as reflecting 'static experience' and an 'identity crisis' which is 'unresolved'. Her relationship to the chronology of poems is refreshing as she maintains that the date of a poem is 'not always relevant', but rather 'the history to which they allude'.[10] Although many critics would argue the opposite, that tying manuscript poems down to dates and following closely the life events of the poems to confer meaning upon them is crucial, Pollak's book is one example of how biographical information can be used in a slightly less prescriptive way alongside criticism and the biographical criticism it produces.[11]

Early biographical input from Martha Dickinson Bianchi and Mabel Loomis Todd, whether intentionally or not, had the effect of perpetuating the myth of Dickinson as the romantic recluse. Jay Leyda's groundbreaking biographical work does much to dispel the sentimental myth of Dickinson as isolated from the world of nation and community. *The Years and Hours of Emily Dickinson* (1960) is often regarded as a reference book, because Leyda presents various, sometimes disparate, materials together to reconstruct the fragments of Dickinson's daily life without imposing an overall structure upon the subject. It is, however, a biography in its purest form. It is perhaps because of this approach, of its wariness of completeness, that his work has provided a lasting resource to Dickinson scholars and indeed biographers over the years. The first volume begins by describing the people in Dickinson's life, mainly family members and friends. Excerpts from the poems and letters of Dickinson, her family and friends, from journals, newspapers, magazines and other biographical materials are provided chronologically, tracing the story of Dickinson's life. This begins with the Intentions of Marriage notice relating to Dickinson's parents held at the records in the Town Clerk's Office at Amherst and ends with recollections of the attendees of the poet's funeral. When quoting anecdotal evidence used by previous biographers such as Martha Dickinson Bianchi and George Whicher, the excerpts are contextualized by placing them chronologically alongside the other relevant material. By assimilating the work of other biographers in this way, Leyda provides as full a picture as possible from the information available to him at that time. He also offers a supplement section at the end of the second volume for anecdotes, remarks and information about Dickinson family traditions which evade the chronology. He lists all 104 sources at the end of volume two, together with the locations of manuscripts, illustrations and memorabilia for future scholars to pursue the various collections and archives at leisure. The fragments of Dickinson's relationships and relation to the world are available here for the reader to observe and to come to their own overall impression of a life as it is laid out within the pages, with Leyda's biographical voice remaining for the most part conscientiously unobtrusive. Such an approach to biography of the poet had not until this point been attempted, and it is still to be paralleled in the unbiased attention to detail it provides. It is a work of true generosity to the Dickinson scholar as it presents the reader with documents and material related to Dickinson's life, but, crucially, they stand alone without any analysis or critical conjecture. Perhaps due to Leyda's background (with an interest in Communist ideology) and experience in film, the biography attempts to allow the reader to 'view' the shape of Dickinson's life much like a documentary approach in cinema. In theory, the reader has the experience of absorbing the material directly and is then more able to form a clearer view about what Dickinson's 'life' looked like, unencumbered by authorial intention. Whether Leyda achieves his aim of representing the 'truth of Emily Dickinson' (as he states in the book's introduction) is up for question, especially as we know so much more about her life and artistic practices now. Leyda's collection of material spans from 1828 to 1886 and thus effectively excludes historical details of before and after the narrative 'window' of her life of 1830–86. However, this method of laying a wealth of material bare for the reader to digest without comment was a welcome and radical departure from the more traditional biographies of Whicher (1938), Johnson (1955) and the highly speculative biography of Taggard (1930) which had preceded them. Leyda includes the broadest range of material from Dickinson's letters, diary entries from various people, contemporary newspaper, magazine and journal articles, to cartoons, book marginalia, sermon notices and plans of Amherst, and presents it all chronologically. Through this material, readers were finally able to read about the various political, theological and literary debates Dickinson would have engaged with and to experience the very cultural texture of Dickinson's milieu minus the critical intervention. Moreover, each piece of material is given equal weight within the book, and as such no one area is privileged over another.

Thomas H. Johnson's *Emily Dickinson: An Interpretative Biography* (1955) was regarded as the definitive biography of its time. This was in many ways in dialogue with George Frisbie Whicher's excellent earlier critical biography of 1938, *This Was a Poet: Emily Dickinson*. Whicher's biography not only got to grips with her cultural landscape but also rigorously defended Dickinson's precise prosody and style. This biography, in turn, was perhaps a response to earlier, more speculative biographies of the 1930s such as Genevieve Taggard's *The Life and Mind of Emily Dickinson* (1930). Taggard's biography makes much of Dickinson's connection to the figure of George Gould, to whom it is thought Dickinson sent a prose Valentine in 1850. Taggard supposes that Dickinson wore white as a sign of fidelity to Gould, who, it was rumoured (by Vinnie after Dickinson's death), proposed to her but was turned away by Edward Dickinson – something which later biographers discredited. Johnson's biography and subsequent three-volume collection *The Letters of Emily Dickinson* (1958) served to capitalize on his success with *The Poems of Emily Dickinson* in two publications (one volume in 1951 and three volumes in 1955). Johnson's *The Complete Poems of Emily Dickinson* (1960) remained the staple primary text for scholars until Franklin's later revised editions of the manuscripts. Although Johnson's scholarship was undoubtedly a milestone in Dickinson studies, Martha Ackmann, along with many other critics, sees Sewall's as the most comprehensive biography of the poet to date, privileging the conveyance of facts and details of the poet's relationships over more openly subjective and psychoanalytical interpretations of her life such as John Cody's *After Great Pain: The Inner Life of Emily Dickinson* (1971).[12] T. H. Johnson's biography glossed over elements of the poet's life which other critics and biographers have since viewed as being crucial for a fuller understanding of her life. For example, the significant role that Dickinson's various relationships with women played in her poetic development is largely unexplored. Ackmann cites one particular example of Johnson's observation of Dickinson's relationship with her cousins, the Norcrosses. She states that they were not simply help for Dickinson with the daily 'trivialities' but were in fact politically and culturally engaged and provided Dickinson with one inlet into these areas.[13]

In comparison with Johnson and Cody, Sewall is not obtrusively selective but is methodical in his approach, interspersing a highly readable narrative with factual evidence from the poet's correspondences and those of others in her social circle as well as excerpts from reading materials of the day such as the *Springfield Republican*. He provides illustrations, an index of first lines of Dickinson poems cited, as well as a comprehensive index of places and people relevant to the story of Dickinson's life. Reassuringly, Sewall is self-reflexive on the nature of biographical writing and begins Volume One by addressing the 'problem' of the biographer. In many ways the structure of the biography over the two volumes is unusual in that we are presented with a full chronology of the poet's life and then treated to a detailed study of topics as opposed to a truly chronological representation of Dickinson's life. Sewall's approach negotiates the biographer's 'problem' of wanting to remain objective whilst recounting and also interpreting the life of the subject by getting all of the background and potentially contentious material out of the way first. Volume One provides detailed information on Dickinson's forbears and cultural heritage and crucially provides hitherto unseen material on the 'war' between the Dickinson household and that of her brother, Austin Dickinson. This section on the 'war' charts the schism within the Dickinson family and ostensibly that between Austin and Susan Dickinson and Mabel Loomis Todd and their respective offspring, which had lasting ramifications in shaping the eventual publication of Dickinson's poems. All of the details Sewall provides are fully documented in the appendices. This work undoubtedly paved the way for future biographers of this aspect of Dickinson's life, such as Lyndall Gordon. Volume Two focuses on Dickinson exclusively and moves chronologically from early childhood to her death. It provides unique insight into Dickinson's early life and relationships and her intellectual development as a poet, utilizing detailed information about Dickinson's education, personal scholarship and reading. However, because of the reluctance to rely upon speculation and to privilege factual evidence, and to see the poet through the prism of the various relationships she had, some critics have argued that Sewall's biography misses something of the everyday detail of the poet's life. However, this second volume concludes with a chapter entitled 'The Poet' in which Sewall finally allows himself to interpret Dickinson as a poet, to 'convey a mystery'.[14] The description of his efforts to convey the quality of Dickinson's greatness to a sceptic is both heart-warming and admirable, beginning with a reference to Shakespeare and then working through comparisons with the metaphysical poets of the seventeenth century. His analyses of the poems are perceptive, and he concludes the chapter and the biographical project *in toto* with the view that Dickinson wrestled with spiritual vision which turned ultimately towards the view of herself as a poet with 'breathtaking authority'.[15] This statement is a reasonable one, although the prior conviction that Dickinson was completely without any social or political agenda is intellectually challenging. Sewall's observation of the poet's achievements is undeniable. However, as the nature of spiritual authority remains to be one of the most startling features of Dickinson's poetry, Sewall's final assessment of her work seems questionable.

Roger Lundin's *Emily Dickinson and the Art of Belief* (1998) charted new territory in presenting Dickinson's life as essentially a religious biography, demonstrating how her experience of faith shaped her work. In many ways this groundbreaking work paved the way for new approaches to writing biographies of Dickinson which, whilst grounded in factual evidence and new material, were also more daring in their reformulations of Dickinson's persona and her wider cultural significance. Lundin sees Dickinson's work and life as a logical trajectory from the Puritan culture of her ancestors and places her work within a historically religious context from the outset. Whilst Lundin is clear that harsh Calvinism had given way to 'Whig republicanism and evangelical moralism' in her lifetime, an arc of development from New England's religious past is constructed nonetheless.[16] He revisits early Dickinson letters which other critics have used as evidence of her religious scepticism and tempers these views with more moderate and careful consideration, observing an ambivalence and then 'disenchantment' and 'estrangement' rather than defiance.[17] Lundin's overarching schema is a view of the poet's vision as essentially and primarily spiritual, and this biography describes the process of that spiritual journey. The poems and letters are interpreted in relation to this and as a result provide the reader with ways of reading Dickinson which are reconsidered creatively through the religious past. The evocation of Dickinson's journey is bookended by descriptions of her funeral, perhaps invoking the tradition of spiritual autobiography and Puritan death-bed tradition in which the onlookers inscribe their witness of a good life at the point of the person's death. Lundin's biography provided a much-needed reassessment of Dickinson's religious engagement, providing a biographical starting point for critical texts and monographs concerned with Dickinson's spiritual development.

In contrast with Lundin's emphasis on religion as an ultimately positive and creative influence, Alfred Habegger's *My Wars Are Laid Away in Books: The Life of Emily Dickinson* (2001) forges a view of Dickinson as an individual battling for intellectual and spiritual independence in the face of the dominant religious culture. From the outset in the book's introduction, he identifies and polarizes two approaches to Dickinson biography – that which sees her as a lone genius working in isolation and that which emphasizes the significance and importance of female networks for her life and work. He argues that both approaches are essentially inadequate and do not provide an accurate enough representation of her life.[18] Habegger's use of materials such as church records, law archives and contemporary women's writing serves to shape a view of Dickinson which, informed by decades of feminist scholarship, had not been seen in its fullest light before. When read against a biography such as Lundin's, it is clear that Habegger's groundbreaking work is also itself contributing to another particular view of Dickinson's life and work – which this time is decidedly secularized. Both biographies break important new ground in bringing together unseen materials and sources for information about Dickinson's life and have proved invaluable in understanding her work more clearly. They manage to persuade the reader respectively of religious and secular readings of Dickinson's life and work whilst crucially avoiding the reductive analyses earlier biographers were perhaps guilty of producing. Reading the two biographies successively, one gathers a truly informed and balanced view of the spiritual, cultural and literary journey which her poems and letters convey.

Lyndall Gordon's extremely readable book *Lives like Loaded Guns: Emily Dickinson and Her Family's Feuds* (2010) is biographical and takes as its focus the story of the so-called family feud which led to the fractured ownership of Dickinson's manuscripts. Gordon brings to life the textures, subtleties and emotional tensions of everyday life in the Evergreens (home of the poet's brother and family) and the Dickinson Homestead (Dickinson's family home), drawing upon her clearly extensive reading of Dickinson's letters, Dickinson family papers, critical and biographical material as well as the poems themselves – a very useful list of primary and secondary sources – are included. This story of a feud has been documented in Sewall's biography, as already discussed. A major strand of this story, which is the adulterous relationship between Dickinson's brother Austin and Mabel Loomis Todd, has been treated singularly before, most notably by Polly Longsworth in *Austin and Mabel: The Amherst Affair and Love Letters of Austin Dickinson and Mabel Loomis Todd* (1984). However, Gordon's richly detailed biography allows us to understand something of the background to the ownership of the manuscript poems or fascicles as discussed in relation to the issue of self-publication in Section 1.2. She sets the scene for readers as to how Dickinson may have worked, piecing her fascicles together for future readers. The biography shows how her poetry was recognized for its brilliance by Susan Huntington Gilbert Dickinson and Mabel Loomis Todd in different ways, and the ways in which their intellectual influence and sense of organization respectively helped to shape what we have today. The biography covers hitherto unexplored ground in its speculation and presentation of an argument that Dickinson suffered from epilepsy, and Gordon provides reasonable evidence for this including a prescription for glycerine and water (it must be noted not the 'chloral' used in combination with the glycerine to treat epilepsy) she acquired from a doctor Jackson in Boston in the 1850s, together with compelling examples where epilepsy may be viewed as described experience in the poems (notable examples include 'I felt a Cleaving in my Mind' (Fr 867, M 423) and 'It Struck me every day' (Fr 636, M 321), and of course the imagery of a volcanic eruption lying in wait which is evident in 'My Life had Stood a Loaded Gun' (Fr 764, M 354) from which Gordon draws the inspiration for the title of her book). She suggests that Dickinson's relatively reclusive life and the fact that she did not marry may also be indicators of her possible epilepsy as those with the condition were discouraged from marrying.[19] The book briefly charts the development of Dickinson's poetic and independent self and the ways she was influenced by the classical and scientific formal education she had as well as the close relationships she had and managed to maintain, but mainly it provides an illuminating picture of what life in the 1880s may have been like for Dickinson. Dickinson's life and work appears as a secondary presence to the central focus of the Austin-Mabel romance in this volume. As such it provides fascinating insight into particular aspects of Dickinson's life rather than attempting to present a chronological life of the poet with its own motivations and struggles. This work stands alongside that of other very readable biographers of Dickinson whose focus on one broad aspect sheds new light on ways to read her work, for example, *White Heat: The Friendship of Emily Dickinson and Thomas Wentworth Higginson* by Brenda Wineapple (2008). Jerome Charyn's *A Loaded Gun: Emily Dickinson for the 21st Century* (2016) is similarly accessible to the more general reader. Entertaining as much as scholarly, it seeks to present a particular view of Dickinson as sexually potent and enthusiastically inspired by her various muses.

Finally, it is worth mentioning Rebecca Swift's *Poetic Lives: Dickinson* (2011), an easy-to-read introductory biography on the poet. Swift is clearly well informed by the work of previous biographers and treats the student and interested casual reader to a lively, fast-paced trip along Dickinson's life. Swift writes in a considered way and is careful to avoid adopting a particular position on various aspects of her life and manages to offer a balanced view of the debates biographer-critics have presented before her. For example, she takes it for granted that Dickinson's life was 'more peculiarly internal than that of most poets' and that 'external events, such as the Civil War of 1861–5, were arguably marginal to her'.[20] She includes excerpts from both letters and poems to illustrate the story and to neatly summarize some of the main critical views on certain aspects of her life, such as the poet's relationship with Susan. For example, 'most commentators agree that Emily's feelings for Sue were more than ordinarily florid and sentimental … Emily's letters to Susan have more in common with the language of longing and suppression.'[21] There is a refreshing absence of a sense of an enforced narrative in this biography. Dickinson's life is conveyed concisely in a balanced way which allows the newcomer to understand the key moments of her life to then approach the poems with some knowledge of their historical and biographical contexts but without the biases which are common in more overtly critical biographies.

Overall, developments in biographies of Dickinson have shown the poet in ways which are informed both by the methods of previous biographers, but also by ideologically based criticism, as well as the desire to appeal to a wider audience. Most recently biographies of Dickinson or aspects of her life seem to be informed by notions of what may be popular with the more general reader. Due to increased access to original textual witnesses through digitization, researching the life of Emily Dickinson has become more fruitful and engaging in recent years. Researchers have a wealth of crosscurrents to pursue with the move to gather the disparate elements of the Dickinson archive and make connections between the life and work more readily accessible. The open-access website for the manuscripts – Emily Dickinson Archive (EDA) (edickinson.org), the Houghton Library collection of papers, Dickinson family reading materials and artefacts and the Dickinson Electronic Archives (DEA) (emilydickinson.org) – a website which gathers critical and creative material on Dickinson and shows new interpretive contexts available – has made forays into biographizing Dickinson far more accessible for us now than they were for earlier biographers. The readily accessible material (such as Sue's obituary of Dickinson) makes the subject of her biography much easier to approach than it has been in previous times. And yet the earlier biographers' sense of where Dickinson's life fits both within time and history alongside the literary canon of other biographized subjects remains invaluable. In addition to offering starting points for the potential reader of Dickinson biography, this brief sketch of biographical history also provides an outline of the ways in which her life and work has inspired writers and critics to think creatively about her in relation to their own implicit or explicit literary motivations. As we shall see in Chapter 6, Dickinson's life has inspired many dramatic and fictional interpretations both on stage and off, where performance of Dickinson's life has itself become part of popular culture in the United States, Europe and throughout the world.

1.2 Dickinson as poet: Self-publication and early publication

To become a poet, one must write and ultimately publish poems, but this is not where the process begins. The moment of self-realization and of affirmation that one is indeed a poet is perhaps even more crucial than the act of publication. With the case of Emily Dickinson, the nature of her relative seclusion meant that this process was an unusually remarkable event. For any reader of her poems and of biographies of her life, Dickinson's conception of herself as a poet appears to be entirely self-generated. We know that she enquired after her poetic correctness and style in correspondence with the editor of the literary magazine the *Atlantic Monthly*, Thomas Wentworth Higginson. However, on closer inspection, her enquiries seem half-hearted at best. At the core of the exchanges there appears to be a much deeper conviction of her own ability and style regardless of convention and type.[22] Dickinson's self-generated conception of herself as poet is something which has been explored by feminist critics such as Adrienne Rich in her essay '"Vesuvius at Home": The Power of Emily Dickinson' (1976), Paula Bennett in her book *Emily Dickinson: Woman Poet* (1990) and by Gilbert and Gubar in their groundbreaking *The Madwoman in the Attic* (1979). As will be discussed in Chapter 3, an important strand within feminist criticism is the role other women writers played in Dickinson's sense of herself as a poet. Cheryl Walker's chapter 'Dickinson in Context: Nineteenth-Century American Women Poets' in *A Historical Guide to Emily Dickinson* (2004), edited by Vivian R. Pollak, places her firmly among her literary contemporaries and suggests ways in which this informs our view of her route to poetic vocation.[23]

However, Dickinson's conception of herself as a poet did not, apparently, compel her to send poems off to magazine editors. Feminist conceptions of Dickinson as a woman whose gender was a source of power throw particular light on the poet's reluctance to publish in a more formalized way. Feminist critics interpret Dickinson's seclusion as a renegotiation of the traditionally female domestic space of the home to a place of poetic work. This also includes her reformulated attitude to poetic output and a form of 'publication' which did not impose limitations upon her work. In 'Vesuvius at Home', Adrienne Rich sees

Dickinson living a life completely dedicated to poetry, and the fact of her being 'at home' as being necessary for this. As often cited by critics, many of Dickinson's poems are concerned with the idea of being a poet, of listening and/or watching the world for inspiration to transpose to language on paper. The notion of being a poet is also mostly always connected with an internal or external struggle for power. Rich's view of Dickinson is one of potentially explosive poetic power, taking the key metaphor of the volcano in one of Dickinson's most often quoted poems as the focus of her argument:

> My Life had stood – a Loaded Gun –
> In Corners – till a Day
> The Owner passed – identified –
> And carried Me away –
> [...]
> And do I smile, such cordial light
> Opon the Valley glow –
> It is as a Vesuvian face
> Had let it's pleasure through –
>
> (Fr.764. M. 354)

Rich draws us into her own journey of self-discovery as she describes her search for Dickinson and provides readings of specific poems which address Dickinson's identification with poetry and being a poet. This essay was central to many discussions of Dickinson's view of herself as a poet and of poetry's ability to mobilize the eruptive power of the self through literary imagination. It remains an important exploration and reminder of Dickinson's unorthodox nature and of her radical approach to self-expression in a deeply patriarchal nineteenth-century culture.[24]

Paula Bennett's *Emily Dickinson: Woman Poet* (1990) takes a similar view to Rich in that Dickinson's work shows us a woman dedicated to poetry as well as to her identity as a woman poet. She argues, as does Rich, that the domestic sphere of the home represented a space in which Dickinson's sense of herself as a poet could be both defined and actively shaped. Bennett argues that the small things present in the everyday existence of the home provided Dickinson with inspiration and a vehicle to express her sense of self on a larger, poetic and abstract scale.[25] It is this view of the poet as self-defined and self-enabled, which both Rich and Bennett helped to underscore, which remains one of the most striking as critics attempt to ascertain the many influences and motivations she gleaned from her social sphere. An essential element of this view is the issue of her self-publication. As will be discussed in the following pages, Martha Nell Smith's convincing arguments about the centrality of Susan Huntington Gilbert Dickinson in this process in *Rowing in Eden: Rereading Emily Dickinson* (1992) are crucial to our understanding of Dickinson's poetic life, both in her perception of herself as a poet and in the organization and dissemination of the poems themselves.

Dickinson did not actively seek the traditional avenues for publication, and yet her method of an alternative, self-publication was on an exceptionally large scale. She was not simply rejecting publication, but the processes necessarily attached to it – editorial excisions, textual reformulations, as well as the constrictive subjects which editors favoured and expected from women poets. Dickinson's ambivalence about publishing her poems and presenting them to the world can be seen in her construction of fascicles or packets of poems. She appeared to shun formal publication in that she did not send manuscripts off to publishers in the way necessary to court publication and she did not as far as we know set up or even encourage prospective meetings with those potentially directly helpful to the publication of her work, with the noted exception of Thomas Wentworth Higginson. There is an ambivalence, however, because she did meet with Higginson, editor and critic, and she did organize her work into the carefully prepared fascicles. This organization has been viewed by many critics as a form of self-publication. Although the history of women's manuscript publication itself is not our subject here, it may be useful to view Dickinson's manuscripts as part of a wider manuscript culture. Increasingly, recent scholarship repositions manuscripts and fragments as taking precedence over printed versions of texts and argues that definitions of publication, and the false dichotomy between printed and manuscript books, should be adjusted to reflect this.[26] The nature of Dickinson's self-publication has been the subject of much critical debate within the field. What was the rationale underpinning the organization of the fascicles? What decisions did Dickinson make about grouping individual poems together? Was there in fact a thematic structure to the vast, seemingly amorphous body of work she produced over her lifetime? Sharon Cameron argues in her essay 'Dickinson's Fascicles' (1998) that referring to Dickinson's production and organization of the fascicles as self-publication or 'private publication' must be used with some caution. Whilst she skilfully describes what Dickinson's fascicles do, and the way they work, she argues that what Dickinson's intentions were with the fascicles can only be 'speculative'.[27] However, the reason this issue has engendered such critical debate is that when we look at what effect Dickinson's own organization had upon the reception of her work it is difficult not to see her actions as a significant form of defiance.

Dickinson arranged her work into packets of poems which were sewn together by herself and put away in a drawer. Critics have argued that this activity was itself a form of self-publication as she sought to give order to the almost 2,000 poems she had written, leaving them thus to be discovered in such a way. However, the existence of the fascicles has been used as a critical tool at times in the absence of other forms of evidence for biographical interpretations. For example, William H. Shurr, in *The Marriage of Emily Dickinson: A Study of the Fascicles* (1983), uses the framework of the fascicles to describe Dickinson's supposed journey through 'love', 'marriage' and 'separation' in which she pursues a romantic affair which ends badly.[28] The existence of the fascicles has invited much indulgent and wild speculation. However, the fact remains that Dickinson's act of creating the fascicles suggests a sequence and trajectory of meaning to them. Fred D. White suggests in *Approaching Emily Dickinson* (2008) that, in creating the fascicles, Dickinson plays with the idea of order to 'amplify the possibilities of sequence'.[29] If the fascicles do describe a sequence, then this raises a series of tantalizing questions, such as: If the sequence does describe a journey, then what kind of a journey, and a journey from what? To what? Also, who were her intended audiences, and with which voices does she speak? If the fascicles describe a journey or imply a set of editorial choices which impart meaning to the poems, then interpretation becomes difficult and invites speculation, of which we ought to be cautious. The rationale for the choices made by editors of her poems posthumously is just as complex to interpret, illustrating their own speculations about Dickinson's presentation of her work and the meanings it may or may not impart. If Dickinson's process of writing was such that it encompassed multiple variants of poems, was able to rest with poems going forever title-less and was fully accepting of 'errors' (e.g. grammatical, syntactical, rhythmical), then this conveys a self-publication which was defiantly against the practices and standards of the publishing world as Dickinson saw them. Many early editors found that they had to regularize and control Dickinson's texts to make them readable, attempting to conceal the 'irregularities' we now recognize as being part of her genius, uniqueness and progressive style.

Millicent Todd Bingham is the first to describe the journey of these fascicles from Dickinson's hands to eventual publication in *Ancestor's Brocades* (1945).[30] Clearly setting out a case for her mother's (Mabel Loomis Todd) intervention in the process and a keen defence of the work she undertook, it is a unique account of Dickinson's organization of her work into 'volumes' as we are told her sister Lavinia referred to them.[31] It also describes, in the account of those who knew her and the work first hand, the various linguistic alternatives she preserved for many poems, simply for the enjoyment and expansiveness of her own mind it seems. Importantly, because of the appearance of the poems being sketchy and unfinished to the uninitiated eye, the book also details the struggle that these first editors had in attempting to organize work that had been defiantly non-finite in its method of execution. The variant readings offered in the manuscripts had to be narrowed down to one reading, and thus certain readings and meanings were sacrificed over others. Moreover, titles were given by editors, where none were given by Dickinson, thus again imposing meaning upon a poem which may be misleading at best. Thomas Wentworth Higginson also suggested section headings to Mabel Loomis Todd for the initial editing of her work, where poems could be grouped under headings of 'Life', 'Love', 'Nature' and 'Time and Eternity'.[32] However, Bingham is clear that her mother and Higginson were 'creative' in their editing, out of necessity.[33] It is interesting that Bingham is at pains to assert that Dickinson's poems were finished, and that her 'workshop' was an effective one. To contemporary ears, an unfinished poem with variant readings provides us with further curiosity and wonder, and this aspect of Dickinson's work has been the subject of much recent scholarship on the manuscripts and their variants as well as their materiality. With variorum editions of her work, Franklin preserves the final version of each poem, showing the alternatives at hand. Bingham writes that Emily's preferred choice for a word or phrase was underlined.[34] However, this was not always the case, as the manuscripts show. The fact that she wrote on scraps of paper, usually on both sides, on envelopes and even on the back of recipes suggests to us a mind always at work, always ready to jot down a poem or a few compressed lines at the very moment they came to her. As Bingham shows, the job of these first editors was to shape her apparently unhewn work into something which would be palatable for the publishing world and could be consigned to the printed book for preservation. However, as we now know, the physical reality of Dickinson's work has much to offer the scholar. Suzanne Juhasz has written on 'Materiality and the Poet' and focuses on the physical reality of the manuscripts in all their forms.[35] Marta Werner's work on Dickinson's late 'Envelope Poems' shows us how the job of collating Dickinson's work and of reaching an understanding of the scale and nature of her writing practices is still ongoing. *Emily Dickinson: The Gorgeous Nothings* (2013), by Marta Werner and Jen Bervin, is a beautiful reproduction of the manuscript fragments, the scraps of envelopes on which Dickinson wrote poems between 1864 and 1886 (during the period from the tail end of the Civil War up until her death). When underscoring the expansiveness and uniqueness of Dickinson's writing practices, Bervin's introduction cites Jerome McGann's point in *Black Riders: The Visible Language of Modernism* (1993) that 'Dickinson's scripts cannot be read as if they were "printer's copy" manuscripts' and that her poetry was:

> not written *for* a print medium, even though it was written *in* an age of print. When we come to edit her work for bookish presentation, therefore, we must accommodate our typographical conventions to her work, not the other way around.[36]

It is easy to see how editorial and typographical conventions such as the very first ones employed by Todd and Higginson were used to bend Dickinson's work to fit within its own prescriptions. Moreover, we can also see that early critical responses to her work were formed by gauging the extent to which her work could accommodate those conventions of print culture.

The method of alternative, self-'publication' and the organization of her poems has led to discussion of possible thematic organization, not merely a chronological grouping of poems as they were composed. Any discernible thematic structure is speculated upon with caution by many scholars. For example, Ruth Miller's (1968) work forges connections between the organization of the fascicles and that of Francis Quarles' *Emblems, Divine and Moral* (1715), arguing that this organization demonstrates a narrative structure to Dickinson's work. Marietta Messmer has summarized Miller's work as identifying a narrative structure consisting of a movement from 'acceptance through suffering and rejection to resolution'.[37] The main problem is that it is almost impossible to know what Dickinson's intentions were with regard to the overall structure of a particular fascicle, or indeed, whether she even conceived of a poem being in relation to others, and in particular, in relation to a wider collection of poems in the form of the fascicle as she composed them.

Dorothy Huff Oberhaus, in *Emily Dickinson's Fascicles: Method and Meaning* (1995), focuses on the construction of Dickinson's poems and the method and meaning of her arrangements as a form of self-publication. She examines Dickinson's material organization of her work and deduces not only a method but a thematic structure of meaning in their organization. In a way reminiscent of Dickinson's first editors, Higginson and Todd, Oberhaus assigns descriptive and proscriptive titles to moments in the poet's canon. Poems appear grouped under headings such as 'The Composition of Place', 'The Poems of Analysis' and 'The Poems of Faith', and there is a special focus on the fortieth fascicle. In this, Oberhaus reads poems where Dickinson alludes to biblical text as being inherently connected and as evidence of her own spiritual journey, and, crucially, as a Christian poetics.[38]

Martha Nell Smith argues forcefully in *Rowing in Eden: Rereading Emily Dickinson* (1992) that Dickinson's publication history should be seen in terms of her alternative publication methods, such as her organization of the work and her sending poems to a network of targeted correspondents. Her analysis of Dickinson's literary production takes in the textual, material 'performance' of the way the poems were put together and self-published in packets whether they were intended for publication or not. She shows how Dickinson's work was a 'cottage industry' which could afford to be unconventional and disregard rules of publication, grammar, syntax, sense, topic and genre because Dickinson did not depend upon writing as a form of income. She was able to be discriminate in her relationship to publication, in the production of the poem itself, as well as in the choice of magazines and editors to whom she sent her work. Smith sees every part of Dickinson's production as akin to a publishing process, for example, looking at the differences in Dickinson's handwriting or 'typeface' across the years as part of her self-fashioning and self-publication.[39] As Chapter 3 of this guide will explain, many critics, including Smith, see Dickinson's relationship with her sister-in-law Susan as crucial to this self-fashioning and alternative publication process. Smith explains Susan's role in getting poems out to editors both during the poet's life and posthumously as well as the numerous ways she influenced Dickinson's work as mentor, muse, editor, critic and lender of books. She also describes how Susan stage-managed Dickinson's image after her death, by presenting a view of Dickinson for posterity in her obituary, stressing, amongst other things, the poet's choice to live a relatively secluded life and emphasizing the point that she was not an 'invalid' or victim of circumstance, but a poet.[40] Reconstructing the relationship between the two women is an important central concern for Smith. She argues powerfully that the love partnership between Dickinson and Susan has been persistently diminished and even erased by critics over time and that the loss this has engendered for readers of her work can never be accurately measured. In returning to Dickinson's relationship with Susan, Smith's book shows us some of the windows into the poet's unique and unconventional creative processes.

The list of poems that Dickinson had published within her own lifetime is lengthier than was first thought, and now strays beyond the several poems Sewall and others described. We know that at least ten poems and one letter were published during Dickinson's lifetime, although some of these poems were also then republished. There are at least twelve published in various publications such as Amherst College's *Indicator*, *Springfield Daily Republican*, *Drum-Beat*, *Round Table*, *Brooklyn Daily Union* and *A Masque of Poets*.[41] It is thought that she did not send these poems off for publication but that they were sent either without her knowledge or on her behalf by someone else. As mentioned, her poems were first put together and edited by Mabel Loomis Todd with the assistance of Thomas Wentworth Higginson and were published as *Poems by Emily Dickinson* in Boston by Roberts Brothers in 1890.[42] They appeared four years after Dickinson's death and with significant revisions.

Cristanne Miller's recent edition of Dickinson's poems, *Emily Dickinson's Poems: As She Preserved Them* (2016), contains a thought-provoking introduction detailing Dickinson's writing processes and a summary of previous editorial practices.[43] It breaks new ground by presenting the poems with Dickinson's own ordering of them in the forty fascicles as she arranged them, and presents the poems alongside Dickinson's textual variations, together with annotations. It is a reading edition as opposed to a variorum which means that it presents one representation of every poem she wrote. The deciding factor in which version to include in the volume to represent the poem is the one which Dickinson herself copied and retained. It is an invaluable text to consult when considering the issue of self-publication and the way editors have shaped our reading of her work. Since her earliest editors Mabel Loomis Todd and Thomas Wentworth Higginson, and the various magazine editors who published individual poems, through to the editors of the major editions of her work, T. H. Johnson, and R. W. Franklin, each has made decisions about the way her body of work is organized and presented to the world. Miller's volume aims to present not only Dickinson's work as *she* 'preserved' it, but also to show her working processes. Miller presents and arranges the material in a fashion which allows the reader to observe what Dickinson did with her texts – what she wrote on, the revisions and various word substitutions she made, which poems she selected and placed together into fascicles, and, crucially, which ones she did not retain. She also clearly shows which poems Dickinson sent out and to whom, and when, and how these versions printed or otherwise differed or not from the ones she kept for herself. Miller organizes this material in a way which is reader-friendly, and she devises five sections: 'The Fascicles', 'Unbound Sheets', 'Loose Poems', 'Poems Transcribed by Others' and 'Poems Not Retained'. When presented in this way, Dickinson's working processes can be more effectively differentiated from the ways in which her work was organized by editors since her death. Miller's volume allows for a deeper analysis than before of Dickinson's self-'publication' and allows us to comprehend more fully the effects of the organizing done by editors of her work. Miller's volume will no doubt become the one which is most often cited in future scholarship, and it is therefore important to include Miller's page numbering alongside Franklin's poem numbers in this guide.

Notes

1. Interview with Jerome Charyn, cited in review of his book *A Loaded Gun: Emily Dickinson for the Twenty-First Century* (New York: Bellevue Literary Press, 2016) in *Kirkus Reviews*, 15th Nov. 2015.
2. *Emily Dickinson: An Annotated Bibliography: Writings, Scholarship, Criticism and Ana 1850–1968*, ed. by Willis J. Buckingham (Bloomington: Indiana University Press, 1970), p. 249.
3. Jay Leyda, *The Years and Hours of Emily Dickinson*, 2 vols (New Haven: Yale University Press, 1960) and Martha Nell Smith, *Rowing in Eden: Rereading Emily Dickinson* (Austin: University of Texas Press, 1992).
4. The Dickinson Electronic Archives (DEA) brings together the manuscript and printed versions of Susan's obituary for Dickinson. See: http://www.emilydickinson.org/writings-by-susan-dickinson/reviews-essays-and-other-criticism/obituary-for-emily-dickinson
5. *The Life and Letters of Emily Dickinson*, ed. by Martha Dickinson Bianchi (Boston: Houghton Mifflin, 1924).
6. Martha Dickinson Bianchi, *Emily Dickinson Face to Face; Unpublished Letters with Notes and Reminiscences* (1932; Hamden: Archon, 1970), pp. 20–1.
7. Millicent Todd Bingham, *Emily Dickinson's Home: Letters of Edward Dickinson and His Family* (New York: Harper, 1955), pp. xi–xiii.
8. Martha Ackmann, 'Biographical Studies of Dickinson' in *The Emily Dickinson Handbook*, ed. by Gudrun Grabher, Roland Hagenbuchle and Cristanne Miller (Amherst: University of Massachusetts Press, 1998), pp. 11–23 (p. 13).
9. Ackmann, 'Biographical Studies of Dickinson', pp. 17–19.
10. Vivian Pollak, *Emily Dickinson: The Anxiety of Gender* (Ithaca and London: Cornell University Press, 1984), pp. 10–11.
11. Ackmann, pp. 11–23.
12. John Cody, *After Great Pain: The Inner Life of Emily Dickinson* (Cambridge, MA: Harvard University Press, 1971).
13. Ackmann, p. 19.
14. Richard B. Sewall, *The Life of Emily Dickinson*, 2 vols (New York: Farrar, Straus and Giroux, 1974), II, p. 707.
15. Sewall, *The Life of Emily Dickinson*, p. 725.
16. Roger Lundin, *Emily Dickinson and the Art of Belief*, 2nd edn (Michigan: Eerdmans, 1998; 2004), p. 13.

17 Lundin, *Emily Dickinson and the Art of Belief*, pp. 45–8.
18 Alfred Habegger, *My Wars Are Laid Away in Books: The Life of Emily Dickinson* (New York: Random House, 2001), p. xii.
19 Lyndall Gordon, *Lives like Loaded Guns: Emily Dickinson and Her Family's Feuds* (London: Virago, 2010). See Chapter Five, 'Snarl in the Brain', pp. 114–36.
20 Rebecca Swift, *Poetic Lives: Dickinson* (London: Hesperus Press, 2011), p. 10.
21 Swift, *Poetic Lives*, p. 79.
22 *Emily Dickinson: Selected Letters*, ed. by Thomas H. Johnson, eleventh printing (Cambridge, MA: The Belknap of Harvard University Press, 2002), pp. 171–8.
23 Cheryl Walker, 'Dickinson in Context: Nineteenth-Century American Women Poets', in *A Historical Guide to Emily Dickinson*, ed. by Vivian R. Pollak (Oxford: Oxford University Press, 2004), pp. 175–200.
24 Adrienne Rich, '"Vesuvius at Home": The Power of Emily Dickinson' *Parnassus*, 5 (1976), 49–74.
25 Paula Bennett, *Emily Dickinson: Woman Poet* (New York and London: Harvester Wheatsheaf, 1990), p. 184.
26 For discussion on the history of women's manuscript publication, see *After Print: Eighteenth-Century Manuscript Cultures*, ed. by Rachel Scarborough King (Charlottesville: University of Virginia Press, 2020). This book explores how 'Invisible books' by women writers such as the manuscript notebooks of Dorothy Wordsworth were ignored by scholars for a long time because of a false dichotomy between manuscript and printed books and because of the perceived 'physical messiness' of such manuscripts (p. 73).
27 Sharon Cameron, 'Dickinson's Fascicles' in *The Emily Dickinson Handbook*, ed. by Grabher, Hagenbuchle and Miller, pp. 138–80 (pp. 139–58).
28 William H. Shurr, *The Marriage of Emily Dickinson: A Study of the Fascicles* (Lexington: University of Kentucky Press, 1983).
29 Fred D. White, *Approaching Emily Dickinson: Critical Currents and Crosscurrents since 1960* (New York: Camden House, 2008), p. 36.
30 Millicent Todd Bingham, *Ancestors' Brocades: The Literary Debut of Emily Dickinson* (New York: Harper, 1945).
31 Millicent Todd Bingham, *Ancestors' Brocades*, p. 17.
32 Millicent Todd Bingham, p. 51.
33 Millicent Todd Bingham, p. 36.
34 Millicent Todd Bingham, p. 38.
35 See Suzanne Juhasz, 'Materiality and the Poet' in *The Emily Dickinson Handbook*, ed. by Grabher, Hagenbuchle and Miller, pp. 427–39.
36 Jerome McGann, *Black Riders: The Visible Language of Modernism* (Princeton, NJ: Princeton University Press, 1993), p. 38, cited in Marta L. Werner, and Jen Bervin, *Emily Dickinson: The Gorgeous Nothings* (New York: Christine Burgin/New Directions, 2013), p. 11.

37 Ruth Miller, *The Poetry of Emily Dickinson* (Middletown, CT: Wesleyan University Press, 1968). Qtd in Marietta Messmer, 'Dickinson's Critical Reception', in *The Emily Dickinson Handbook*, ed. by Grabher, Hagenbuchle and Miller, pp. 299–322 (p. 318).
38 Dorothy Huff Oberhaus, *Emily Dickinson's Fascicles: Method and Meaning* (University Park: Pennsylvania State University Press, 1995), pp. 169–87.
39 Smith, *Rowing in Eden*, pp. 61–75.
40 Smith, pp. 207–20 (p. 210).
41 https://www.emilydickinsonmuseum.org/publications_lifetime
42 *Poems by Emily Dickinson*, ed. by Mabel Loomis Todd and Thomas Wentworth Higginson (Boston: Roberts Brothers, 1890).
43 *Emily Dickinson's Poems: As She Preserved Them*, ed. by Cristanne Miller, pp. 1–22.

2

Style and meaning

| 2.1 Early criticism | 39 |
| 2.2 Later revaluations | 45 |

Dickinson's poetic innovation is something which often placed her at odds with her contemporary readers and critics. As explored in the previous chapter, Dickinson was radical in her approach to publication and in the writing processes she chose. Questions about Dickinson's style include a consideration of her attitude to the poems as material things, and implicit in this is the fundamental question of what constitutes as a poem. As Cristanne Miller's recent work has shown, in both *Reading in Time: Emily Dickinson in the Nineteenth Century* (2012) and in her superlative edition of the poems, *Emily Dickinson's Poems: As She Preserved Them* (2016), Dickinson's 'style' is evident in her writing practices as well as in her experiments with language. As we have seen, Dickinson wrote poems on whichever scraps of paper were available to her, such as the backs of recipes or envelopes, and she frequently included poems within her letters. She chose to edit and organize many of her poems but apparently disregarded others; her poems are sometimes longer than her usual two or three stanzas, whereas others appear as only one or two lines and are epigrammatic. Frequently, especially towards the end of her life, Dickinson could convey much with only a few words. The materiality of her poems, and of her writing processes, is now widely available to view as an object of study in itself. Facsimile copies of her manuscript poems in their 'fascicles' were published in 1981 and edited by R. W. Franklin. Her manuscript archive is now available to view online at the open-access website edickinson.org. The poems she composed on envelopes exclusively have been reproduced in colour facsimile (Bervin and Werner, 2013).[1] Early criticism of her work as being haphazard or disorganized could equally be applied to these kinds of writing practices. Her progressive approach, and her mode or 'style' of working, also inevitably extend to the style of her poetry, and to the various ways in which she manipulated poetic and literary conventions to convey meaning in her poems. Her disregard for giving poems titles, for example, caused headaches for editors who felt that they should invent some. Most notably, Mabel Loomis Todd and Thomas Wentworth Higginson found it their task to categorize and give titles to her poems in their early printed editions of her work. Moreover, early editors also felt the need to 'correct' her punctuation, grammar and spelling and to 'regularize' her rhythms. I use inverted commas here as such revisions were subject to the barometers of taste and of what was deemed acceptable to editors, critics and ultimately, readers of the period. As we shall see in this chapter, Dickinson's use of language and form was highly sophisticated and inventive, and anticipated future literary forms. David Porter, for example, set out one of the first full expositions on the relationship between Dickinson's style and modern literary techniques in *Dickinson: The Modern Idiom* (1981). He argues compellingly that Dickinson's idiosyncratic use of ellipsis, unusual syntax and grammatical irregularity, amongst other striking features of her work, is a crucial poetic precursor to the linguistic and semantic playfulness of modern and postmodern literature. He turns again to her modern approach to 'themes' or, rather, the absence of such discernible thematic structure in 'Searching for Dickinson's Themes' (1998).[2] Her characteristic 'style' includes line breaks, a (now iconic) unique use of dashes, a broad range of diction, experiments with rhythm, grammar, punctuation and syntax, and the use of rhetorical devices such as metonymy and synecdoche. Her use of dashes sometimes indicates a break in thought and/or a radical shift in sense, but they are also sometimes used to connect seemingly disparate elements in a poem. Dickinson used the linguistic tools she knew to forge a unique way of writing poems and to allow for a new way of reading. Her poetic strategies engage the reader fully, inviting and instructing us to read creatively and to follow her multiple, suggestive voices. In examining the relationship between style and meaning in Dickinson's work, many critics have concluded that her complexity and sophistication provides us with (and requires of us) entirely new ways of thinking. For example, Robert Weisbuch (1998) has described how Dickinson's work demands that we 'let go' of received ways of interpreting and reading poetry, prescribing instead what he calls a 'poetic Bauhaus', or a 'less-is-more' approach, where there is a cathartic 'releasing of interpretive habits and idiot-questioner demands'.[3]

Helen Vendler writes in *Poets Thinking: Pope, Whitman, Dickinson, Yeats* (2004) that Dickinson's invention of poetic temporal structures 'channels our reactions, stylizes our pace to hers, and constructs our thinking after her own'.[4] By reading Emily Dickinson's poetry, we are coaxed into following the shape of her thought and retracing her cognitive leaps – making our own thought processes stretch to meet hers.

Her literary sophistication can be seen, for example, in the ways she uses synecdoche to infer theological meanings, and the simultaneous subversion of them.[5] For example a statement such as 'I wish I were a Hay' (the final line of 'The Grass so little has to do', Fr 379, M 202) highlights the relation of part to whole which is inextricable from the human-God relation in theological discourse.[6] In this example, she uses an indefinite article 'a' (singular) to describe the noun 'Hay' (collective) which, in its complexity, highlights the difficulty in being a part of a whole when it no longer seems appropriate or entirely logical. Her literary skill can also be seen in the ways she plays with metre, in pushing the parameters of the forms she used, such as the common hymnic metre, short and long metre, the ballad stanza, and very infrequently the common particular metre (a double tercet rhythm of 8-8-6/8-8-6 syllables and 4-4-3/4-4-3 metrical feet). The common hymnic metre, which is often cited as her most used form, has alternating lines of 8/6 syllables and alternating lines comprising 4 and then 3 metrical feet (tetrameter and trimeter). For example:

   /   /   /   /
A transport one cannot contain
   /   /   /
May yet, a transport be –

(Fr 212, M 136)

Although it is frequently cited that Dickinson often used the common hymnic metre, it should be noted that her metrics are rarely strictly regular. Dickinson's use of such metres seems salutatory, as if she wants us to remember the regularized metres and compare them with her own version or distorted echoing of them. By employing metres and frequently, simultaneously, interrupting their 'logical' rhythm with irregular lines, Dickinson's poetic style illuminates those moments at which style and meaning collide to produce new meanings. For example, sometimes we are expecting 8 syllables in a line but read 7, and we are encouraged to read a dash as a syllable, thus conferring meaning to the dash itself. We are encouraged by her (ab)use of metre to linger over certain words where we would not ordinarily pause. This has the effect of reconsidering the importance of words which at first seemed relatively insignificant in any given poem. For example, in the poem 'Why – do they shut me out of Heaven?' (Fr 268/ M 133) stressed syllables which are followed by a dash emphasize the tension between loud and quiet voices, between speaking and remaining silent, and, ultimately, between having access to the divine and being excluded – the opposing positions which the poem explores. Dickinson also sets up and exploits a tension between the reader's knowledge of formal conventions and the unconventional ways her poem deviates from them. In each of the three stanzas, the poem suggests and approximates the alternating tetrameter and trimeter lines (4 and 3 metrical feet) of the hymnic form. However, the syllables are irregular in each (9/5, 7/3 and 7/5, then 8/4 and 9/4) and therefore the form Dickinson chooses does not strictly adhere to the 8/6 syllable structuring traditionally associated with the common hymnic metre. The second line of the second stanza is unexpectedly shorter than the second and last lines of the first stanza which have five syllables. It has three syllables and the trimeter has the effect of making the reader linger over the dashes to consider the drawing out of the speaker's time and effort: 'Just – once – more –'. A similar effect is achieved in the poem's final line, 'Could – I – forbid?' Dickinson's use of rhythm and metre forces us to confront the pauses that the dashes invite. The rhythm and pace of the lines manipulate moments of reflection throughout the poem where space is created for possible answers to a series of questions. The form of the poem communicates meaning by throwing these questions into relief, where stressed syllables are followed by a dash:

> /   /   /   /
> Why – do they shut me out of Heaven?
> /   /   /
> Did I sing – too loud?

(Fr 268, M. 133)

The stress on 'sing' is followed by a dash which invites us to consider the reason for the exclusion from 'Heaven', echoing the initial 'why' of the first line. The speaker surmises, not without irony, that the banishment may be connected to a form of devotion itself – singing. Dickinson uses metre to highlight particular words as well as to voice the gaps and pauses where the opportunity for meaning within the poems often lies. The subtle and complex relation between style and meaning in Dickinson's work is something which critics have at turns focused on, and, in the case of the earlier critics and reviewers, frequently misunderstood. She has arguably been one of the most misconstrued poets of her generation, as the history of her publication and the subsequent editing of her work has shown.

Dickinson's work demands a high level of engagement from the reader. As David Porter so eloquently puts it:

> What is required of Dickinson readers, then, is patience of mind, the ability to live with indefiniteness and indeterminacy, more so than with any other major American poet before the postmodern onset of pastiche as a form and the deliberate evasion of linguistic closure as communication.[7]

Perhaps the modern reader is more readily attuned to her indefiniteness as well as to her sophisticated rhythms.

2.1 Early criticism

This chapter draws upon early criticism of Dickinson's poetry and summarizes the main arguments that such early criticism of her writing style generated. In the first section, early reviews from Caesar R. Blake and Carlton F. Wells's *The Recognition of Emily Dickinson, Selected Criticism Since 1890* (1968) are considered as well as texts which include commentaries upon early criticism such as Willis J. Buckingham (ed), *Emily Dickinson: An Annotated Bibliography: Writings, Scholarship, Criticism and Ana 1850-1968* (1970) and *Emily Dickinson's Reception in the 1890s: A Documentary History* (1989).[8] The second section of this chapter will then go on to examine the later critical revaluations of Dickinson's poetic style and her eschewing of poetic and publishing conventions. It will summarize the arguments made in key articles such as Shira Wolosky 'Rhetoric or Not: Hymnal Tropes in Emily Dickinson and Isaac Watts' (1988) and discuss Cristanne Miller's critical innovations with regard to the mechanics of Dickinson's work in both *Emily Dickinson: A Poet's Grammar* (1987) and *Reading in Time: Emily Dickinson in the Nineteenth Century* (2012).[9] The availability of Dickinson's manuscripts in facsimile form and later online has led to renewed debates about the editing of her work and how the obfuscation of her creative processes has shaped our readings. Emphasis on the manuscript variations has led to an ongoing debate about whether Dickinson's poems can be better understood primarily as visual or aural presentations – whether the fullness of Dickinson's poetic effects can be registered most effectively by being seen (read) or heard. This debate in evident in texts such as Susan Howe's *The Birth-Mark: Unsettling the Wilderness in American Literary History* (1993) and Domhnall Mitchell's *Measures of Possibility: Emily Dickinson's Manuscripts* (2005). The critical texts in this section provide key examples of twentieth- and twenty-first-century criticism which focuses upon the construction and mechanics of the poetry as laid out in the manuscripts, bringing together historicist as well as feminist perspectives which serve to deconstruct the criticisms made in early commentaries on her work.

The main 'problems' early reviewers of Dickinson's work found were those related to her style, followed closely by those connected with her choice of subject matter. One early English review, attributed to Andrew Lang, then editor of the *London Daily News*, was such that it warranted a reply from an American counterpart. Lang's review of *Poems* (1890) ('An American Sappho') appeared in the *London Daily News*, 3 October 1891 (preceded by an earlier review, also probably by Lang, in the same publication on 2 January 1891) and described Dickinson's work thus:

> It is easy to see the interest of a character like this, but it is really next to impossible to see the merit of poetry like Miss Dickinson's. She had thought a great deal, she did little but think, yet the expression of her thought is immeasurably obscure, broken, unmelodious, and recklessly willful. Like other very retiring persons, she was often in her correspondence extremely effusive. Her verse, at its absolute best, has a distant echo of Blake's, though it is highly probable that she never read anything of his. Poetry is a thing of many laws – felt and understood, and sanctioned by the whole experience of humanity, rather than written. Miss Dickinson in her poetry broke every one of the natural and salutary laws of verse. Hers is the very anarchy of the Muses, and perhaps in this anarchy lies the charm which has made her popular in America and has caused Mr. Howells to say that she alone would serve to justify American literary existence. Fortunately, that continent has a much more valid *raison d'être*. Readers of Miss Dickinson's letters will perhaps regret that the lines of this curious, shy, self-conscious, and expansive lady were ever published at all. She seems to have been a kind of unfinished, rudimentary Brontë, and her character is so unusual and interesting, that it is a pity her rhymes should make matter for mirth. Yet it is impossible for most people to avoid laughing at what is, frankly, so laughable. Unless all poets, from the early improvisers to the Laureate, have been wrong in their methods, Miss Dickinson cannot possibly have been right in hers. [...] It is much to be wished that her admirers will not become her imitators, defying grammar, rhyme, sense, and prosody. Critics who are asked to be candid about such effusions will be wise if they bid the writers 'drop the paste and think themselves a fool,' as Miss Dickinson puts it, for coming to the festival of the Muses in such scandalous lack of a wedding garment.[10]

Benjamin Franklin Sanborn's American response to this English review suggests that Lang was unusually scathing in his tone, calling it 'mere Philistinism'.[11]

Early reviewers such as Lang were openly scathing about Dickinson's stylistic presentation, and there was also an implication that she did not read Blake (Lang states simply, minus any suggestion of evidence, that it was 'highly probable' Dickinson did not read Blake). For him, her expression was 'immeasurably obscure, broken, unmelodious, and recklessly willful'. There is no suggestion that her 'recklessly willful' style or 'anarchy' was in any way the hallmarks of an avant-courier, or a poetical pioneer. What is more damaging, however, is the suggestion that there would be no literary legacy for her (presumably female) 'imitators', only folly and an unpreparedness for literary success. It is no accident that literary success is expressed in terms of a betrothal. There were, of course, other factors at play in the early reviews, which were extraneous to the merit of the work being considered. Marietta Messmer has written about the politics of Dickinson's critical reception in the 1890s, arguing that it is more complex than a discussion of those who believed poetry could survive without traditional form and those who could not. She argues that existing rivalries between the literary centres of Boston and New York, and those of British and American critics, affected reviews of Dickinson's work and that such rivalries can be read as 'discriminations against female-gendered forms of reception that attempted to transcend the narrowly defined genre of "critical review"'.[12]

Even a more generous early-twentieth-century review by Martha Hale Shackford in the *Atlantic Monthly* (1913) conveys how it was deemed necessary to acknowledge at once the common 'complaint' of Dickinson's reviewers:

> There is no doubt that critics are justified in complaining that her work is often cryptic in thought and unmelodious in expression. Almost all her poems are written in short measures, in which the effect of curt brevity is increased by her verbal penuriousness. Compression and epigrammatical ambush are her aids; she proceeds, without preparation or apology, by sudden, sharp zigzags. What intelligence a reader has must be exercised in the poetic game of hare-and-hounds, where ellipses, inversions, and unexpected climaxes mislead those who pursue sweet reasonableness. Nothing, for instance, could seem less poetical than this masterpiece of unspeakable sounds and chaotic rhymes.[13]

The poem with 'unspeakable sounds and chaotic rhymes' is 'Drab Habitation of Whom?' (Fr 916/M 431). Despite this caveat, Shackford understands what is expansive and generous about Dickinson's poetry and that her poetic style ('expression') *is* intimately connected with its meaning ('idea'):

> The essential qualities of her music are simplicity and quivering responsiveness to emotional moods. Idea and expression are indissolubly fused in her work

that no analysis of her style and manner can be attempted without realizing that every one of her phrases, her changing rhythms, is a direct reflection of her personality. The objective medium is entirely comfortable to the inner life, a life of peculiarly dynamic force which agitates, arouses, spurs the reader.

However Shackford is so keen to stress the wealth of Dickinson's 'personality', her 'capacity for feeling', that she misses the artistry of Dickinson's manipulations with formal aspects such as rhyme, metre and language – of the various and complex ways her style does reflect the meaning, in this case, identified as 'personality' which 'agitates, arouses, spurs the reader'. Instead, the review culminates with references to her work being less than 'precise' or 'flawless', suggesting that the power and artistry are somehow 'deeper', 'intrinsic' and obscured rather than 'external':

> A poet in the deeper mystic qualities of feeling rather than in the external merit of precise rhymes and flawless art, Emily Dickinson's place is among those whose gifts are 'Too intrinsic for renown.'[14]

The review misses much, not least because Dickinson's linguistic art was so visually showy, as later-twentieth-century critics would go on to illustrate. Shackford's review demonstrates that the elements of Dickinson's work early critics were at pains to identify and decry as poetically heretical (the 'poetic game of hare-and-hounds, [...] ellipses, inversions, and unexpected climaxes') were also the very tools which made the expression of such 'deeper mystic qualities' possible.

Nineteenth-century critics who found themselves favouring Dickinson's work despite the frequently bad reviews it received were unsure how to refer to the quality of her verse. Their points of reference hark back to a vaguely 'mystical' or 'mediaeval' type of verse perhaps, paradoxically, because there was no available language to expertly express the entirety of its newness and progressiveness. Blake and Wells point out in their selection of criticism since 1890, *The Recognition of Emily Dickinson* (1964), how ironic it is that the then Professor of English at New York University, Francis H. Stoddard (1847–1936), who wrote a defence of Dickinson's verse in *The Critic* ('Technique in Emily Dickinson's Poems', XX, 9 January 1892), 'looks backward for his justification, calling the form he sees in her "mediaeval"'. They see this reference as 'ironic' because Stoddard's analytical approach to Dickinson itself suggests, in their view, the 'New Criticism of the 1940s':

> His letter to *The Critic* answers the reviewer who had made the usual complaints about Emily Dickinson's flawed technique. His defense of her poetic form employs a method of analysis unusual in 1892, but suggesting the critical approach of the

'New Criticism' of the 1940s. It is ironic, perhaps, that Stoddard looks backward for his justification, calling the form he sees in her as 'mediaeval.'[15]

It is unsurprising to twenty-first-century readers of Dickinson to learn that nineteenth-century critics were necessarily forming new modes of criticism through engagement with her work. Stoddard's defence of Dickinson challenges the accusation of 'absolute formlessness' levelled at her work by an anonymous reviewer in the previous issue of *The Critic* (XVI, 19 December 1891). He argues:

> Miss Dickinson's poems may be formless, or they may be worded to so fine and subtle a device that they seem formless, just as the spectrum of a far-off star may seem blankness until examined with a lens of especial power.[16]

Presumably, Stoddard flatters his own critical prowess in this declaration. However, his careful attention to contrast and parallel in Dickinson's 'I died for beauty' (Fr 448, M 225) draws out the relation between style and meaning, here between matching rhymes and what Stoddard calls 'slurred' rhymes to open out the wider debate about the relation between 'truth' and 'beauty' in the poem:

> Now the notion here is the notion of the unity of truth and beauty. If harmony with the thought is to prevail in the verse we should expect a closely parallel structure with a figure in dual accent – i.e., based upon two factors. Such a figure we get:-
> > I died for beauty, but was scarce
> > Adjusted in the tomb,
> > [...]
>
> Two pairs of lines, each with two accents, the similar words being matched in pairs – justed: joining, died: died, tomb: room. Beauty and truth do not perfectly match, of course, because not yet proved to be one in nature. These exact correspondences would produce mechanical regularity, overprove the proposition by overemphasizing the innate notion of harmony, if care were not taken. So care is taken to contrast the positions of the members of the separate pairs. That is, in the first line, the slurred words *but was scarce* are at the end, while in the corresponding line the slurred words *when one who* are at the beginning. Similarly, the slurred words *in an* in the fourth line.[17]

He concludes:

> The rhyme changes to alliteration which is beginning-rhyme instead of end-rhyme – *night: names.* Our earthly names are lost in the endless night of death; ourselves, at one with each other, at one with truth and beauty, entered into the endless day of beauty and of truth. I submit that such art as this may be subtle and mediaeval, but it is not formlessness.[18]

By focusing on the formal aspects of her work, Stoddard is lyrically engaged with Dickinson on the relation between truth and beauty; his prose becomes lyrically charged, clearly thinking seriously about the poem's probing questions and above all taking Dickinson's artistry as seriously as it deserves to be. His attention to what he calls its 'subtlety' allows him to consider its meanings. His focus on the stylistic concerns of off-rhymes and alliteration elicits a critical seriousness which eluded many of her early critics and, as such, is an exemplary precursor for twentieth-century reviewers and critics and beyond.

The effects of Dickinson's uniqueness rippled outwards to those interested not merely in her 'personality' as a mythical/mystical figure of New England literary legend, but to those most interested in the process of writing poetry, namely poets, writers and critics. Andrew Lang's fear that Dickinson's 'admirers' would become her 'imitators' displays an anxiety about the force of her radical approach to poetry and the route that that force could potentially take. Lang's anxiety was justified because although Dickinson's 'admirers' since the early editions could not successfully replicate her poetic uniqueness, the influential effects of her radical style and approach to poetry have since been, and continue to be, diffuse and manifold.

It has been widely accepted that Dickinson's style positions her, along with Whitman, as a nineteenth-century precursor to literary modernism. Connections between Dickinson's style and that of literary modernism have been most notably explored by David Porter in *Dickinson: The Modern Idiom* (1981), laying the groundwork for this area of interest in Dickinson to place her more properly as a forbear to both modernism and postmodernism within the history of American literary culture.[19] Twentieth-century reviewers seemed ready to accept her formal irregularities. Early-twentieth-century reception of her work shifted away from the many formalistic difficulties nineteenth-century reviewers of her work encountered. One reason for this shift is that the linguistic and semantic experiments to be found in the modern poetry and prose of the twentieth century afforded critics a lens through which to view Dickinson more solidly as a poetic forerunner. However, Patricia Chaudron has argued recently that it was only once Dickinson's work was de-regionalized by early-twentieth-century critics that it could be viewed as anticipating modernism.[20] For example, an early-twentieth-century review of Dickinson's poetry – the collection of Dickinson's poems put together by her niece, Martha Dickinson Bianchi, entitled *The Single Hound* (1914) – sees her work as instructive to the imagist school of poets, and as throwing a 'searching light on the revolutionary volumes of 1915'. The review is called 'An Early Imagist':

'Criticism is timid,' writes Emerson. 'When shall we dare to say only that it is poetry which cleanses and mans me?' 'The Single Hound' is poetry of this tonic sort, and – though the lifetime it records ended nearly thirty years ago – throws a searching light on the revolutionary volumes of 1915. For starkness of vision, 'quintessentialness' of expression, boldness and solidity of thought, and freedom of form, a New England spinster who flourished between 1830 and 1886 in an elm-shaded college town above the Connecticut valley, might give the imagists 'pointers': here is a discovery to quicken the modern New England heart.[21]

The reviewer, Elizabeth Shepley Sergeant, sees connections between Dickinson and the imagists in the 'freedom of form' and a 'boldness and solidity of thought'. She sees Dickinson as thoroughly modern and revolutionary: her economy of language and willingness to experiment is seen here as a precursor to the 'revolutionary volumes of 1915' and as something radically different from the lyrical discursiveness which the imagists were also keen to jettison. Her uniqueness amongst her puritan heritage, as 'one of the rarest flowers the sterner New England ever bore', sets her apart in Sergeant's view as an outsider, a 'white, fearless New England spinster'. Here we see a reviewer attempting to account for Dickinson's uniqueness *despite* her New England environment, making a comparison with Carlyle and his 'narrow Scotch inheritance'.[22] Here we see a move away from the delimited, regionalized 'local colour' view of her poetry, which, Chaudron has argued, was necessary for Dickinson's anticipation of literary modernism to be fully realized. Dickinson's poetic innovations were not simply employed to represent a localized, restricted life, but, rather, served as a means of expansion, to draw upon universalized, rather than localized, meanings alone. A key feature of modernist poetry, and especially that of the imagists, was a keenness to move away from the use of rhetoric in their work. Clarity of thought and economical expression took priority over intuited meanings and shared knowledges which seemed to be extraneous to the immediate concerns of the poem. As we shall see, many discussions of the formal aspects of Dickinson's work and the later studies of style and meaning in the poems focus on her uses of rhetoric, and this is a poetic feature which many discussions of her 'pre-modernism' seems to miss.

2.2 Later revaluations

As her work continued to influence poets and writers beyond the nineteenth century into the modern era, later-twentieth-century critics of Dickinson's work inspired by New Criticism were keen to focus on the relation between style and meaning in the poems. Part of this formalist approach involved rigorously analysing Dickinson's various (ab)uses of and experiments with grammar, punctuation, structure, syntax, form, metre, rhythm to name a few formal concerns – the very things early reviewers found so disagreeable. Critics such as Gary Lee Stonum (1990) insisted upon the importance of Dickinson's style, evidenced by the fact of its 'aggressive idiosyncrasy'. In Stonum's view, it is Dickinson's invention of a unique style which can be seen as her main literary goal, and as the poems' 'single most persistent and deliberate aspect'.[23]

This concern with the formal aspects of her work and the ways Dickinson uses specific linguistic techniques often comes under the heading of 'rhetoric' in many critical enquiries. Her poetic 'style' is seen as a feature of a broader system of rhetoric (Stonum's book includes a chapter on 'The Rhetoric of Stimulus'). The term 'rhetoric' is properly used to describe the variety of figures of speech employed in persuasive writing or speech, as well as the categorization of these figures of speech. Many critics, including Shira Wolosky, have analysed the position and importance of 'rhetoric' in Dickinson's poetry. Stonum identifies three categories of Dickinson's 'rhetoric of stimulus' which can be briefly summarized as an interest in the relation between cause and effect, natural symbolism and a non-singular, literary voice which is developed within her letters.[24] Stonum's categories describe the ways in which her deliberate use of language elicits a series of responses from the reader according to their shared knowledge of the above criteria (on the 'relation of cause to effect' for example), in the manner of rhetorical persuasion. He makes it clear in describing her use of metonymy, for example, that Dickinson's rhetoric, like all rhetoric, demands a great deal of engagement from the reader. Dickinson's use of metonymy conveys an 'extravagantly free responsiveness' to 'extraverbal stimuli'.[25]

Fred D. White (2008) provides a useful précis of the origins of rhetoric in Dickinson's work and of the various influences that Belletristic rhetoric had in New England at the time, as well as a good introduction to the style of her poetry more generally.[26] He refers to texts on rhetoric throughout the first section of the chapter dedicated to style and considers the argument of whether Dickinson is engaging in oratory. Related to performance and oratory tradition, the issue of the presence and use of rhetoric in her work opens a debate about whether Dickinson's poetry was ever intended for an audience or not. Texts which are concerned with the voice or voices in Dickinson's work and correspondence and the nature of audience more directly are Dolores Dyer Lucas's *Emily Dickinson and Riddle* (1969), Brita Lindberg-Seyersted's *The Voice of the Poet: Aspects of Style in the Poetry of Emily Dickinson* (1968) and Marietta Messmer's *A Vice for Voices: Reading Emily Dickinson's Correspondence* (2001). Messmer's study examines Dickinson's letters and considers the literary status conferred upon epistolary prose in texts such as Samuel Philips Newman's *Practical Systems of Rhetoric* (1834).[27] White cites Carlton Lowenberg's bibliography *Emily Dickinson's Textbooks* (1986) to provide examples of American rhetoricians from whom Dickinson would have learned, namely, Newman's *Practical Systems of Rhetoric*; Henry Home, Lord Kames's *Elements of Criticism* (1796; new edition 1849) and Ebenezer Porter's *Rhetorical Reader* (1832; new edition 1841). He utilizes an article by Bryan C. Short to present the argument for the presence of Scottish New Rhetoric in Dickinson.[28] He then cites Clark Griffith, *The Long Shadow: Emily Dickinson's Tragic Poetry* (1964), as an example of a text which argues in the opposite direction, that Dickinson deliberately kept away from forms of rhetoric and devices because they were 'totally at odds with her pattern of ironic thought'.[29] The persistent critical interest in Dickinson's use of rhetoric, however, does not seem to support Griffith's view. Furthermore, White argues that one of the main ways in which we can see Dickinson's poetry as employing rhetoric lies in her uses of irony.

White and other critics of Dickinson's work have thus found it necessary to explain the central features of rhetoric. White describes 'macro' features such as 'definition, example, arrangement, paragraph (or stanza) pattern and progression, and voice'. And then 'micro', stylistic elements, such as 'diction, syntactic structures, punctuation, inflection, sound, rhyme, meter, and rhythm'.[30] One of the main ways in which Dickinson can be seen as rhetorical, White argues, is in her use of irony. He cites Blasing, who argues that Dickinson's irony can best be seen in her subversion of traditional uses of symbolism, by reducing the metaphorical to the literal, in a poem such as 'Those – dying then' (Fr 1581/ M 638), where God's right hand is 'amputated'.[31] This leads White to consider the ways in which Dickinson's use of rhetoric relates to her engagement with orthodox religion, citing many critics who attend to this idea, such as James McIntosh's *Nimble Believing: Dickinson and the Unknown* (2000) and Cynthia Griffin Wolff's *Emily Dickinson* (1986), and on the issue of hymn metre specifically, Martha Winburn England and John Sparrow's *Hymns Unbidden: Donne, Herbert, Blake, Emily Dickinson and the Hymnographers* (1966), and Shira Wolosky's essay, 'Rhetoric or Not: Hymnal Tropes in Emily Dickinson and Isaac Watts' (1988). However, White does not consider in his discussion of rhetoric the place it held within the Dickinson household. The rhetorical figures of speech and linguistic features commonly applied in law to persuade (and specifically those techniques her father most likely learned and used as a lawyer) would have been an obvious influence on her linguistic style and use of rhetorical figures of speech such as metonymy.

One of the main ways in which style relates to meaning in her work is in the way the poems draw upon shared meanings to destabilize them, particularly the notions of religious certainty and trusted logic. Shira Wolosky's article (1988) is perhaps one of the most crucial strands in this area of criticism. Wolosky argues that Dickinson uses rhetorical tropes to destabilize religious certainties and uses many well-chosen examples from poems to describe the ways in which Dickinson plays with metre, rhyme, punctuation, grammar and imagery to echo the eighteenth-century Protestant hymnody of Isaac Watts, whom she read and sang as a child in church and at school, whilst also exercising rhetorical strategies to highlight the flaws in Wattsian attempts at spiritual clarity. For example, Wolosky argues that her challenging use of synecdoche directly confronts the doctrinal relation of whole and part (which figures the relation of God and man) to scrutinize the nature of that relation. She cites poem Fr 379, M 202, with its final line as a clear example, where Dickinson states, 'I wish I were a Hay – ':

> And then to dwell in Sovreign Barns,
> And dream the Days away,
> The Grass so little has to do,
> I wish I were a Hay –
>
> (Fr 379, M 202)

Hay is the collective noun of the individual straws of hay. The definite article 'a' frustrates the relation between the part and whole, thus echoing and mirroring a tension she observes in the God-man relation presented in the protestant hymnody of Watts. Thus, her use of rhetorical devices can be seen as a strategy to generate meanings beyond the immediately obvious. Moreover, where Watts believes wholly in the relation between rhetoric and assertion, between the representation of biblical figures and their ability to convey truths, Dickinson is doubtful and questions their status as such. For Dickinson, the biblical trope exists to structure the text and the experience it describes as much as the text or experience produces the trope. Wolosky points out that Dickinson's poems work in two directions rhetorically, 'from theology to tropes and from tropes to theology'. In this way Dickinson makes explicit the tension in hymnody which Wolosky argues is suppressed. The inconsistency between biblical figures and doctrine and between rhetoric and assertion in Watts's hymns is a tension which is observed and then amplified by Dickinson. Wolosky's article brilliantly shows how Dickinson uses unique phrases, idioms and the distinctive openings found in Watts's hymns to illustrate the point that her interest in his work goes some way beyond the subversion of conventional forms. Her various uses of aspects of his style and form create new meanings within her poetic world and carry with them far-reaching personal and theological implications.[32]

By focusing on Dickinson's critical engagement with religious culture, such work has highlighted the ways in which Dickinson's style expands not only the possibilities for self-expression but also how the divine in nature and in humanity might be reconceptualized. Such critical work is an example of the way in which Dickinson's uses of form, rhythm, metre and her idiosyncratic 'style' can be interpreted and drawn across wider meaning in her poetry as an 'aesthetic' or 'project'. As Christine Ross (2001) explains in her incisive essay 'Uncommon Measures: Emily Dickinson's Subversive Prosody':

> Dickinson's uncommon measures are therefore open to an interpretive process as opposed to standard scansion only. While Dickinson knew and used stanzaic patterns inherited from hymnal and literary tradition, it is unlikely that she left those forms entirely unmarked by her projects, where she so clearly arranged everything else in the poetry to suit her distinctive aesthetic.[33]

As will be discussed in more detail in Chapter 5, Ross details carefully the ways in which Dickinson's use of form can be used as an indicator of her 'subversive' approach to poetry and locates her literary and hymnal influences within the context of their nineteenth-century reception.

Dickinson's poetic style, which includes the use of rhetoric, has also been examined in terms of its production of a new kind of 'grammar'. Cristanne Miller's work on the mechanics of Dickinson's poetry has been groundbreaking, not least because her deft explorations illuminate how the formal construction of Dickinson's work is entirely connected with the meanings her poems generate. In *Emily Dickinson: A Poet's Grammar* (1987) Miller was one of the first critics to seriously examine her poetic style, finding both consistency and intention in her apparent 'abuses' of language, calling it Dickinson's 'grammar'. In this key critical text Miller makes clear for us the ways Dickinson's unique 'grammar' is being used, and how her style and poetic techniques operate. This 'grammar' is explained in terms of compression, disjunction, repetition, syntax and speech. This is followed by an application of these identified areas of her technique in a close reading of four of Dickinson's poems (Fr 477/M 237, Fr 446/M 224, Fr 764/M 354 and Fr 1353/M 713). She examines Dickinson's literary and religious influences as well as the patterns of women's speech to show how these linguistic, literary and biblical styles of expression enter her poetry. She draws upon feminist theories of language and feminist literary theory to demonstrate how Dickinson was creating a new women's poetry. She shows how Dickinson's radical style relates to her own literary identity as a woman poet. It also illustrates how her style influenced modernist poets and how her techniques or her unique 'grammar' can be used as a tool to read other (including modernist) poets. Miller builds upon this earlier identification of Dickinson's 'grammar' in her more recent book *Reading in Time: Emily Dickinson in the Nineteenth Century* (2012). This work is concerned with Dickinson's 'time', both the historical period in which she was most prolific (1860–5) but also the rhythms and forms (the 'time') of her poetry. Here Miller examines formal aspects of Dickinson's style in chapters such as 'Lyric Strains', 'Hymn, the "Ballad Wild," and Free Verse', and 'Spoken Poetry and the Written Poem'. Miller argues that Dickinson's conception of 'music' is extremely fluid and embraces religious and secular versions of lyrical expression. She demonstrates, most notably with detailed examples of syllabic patterns from the poems, how this fluidity is tethered precisely by a compositional foundation of metre, stanzaic time and rhythmic tunes. Miller underscores the flexibility which the metred lines allowed Dickinson, and the 'capacity for thought experiments' through 'set and shifting, competing and interlocking rhythms and tunes'. Such flexibility, she argues, was a:

> function of the cultural context in which hymns, ballads, popular songs, and poems [...] enjoyed wide circulation, using similar forms with great variety.[34]

Dickinson's ability to utilize simple forms such as the hymn or the ballad stanza in a flexible way to generate complex and powerful lyricism is part of her genius. Miller's work consistently shows how crucial style was to the production of meaning(s) in Dickinson's work and the various ways Dickinson utilized aspects of poetic style and through this produced a veneer of simplicity to generate powerful and complex lyrical expression.

Virginia Jackson's influential book, *Dickinson's Misery: A Theory of Lyric Reading* (2005), served to spark the debate on whether Dickinson was writing lyric poems or not. As will be discussed in Chapter 4, Jackson shows how Dickinson's work encompasses many disparate elements, styles and forms which would now be considered outside the realm of the lyric genre and also beyond our estimations of what reading lyric poetry should be like.[35] She argues that 'the framing of Dickinson's writing as a set of lyrics is not only an ongoing collective, historical process, but also a mistake'.[36] Critics then considered what Dickinson's style and forms were if they weren't 'just' lyrical poems. The many niche presentations of the manuscript poems and fragments and the unique ways in which these materials generate meaning became the focus within Dickinson criticism as well as an ongoing debate about whether they should be read primarily as visual or aural presentations. These disputes focus on whether Dickinson was concerned mainly with the way her poems looked on the manuscript page or with how they sounded. Scholars such as Susan Howe have stressed the visuality of Dickinson's manuscripts, paying particular attention to the lineation, variants and punctuation. Howe argues in *The Birth-Mark: Unsettling the Wilderness in American Literary History* (1993) that Dickinson's radicalism and experimentation can be seen in her refusal to conform to the standards of print culture and insists that the manuscript poems (then only available in facsimile) are the only reliable texts. The idiosyncrasies of metre, lineation, rhyme, grammar and punctuation laid bare in the manuscripts allow readers to fully appreciate the scope and extent of her unconventional project.[37] Whilst other critics, such as Cristanne Miller in *Reading in Time*, and Domhnall Mitchell in *Measures of Possibility: Emily Dickinson's Manuscripts* (2005), have prioritized their aural features when considering meaning.[38] Their concern with rhythm, rhyme and metre has caused renewed attention to be given to the sonics of Dickinson's metrical practices. Christina Pugh's essay 'Ghosts of Meter: Dickinson, after Long Silence' (2007) argues that:

> Meter in Dickinson is part and parcel of her achievement of an extremely sophisticated indeterminacy, and it is important to acknowledge the degree to which her work depends upon literary convention in order to reveal the uncanniness that may inhere in convention itself.[39]

Pugh sees Dickinson's use of metre as central to her poetry's uniqueness, and in creating their 'sophisticated indeterminacy'. Dickinson's style of poetry depends upon literary convention and conventional ways of making rhythm and rhyme to register her own 'indeterminate' sounds, and, therefore also, her own experimental ideas.

Meanwhile, recent criticism which draws upon the earlier New Critical mode and formalist approaches to reading is concerned with elements of Dickinson's style in relation to a particular aesthetic within a poem. For example, Helen Vendler's book *Dickinson: Selected Poems and Commentaries* (2010) shows how considered attention to Dickinson's poetry through detailed close reading and scrutiny of individual poems can elicit meaning and illuminate her aesthetic. As a counterpoint to this, it is important to mention here some examples of historical approaches to Dickinson's work in relation to her poetic style. Barton Levi St. Armand's *Emily Dickinson and Her Culture: The Soul's Society* (1984) is a landmark study which places Dickinson's poems on death, the afterlife, romance, art and nature within their specific nineteenth-century cultural contexts. St. Armand's study shows the ways in which Dickinson's style reflects many aspects of her own culture at a time when there was a critical tendency to highlight both her uniqueness and her apparent social dislocation. The connections St. Armand makes between aesthetics in Dickinson's work and elements of American and Victorian popular culture such as the Victorian 'way of death' and the 'folk forms' of the American Grotesque are insightful, showing how Dickinson was alert to these popular forms and preoccupations and how they were incorporated into her own aesthetics. His chapter on the inheritance of John Ruskin and Victorian aesthetics in Dickinson's poems on landscape shows their influence on her poetic style as well as her justification for poetic perception of the divine, something St. Armand argues comes directly out of John Ruskin's *Modern Painters* (1843–60).[40] It is clear to see how St. Armand's important and wide-reaching work paved the way for critics interested in Dickinson and visual art, such as Judith Farr. Farr's exceptional study of the relationship between nineteenth-century visual art and its impact on Dickinson's work, *The Passion of Emily Dickinson* (1992), is extremely useful when considering her style and how it relates to meaning in the poems.[41] This book is also especially important to those seeking to bring further background and context to some of the twentieth-century critical reception of Dickinson as being a precursor to Modernist and Imagist poetics and the turn to the visual and material more generally applied in Dickinson criticism. Farr skilfully revisits poems such as 'Just so – Christ – Raps' (Fr 263/M 130) considering the huge popularity of British Pre-Raphaelite paintings such as Holman Hunt's 'The Light of the World' (1853) to show how specific imagery and treatment of biblical and literary subjects made their way into her work via the art she admired. She makes a convincing case for a close connection between Dickinson's style and the methods employed by contemporary nineteenth-century artists. Dickinson's uses of 'light' as a motif and her scrutiny of nature to capture moments of reality and 'eternity' in time can be compared with the methods of the Luminist and Hudson River Schools of painters operating in New England in the mid-nineteenth century as well as the British and American devotees of the Pre-Raphaelite movement she knew about. Farr rightly argues that many of the poems in the Dickinson canon are concerned with 'anatomizing the nature of light'. American so-called 'Pre-Raphaelites' such as William Stillman, John Henry Hill, William Trost Richards and Thomas Farrer are mentioned alongside British Pre-Raphaelites William Holman Hunt and Dante Gabriel Rossetti and are described as following the same 'strict, scientific attention to the appearance of objects' as their British counterparts. Luminists and Hudson River painters, largely painters of landscapes and followers of Constable and his method of 'skying' – studying the sky as the primary source of light – are also referred to as being influential to Dickinson's work such as Thomas Cole, Frederic Edwin Church, Albert Bierstadt, Jasper Cropsey and Martin Johnson Heade. Farr cites the Pre-Raphaelite exhibition in Boston in 1857 organized by Dante Gabriel Rossetti as generating much of the interest in the British Pre-Raphaelite painters in New England at the time and argues that Dickinson probably saw reproductions of the paintings in magazine reviews of the exhibition.[42] She would have read about art theories and movements in magazines her family subscribed to and most likely read John Ruskin's *Modern Painters*, which appeared in America in 1847.[43] Thomas Cole's series of paintings entitled 'The Voyage of Life' were extremely popular and provided a moral trajectory for New England society to meditate upon. Farr's work illustrates how Dickinson was far more interested in art in ways we had previously not understood or accurately estimated. She provides fascinating detail from letters and poems to provide the evidence of Dickinson's avid interest in the visual arts, such as her signing a letter (perhaps not without irony) 'Cole' – the surname of the prominent American Luminist landscape painter and writer with whom Dickinson would have been familiar.[44]

Farr's study makes a concrete connection between style and meaning in Dickinson's poetry. She shows how Dickinson's style most vividly animates her poetic meanings by analysis of individual poems and their references to art and the way they enact the modes of visual art. Farr refers to Dickinson's treatment of 'light' as a theme in her poems as well as her frequent references to art and to painting specifically. ('I would not paint a picture' (Fr 348/M 184) is a choice example.) Another way in which Farr shows how style and meaning are connected in Dickinson's work is by drawing upon her letters and what we know of her biography to gain an understanding of Dickinson's sense of herself as a poet and of her own poetic production. Crucially, Farr argues against David Porter's claim in *Dickinson: The Modern Idiom* (1981) that Dickinson was without a project, and states simply that Dickinson's 'poetic aimlessness' is part of her project. She foregrounds Dickinson's interest in art by reminding us of her declared preferences for and reading of artists-poets-critics Ruskin and William Blake. Quoting from her letters, in which Dickinson echoes Blake, Farr argues that Dickinson's project was to:

> depict 'Eternity in Time' (L 3. 689). To carry out this design she became herself a kind of painter, according to the Ruskinian traditions of her day. She dramatized the beautiful, the sublime, and sometimes the picturesque, eternizing the 'wayward Light' of immortality as it surrounded and clarified the forms she saw.
>
> (L 2.840)[45]

Farr then goes on to argue that:

> Emily Dickinson's passion for exactitude in language was matched by the joyful delight with which she drew pictures of objects or scenes. She evidently sought to reveal the secret inner nature of the thing observed. This was the special mission of the still life painter. It is in her careful creation of a world of birds, beasts, flowers, and hills that her technique most resembles that of the American Pre-Raphaelites.[46]

Another important aspect of Farr's book is the way in which she takes the various critical 'narratives' of 'master' and of 'sue' (the nameless correspondent of some of her letters and Susan Dickinson) to show how these relationships were important to Dickinson in terms of her development as an artist-poet, expanding the debate to reorient it towards her intellectual and artistic networks. Farr's work shows us how Dickinson's style of poetry was informed by theories of art and the paintings she saw and how that affected her observations of nature and objects. Like the painters she admired, her intense linguistic scrutiny of what she saw, thought and felt produced an extraordinary type of poetry which animates the 'secret inner nature' of the things she scrutinized. In this way, she provides a more thorough understanding of the relationship between Dickinson's style, her engagement with both nature and art, and the meanings with which her poems wrestle.

The tradition of Dickinson as a nature poet has led to a wealth of ecocritical readings of her work in recent years, from the early 2000s to the present. These readings view Dickinson's poetry in relation to such topics as ecology, environmentalism, the Anthropocene and the representation of the non-human. Much ecocriticism responds to the various contextual approaches to Dickinson's work and analyses her engagement with nature to assess her views on the political, social, cultural and religious cultures of her day. However, much of it also maintains a specific trajectory towards ecology as much as culture, where nature can be seen as having a variety of cultures within itself. In 2017 Paul Crumbley edited a special issue of the journal *ESQ: A Journal of Nineteenth-Century American Literature and Culture* entitled 'Dickinson's Environments', which brought together essays showcasing the existing tensions within ecocritical readings of Dickinson.[47] While some critics focus on Dickinson's engagement with nature to illuminate the ways in which she was historically and culturally engaged, other ecocritical readings of Dickinson seek to implement perspectives heavily influenced by environmental science and ethics. Initially, ecocritical readers of Dickinson reacted against the idea of nature being cast as a vehicle for thought, where human perception and an abstract notion of the sublime were privileged over non-human material reality.⁴⁸ Later ecocritical and environmental readings of Dickinson have emphasized the ways in which her engagements with nature do not deny the realities of a non-human, biological world or relegate them to a lesser significance within the poem's meanings.⁴⁹ For example, critics have emphasized the presence of the non-human in Dickinson's work and the ways in which nature and its correlative symbolism wrestle within a poem. Cody Marrs's essay 'Dickinson in the Anthropocene' (2017) poses the question as to whether we can read Dickinson as a poet of the Anthropocene.⁵⁰ Citing a definition of the Anthropocene as beginning with the Industrial Revolution and the restructuring of human society caused by both the extraction and use of fossil fuels, Marrs then discusses the ways in which Dickinson's work anticipates our own culture's struggle with an estrangement from nature. He argues that Dickinson's poems both 'locate *and* abstract natural scenes, imparting a sense of elusive rootedness that prefigures twenty-first-century reckonings with our estrangement from the once-familiar earth'.⁵¹ This simultaneous othering and recognizing of nature as its own culture and system is indicative of what Marrs terms Dickinson's 'negative ecology'. This can most readily be seen in her depictions of 'nature's epistemological foreignness' and in her poems of the Civil War which delineate an 'ecological upheaval', arguing that:

> Across these poems Dickinson cultivates a *negative ecology*, an ethic of care that proceeds from, rather than contests, nature's otherness.⁵²

In Marrs's view, Dickinson's depictions of nature and the style in which she represents it can be read as a negative ecology positing an 'ethic of care'. This, paradoxically, comes out of the nineteenth-century tendency to view nature as other. Dickinson's representational mode encompasses both the 'rootedness' of nature and its cycles, as well as its 'elusiveness'. For example, Marrs discusses poem Fr 465/M 233 as a way of reading Dickinson framing the Civil War as an ecological event, where the destruction of human bodies and the landscape are conjoined in her description of autumn's bloody hues:

> An Artery – opon the Hill –
> A Vein – along the Road –
>
> Great Globules – in the Alleys –
>
> (Fr 465, M 233)

Here Dickinson uses human biological terms to describe the geographical features of the autumnal landscape, thus connecting humanity and nature in a dramatically visual and visceral way. Cody suggests that this description of autumn might be less metaphorical than we first interpret it to be, where the violence of war that it also suggests impacts the landscape as much as it would a human in battle. The landscape and ecological systems are also ruptured with humanity's effects upon it. In Marrs's view, the style of Dickinson's depictions of nature can be seen as constructing a 'negative ecology' which asserts a 'perspective of care rooted in difference'.[53] By reading the style of Dickinson's poems of the Civil War through this negative ecology, Marrs shows how Dickinson frames the war as an ecological event as much as a moment in human history.

Finally, Helen Vendler interrogates Dickinson's 'style' and her 'art' by examining the processes of thinking in her book *Poets Thinking: Pope, Whitman, Dickinson, Yeats* (2004), where the 'style of thinking' of each of the four poets is assessed. Instead of discussing well-worn 'themes' in Dickinson's work, Vendler's chapter 'Emily Dickinson Thinking: Rearranging Seriality' begins by asserting Dickinson as the go-to poet for evidence of thinking in poetry and that 'vocabularies have been invented' by critics to describe her 'style of thinking'.[54] For example critics use terms such as 'cryptic ellipses', 'compression', 'enigmatic subjects', 'absent centres' and its 'abstraction' when describing her style. However, Vendler's concern in this book is with Dickinson's 'invention of poetic temporal structures that mimic the structure of life as she at any moment conceives it' and to scrutinize 'her thinking as she invents ways to plot temporality'. It is by these poetic temporal structures she argues that Dickinson 'channels our reactions, stylizes our pace to hers, and constructs our thinking after her own'. Arguing that Dickinson's 'larger ideas' or 'themes' are not in fact that unusual or obscure, Vendler asserts that it is Dickinson's rearrangement of seriality, of temporal structures, which best helps us to identify her particular style of thinking.[55] The formal aspects of her style such as her idiosyncratic uses of grammar, syntax and metaphor are indicators of her style of thinking, but Vendler argues that in order to 'understand her imaginative thinking' we should look to her treatment of '"normal" temporal organization'. Vendler then sets out to plot Dickinson's temporal map. Her early and 'natural' style of thinking tends towards presenting the reader with a complete picture, aiming at a 'temporal exhaustiveness' where poems have a definite beginning and end and unscroll a 'ribbon at a time'. Vendler refers to this sequential 'unscrolling' as a series of '*and then's*'. Early poems aspire 'to leave no gaps in event or perception before arriving at the end of the sequence' and follow what Vendler terms a 'chromatic' experience, in that the poems attempt to chart each event as it happens, to 'sound' each 'note' in sequence, to appear 'merely transcriptive'.[56] The construction of the poem itself and the designation of the poem's moments in time are obscured in these early poems. This earlier mode is brilliantly contrasted with Vendler's examination of a later poem (Fr 588/M 268; 1863) to show how loss of control over sequence, and ultimately of how the sequence will end, is played out with terrifying consequences in Dickinson's later poems. The poem begins:

> The Heart asks Pleasure – first –
> And then – excuse from Pain –
>
> (Fr 588, M 268)

However, there is no 'peaceful slot-filling seriality' in this poem as Dickinson had been able to achieve in earlier poems. The heart asks only for the 'privilege' of death in the poem's final line. As Vendler argues, in later Dickinson poems such as this Fate has taken over and applied its own plot and 'thought has lost not only existential mastery of sequence but also cognitive dominion over sense perception'. Instead of 'sequential comprehensiveness' where one perception is allocated its own temporal slot and each successive slot is noted and filled, the later poems convey a crowding of perceptions which cannot be registered, accounted for, and therefore controlled in any conscious way, leading to 'ignorance' and a 'confusing multiplicity'.[57]

Vendler sees Dickinson's thought as 'chromaticism', as a way of thinking which seeks always to organize perception into a chromatic serial, logical set of impressions: 'A seriality without gaps remains forever, I believe, the first resort of her mind when she begins to think.' She argues that the 'great crisis' in Dickinson's work appears when her 'serial chromaticism' breaks down and 'encounters unavoidable fissure, fracture, rupture, or abyss' and provides examples of later poems where sequence is referred to specifically and/or alluded to (Fr 867/M 423, Fr 340/M 179) to demonstrate sequence unravelling in tandem with thought itself.[58] 'I felt a Funeral, in my Brain' exemplifies this synchronicity:

> I felt a Funeral, in my Brain,
> And Mourners to and fro
> Kept treading – treading – till it seemed
> That Sense was breaking through –
>
> (Fr 340. M 179)

The repetition of 'treading' brilliantly conveys the idea of a sequence (or ceremony, as 'Funeral' denotes) which may in this instance be the passing of time as much as the persistence of thought and memory. The effect of the 'treading' might be that 'Sense' may or may not emerge. As the poem progresses, the sequence of the ceremony unravels alongside the thought of the speaker, where a 'Plank in Reason, broke'. After tracing the destabilized linear sequencing of her earlier poems, Vendler shows how Dickinson's later poems display instead a circularity, where the '*and thens*' are replaced with '*ors*' which carry with them a breakdown in meaning. Poems such as 'After great pain' (Fr 372/M 198) display such uncertain '*ors*', where 'Chromatic linear advance has vanished in favour of repetitive circling' and Dickinson displays her knowledge of the difference between such 'chromatic *advance* (marked by the *and then* of true sequence) and the faux-chromatic *repetition* of aftermath'.[59] Vendler continues to trace the breakdown of sequence to a 'nonsequential vibration' exemplified by the 'giggling' brain which she finds in Fr 423/M 168:

> My Brain – begun to laugh –
> I mumbled – like a fool –
> And tho' 'tis Years ago – that Day –
> My Brain keeps giggling – still.
>
> (Fr 423, M 168)

Here the brain is out of sequence, still reeling from an experience which is chronologically 'years ago' but at the same time still present within the vibration. She then goes on to argue that Dickinson finds it hard to relinquish sequence even in the knowledge that it has broken down, asserting that poem Fr 1550/M 631 (a late poem which imagines the dead body resurrected back into life with a creation sequence) shows 'what a strong hold chromatic sequence retained on Dickinson's imagination; she would rather run sequence backward in fantasy than lose it altogether'. When death ultimately makes sequence meaningless in Dickinson's work what does she do with it? Vendler's answer is to focus on Dickinson's use of 'the invariant present tense' which, she argues, Dickinson turns to after she has 'given up on seriality'. There are many present tenses in Dickinson to distinguish between, such as the present tense of stasis and routine (of '*is*' and '*has*') to be found in poems such as 'After great pain' (Fr 372/M 198) and 'The Bone that has no Marrow' (Fr 1218/M 505). However, Vendler argues that it is the 'philosophical present tense (an "eternal" present, and therefore not a true tense) appearing in axiom and definition' which is 'dearer to Dickinson's thinking'.[60] This philosophical mode is wedded to abstractions and is also 'tenseless'. Having established the importance of chromatic tensed feeling to Dickinson, Vendler now explains the ways in which the tenseless, philosophical mode is, although different, still related to the chromatic sequencing of the earlier poems. To do this she compares two poems, one tensed, one untensed, concerned with the same metaphor of eye blindness; the tensed poem 'Before I got my eye put out' (Fr 336/M 177) and the philosophical untensed poem 'Renunciation – is a piercing Virtue' (Fr 782/M 384). Vendler shows how the former poem is 'rewritten' in the latter, where each of the tensed moments of the first are merged into a 'single definitional "now" and "here"' in the second, where Dickinson 'turns the events into gerunds ("The letting go/A Presence," "The putting out of Eyes," "the Choosing")'.[61] Through her explorations of Dickinson's 'thinking' in terms of a 'chromatic seriality' and the multiple mutations of it Vendler shows us how the different intellectual models she uses illuminates the 'style' and 'art' of her poetry:

> by constructing so many versions, evasions, and revisions of the seriality that was her original defense against anxiety, Dickinson makes us conscious of the extent to which examining a poet's intellectual models of experience is indispensable to the understanding of art.[62]

Vendler's chapter on Dickinson is a powerful examination of those models of experience and also offers a critique of the search for definitions of 'style' in Dickinson's work. Jed Deppman has done further work on the intellectual models and areas of philosophy which have affinities with Dickinson's unfinished or open-ended modes of representation and modes of thinking in *Trying to Think with Emily Dickinson* (2008) and also in the co-edited volume *Dickinson and Philosophy* (2013). Deppman's work examines Dickinson's intellectual culture, exploring areas of philosophy, science, religion as well as literature to show how Dickinson's 'conversational' and 'thinking in progress' poetic style enables her to question the authoritative discourses of her time.[63]

Such critical enquiries into the style of Dickinson's poetry and the forms she chose to use show us how we cannot privilege the search for meaning over the search for modes of meaning in Dickinson's work. To strive to arrive at 'a particular' meaning would be to some extent to miss the point. Enquiring into the mechanics of Dickinson's poetry allows us to escape the traps her early editors fell into. Themes and subjects are elusive and changing across her vast body of work, as one would expect. Critics agree and disagree over their content and meaning. However, the mode in which Dickinson represents life and her own perception of it is rigorously controlled by the poet herself as the critics discussed in this chapter have shown. Moreover, some critics such as Stonum have argued that it is the poems' mode of representation itself, the 'aggressively idiosyncratic' poetry she produced, which engages the reader to consider the 'extraverbal stimuli' which is perhaps their main identifiable 'meaning'.[64] So form becomes something which is crucial to the 'meaning' of the Dickinson oeuvre. Critical emphasis on Dickinson's style shows the reader in different ways the shape of her idiosyncrasies. It is by probing these 'aggressive' idiosyncrasies that critics have revealed the wealth and breadth of Dickinson's references and of her deep cultural engagement.

Notes

1. Jen Bervin and Marta L. Werner, *The Gorgeous Nothings: The Envelope Poems of Emily Dickinson* (New York: New Directions, 2013) See also: *The Manuscript Books of Emily Dickinson: A Facsimile Edition*, ed. by R. W. Franklin (Cambridge, MA: The Belknap Press, 1981). edickinson.org is the open-access website for the Emily Dickinson archive which is an ongoing collaborative project.
2. David Porter, 'Searching for Dickinson's Themes', in *The Emily Dickinson Handbook*, ed. by Gudrun Grabher, Roland Hagenbuchle and Cristanne Miller, pp. 183–96.
3. Robert Weisbuch, 'Prisming Dickinson; or, Gathering Paradise by Letting Go', in *The Emily Dickinson Handbook*, ed. by Grabher, Hagenbuchle and Miller, pp. 197–223 (p. 197).
4. Helen Vendler, *Poets Thinking: Pope, Whitman, Dickinson, Yeats* (Cambridge, MA: Harvard University Press, 2004), p. 64.
5. Synecdoche is a special kind of metonymy in which the part-whole substitution works in both directions – part is substituted for whole or whole is substituted for a part. Something can be alluded to by referring to a part or constituent of a whole, for example, 'hands' for manual labourers *or* by referring to a whole, of which it is a part, for example, 'the law' for a police officer. Metonymy simply replaces the name of one thing with the name of something else strongly associated with it, for example, 'the press' for journalism. These examples are taken from Chris Baldick, *The Concise Oxford Dictionary of Literary Terms* (Oxford: Oxford University Press, 1990), p. 221 and p. 135.
6. This example of Dickinson's use of synecdoche is used by Shira Wolosky in 'Rhetoric or Not: Hymnal Tropes in Emily Dickinson and Isaac Watts', *The New England Quarterly*, 61.2 (1988), 214–32.
7. David Porter, 'Searching for Dickinson's Themes', p. 184.
8. See also Jeanetta Boswell, *Emily Dickinson: A Bibliography of Secondary Sources, with Selective Annotations, 1890 through 1987* (Jefferson: McFarland, 1989) and Anna Mary Wells, 'Early Criticism of Emily Dickinson', *American Literature*, 1.3 (1929), 243–59. For an excellent survey of texts collating and commenting on early criticism of Dickinson's work, see Marietta Messmer, 'Dickinson's Critical Reception', in *The Emily Dickinson Handbook*, ed. by Grabher, Hagenbuchle and Miller, pp. 299–322.

9   Shira Wolosky, 'Rhetoric or Not: Hymnal Tropes in Emily Dickinson and Isaac Watts', in Cristanne Miller, *Emily Dickinson: A Poet's Grammar* (Cambridge, MA: Harvard University Press, 1987) and *Reading in Time: Emily Dickinson in the Nineteenth Century* (Massachusetts: University of Massachusetts Press, 2012).

10 Andrew Lang, 'An American Sappho', *London Daily News*, 3 October 1891, pp. 4–5. Reproduced in Willis J. Buckingham, *Emily Dickinson's Reception in the 1890s: A Documentary History* (Pittsburgh: University of Pittsburgh Press, 1989), pp. 201–4 (p. 204).

11 Franklin Benjamin Sanborn, 'The Breakfast Table', *Boston Daily Advertiser*, 27 October 1891. In Buckingham, *Emily Dickinson's Reception in the 1890s*, pp. 219–20 (p. 220).

12 See Marietta Messmer, 'Reviewer's Despair: The Politics of Dickinson's Critical Reception during the 1890s', *Amerikastudien/American Studies*, 45.3 (2000), 373–86 (p. 373).

13 Martha Hale Shackford, 'The Poetry of Emily Dickinson', *Atlantic Monthly*, CXI, January 1913, pp. 93–7. This review is reproduced in *The Recognition of Emily Dickinson: Selected Criticism since 1890*, ed. by Caesar R. Blake and Carlton F. Wells (Ann Arbor: The University of Michigan Press, 1964), pp. 79–88 (p. 79, p. 81 and p. 88). For details of early reviewers, see also *Emily Dickinson: An Annotated Bibliography*, ed. by Willis J. Buckingham (Bloomington and London: Indiana University Press, 1970), pp. 13–28.

14 Martha Hale Shackford, 'The Poetry of Emily Dickinson', in Blake and Wells, pp. 93–7.

15 Blake and Wells, p. 51.

16 Francis H. Stoddard, 'Technique in Emily Dickinson's Poems', *The Critic*, XX.9 (1892), Blake and Wells, p. 52.

17 Blake and Wells, p. 52.

18 Blake and Wells, p. 53.

19 David Porter, *Dickinson: The Modern Idiom* (Cambridge, MA: Harvard University Press, 1966).

20 Patricia Chaudron, 'From Local Colour to Modernist Poet: Revisiting Emily Dickinson's Critics in the 1890s', *The Emily Dickinson Journal*, 25.1 (2016), 1–28.

21 Elizabeth Shepley Sergeant, 'An Early Imagist', *The New Republic*, IV, 14 August 1915. In Blake and Wells, pp. 88–93 (p. 88).

22 Blake and Wells, pp. 89–93.

23 Gary Lee Stonum, *The Dickinson Sublime* (Madison: The University of Wisconsin Press, 1990), p. 22.

24 Stonum, *The Dickinson Sublime*, p. 81.

25 Stonum, p. 90.

26 Fred D. White, *Approaching Emily Dickinson: Critical Currents and Crosscurrents since 1960* (Rochester, N.Y: Camden House, 2008), pp. 12–39.

27 Marietta Messmer, *A Vice for Voices: Reading Emily Dickinson's Correspondence* (Amherst: University of Massachusetts Press, 2001), pp. 27–8.
28 Bryan C. Short, 'Emily Dickinson and the Scottish New Rhetoric', *The Emily Dickinson Journal*, 5.2 (1996), 261–6.
29 White, *Approaching Emily Dickinson*, p. 14, cites Clark Griffith, *The Long Shadow: Emily Dickinson's Tragic Poetry* (New Jersey: Princeton University Press, 1964), p. 62.
30 White, p. 14.
31 White, pp. 16–17, cites Mutlu Konuk Blasing, *American Poetry: The Rhetoric of Its Forms* (New Haven and London: Yale University Press, 1987).
32 Wolosky, 'Rhetoric or Not', pp. 215–17.
33 Christine Ross, 'Uncommon Measures: Emily Dickinson's Subversive Prosody', *The Emily Dickinson Journal*, 10.1 (2001), 70–98 (p. 92).
34 Miller, *Reading In Time*, p. 81.
35 Virginia Jackson, *Dickinson's Misery: A Theory of Lyric Reading* (Princeton: Princeton University Press, 2005), p. 1 and p. 6. See Chapter 4's discussion on historicizing Dickinson versus the 'lone genius' view of her creative engagement and practices.
36 Jackson, *Dickinson's Misery*, p. 235.
37 Susan Howe, *The Birth-Mark: Unsettling the Wilderness in American Literary History* (Hanover: Wesleyan University Press, 1993).
38 Domhnall Mitchell, *Measures of Possibility: Emily Dickinson's Manuscripts* (Amherst: University of Massachusetts Press, 2005). For discussion of rhythm, rhyme and metre in the manuscripts, see Chapters 5 and 6, pp. 191–264.
39 Christina Pugh, 'Ghosts of Meter: Dickinson, after Long Silence', *The Emily Dickinson Journal*, 16. 2 (2007), 1–24 (pp. 19–20).
40 Barton Levi St. Armand, *Emily Dickinson and Her Culture: The Soul's Society* (Cambridge: Cambridge University Press, 1984), pp. 219–58 (p. 231).
41 Judith Farr, *The Passion of Emily Dickinson* (Cambridge, MA: Harvard University Press, 1992).
42 Farr, *The Passion of Emily Dickinson*, pp. 262–7.
43 Farr, p. 369, n. 5. Farr notes that *Modern Painters* was reviewed in the *Atlantic Monthly* and again by *The Crayon* in 1860.
44 Farr, p. 248.
45 Farr, pp. 246–7.
46 Farr, p. 271.
47 Paul Crumbley, ed., 'Dickinson's Environments', *ESQ: A Journal of Nineteenth-Century American Literature and Culture*, 63.2 (2017), 198–358.
48 See: Rebecca Patterson, *Emily Dickinson's Imagery* (Amherst: University of Massachusetts Press, 1979) and Joanne Feit Diehl, *Dickinson and the Romantic Imagination* (Princeton: Princeton University Press, 1981).

49 See: Robert Kern, 'Birds of a Feather: Emily Dickinson, Alberto Manguel, and the Nature Poet's Dilemma', *Interdisciplinary Studies in Literature and Environment*, 16.2 (2009), 327–42; and Aaron Shackelford, 'Dickinson's Animals and Anthropomorphism', *Emily Dickinson Journal*, 19.2 (2010), 47–66.

50 Cody Marrs, 'Dickinson in the Anthropocene', *ESQ: A Journal of Nineteenth-Century American Literature and Culture*, 63.2 (2017), 201–25.

51 Marrs, 'Dickinson in the Anthropocene', p. 203.

52 Marrs, p. 203.

53 Marrs, p. 218.

54 It is useful to look at this book when discussing 'style'; however, Vendler's *Dickinson: Selected Poems and Commentaries* (Cambridge, MA: Harvard University Press, 2010) is an extremely useful collection of essays for further detailed readings of Dickinson's poems within Vendler's New Critical mode.

55 Vendler, *Poets Thinking*, pp. 64–91 (p. 64).

56 Vendler, pp. 65–7.

57 Vendler, p. 68.

58 Vendler, pp. 70–1.

59 Vendler, p. 75.

60 Vendler, pp. 77–8.

61 Vendler, p. 81.

62 Vendler, p. 91.

63 See: Jed Deppman, *Trying to Think with Emily Dickinson* (Amherst: University of Massachusetts Press, 2008) and Jed Deppman, Marianne Noble and Gary Lee Stonum, eds, *Dickinson and Philosophy* (Cambridge: Cambridge University Press, 2013).

64 Stonum, *The Dickinson Sublime*, p. 90.

3

The female tradition, gender and sexuality

3.1 The female tradition	68
3.2 Writing the body	73
3.3 Queering Dickinson	82

This chapter examines the central concerns of the largely feminist perspectives which dominated twentieth-century critical writing on Dickinson. Much contemporary criticism now assumes as a given the careful arguments painstakingly carved out by feminist critics during this important and hugely creative era for the reception of Dickinson. This era, and area of feminist critical reception, has rightly been labelled as a 'revolution' in Dickinson studies.[1] The highly politicized readings of the 1970s–90s have served to inform the relatively recent historical turn in Dickinson criticism, and issues of gender, sexuality and those surrounding the notion of a female tradition are now generally well assimilated. It took a long time to get to this point. What is striking about the essays and book-length arguments about gender, sexuality and/or the female tradition in relation to Dickinson's poetry from this period is how creative the critics were prepared to be. This wave of critical imagination re-envisioned a future for Dickinson scholars, and the shaping force of Dickinson's poetry appeared to be directing the critical trajectory. The critical landscape we have now inherited is one where such ideas are fundamental to our understanding of how to approach her work. Moreover, in writing about what they saw in Dickinson's poems, feminist scholars brought to bear a great number of disciplines from within the Academy, including some modern-day equivalents of those which Dickinson herself had employed; drawing from literature and history, grammar, philology, linguistics, music, philosophy, psychoanalysis, science, religious studies, art history, law and geography, to name a few. This creative surge had the effect of reshaping not only the way we read Dickinson but also the way we may read and understand literature through the lens of more comprehensively intellectual and politically enlightened perspectives.

There has been so much criticism written on the work of Dickinson from an explicitly feminist perspective throughout the various decades that it would be impossible to attend to each one in detail here. The first feminist critics of Dickinson's work established a strong foundation upon which to build an area of enquiry and created a critical trajectory which made it possible to ask politically inflected questions about the poet and her work. Early-twentieth-century feminist criticism explored the notion of a female tradition and its features by examining the work of women writers, mostly, but not exclusively, from the nineteenth and early twentieth centuries, and included Dickinson within these broader studies. It is perhaps testament to the richness of Dickinson's work that feminist critics found much to be explored in relation to issues such as social constructions of gender, and the intersection between identity, bodies and politics. Therefore, a handful of some of the oft-cited early feminist critics of the 1970s and 1980s and their respective works (mostly books, with the exception of Rich) should not go unmentioned here, including Suzanne Juhasz's *Naked and Fiery Forms: Modern American Poetry by Women, A New Tradition* (1976) and her edited collection *Feminist Critics Read Emily Dickinson* (1983); Adrienne Rich's 'Vesuvius at Home: The Power of Emily Dickinson' (1976); Sandra M. Gilbert and Susan Gubar's *The Madwoman in the Attic: The Woman Writer and the Nineteenth-Century Literary Imagination* (1979); Margaret Homans's *Women Writers and Poetic Identity* (1980); Cheryl Walker's *The Nightingale's Burden: Women Poets and American Culture before 1900* (1982); Wendy Martin's *An American Triptych: Anne Bradstreet, Emily Dickinson and Adrienne Rich* (1984) and Vivian Pollak's *Dickinson: The Anxiety of Gender* (1984). By including Dickinson in their multi-author studies, these late-twentieth-century feminist critical texts helped to establish Dickinson's canonicity as well as underscore the continuum of a female tradition. For further reading on Emily Dickinson and feminist criticism which cannot be covered in detail here, see the Bibliography.

The objective of this chapter is to approach the area thematically and to look at the key texts which have forged critical paths in these three, interrelated areas: the female tradition, representations of the body in Dickinson's poetry and queering Dickinson. These three areas are of course not the only areas of interest for readers of Dickinson who are concerned with feminist and/or LGBTQ+ perspectives, for example, but they are indicative of some of the central and ongoing foci. To this end, the first section will summarize the arguments of critical texts which explore Dickinson as being part of a literary tradition; first, in her reading of and responses to a masculine tradition, such as Benjamin Lease *Emily Dickinson's Reading of Men and Books* (1990), and then in her proximity to other women poets, both contemporary and more recent. Texts such as Cheryl Walker's *The Nightingale's Burden: Women Poets and American Culture Before 1900* (1982), Joanne Dobson's *Dickinson and the Strategies of Reticence* (1989), Sharon Leder and Andrea Abbott's *The Language of Exclusion: The Poetry of Emily Dickinson and Christina Rossetti* (1987) and Elizabeth Petrino's *Emily Dickinson and Her Contemporaries: Women's Verse in America 1820–1855* (1998) helped to establish Dickinson within a tradition of nineteenth-century women poets. The second wave of feminist criticism is explored in texts such as Sabine Sielke's *Fashioning the Female Subject: The Intertextual Networking of Dickinson, Moore and Rich* (1997) and in those texts which, in addition to utilizing psychoanalytic theories of the body (in the case of Sielke, as Section 2 in this chapter explores), seek to align Dickinson with other female writers, thus underscoring a continuum of the female tradition in writing. The second section in this chapter will examine critics who utilize psychoanalytic theory and concepts of the pre-oedipal semiotic, binary opposition and 'difference', and place emphasis on the body as a focus for critical debate on Dickinson, such as Paula Bennett's *Emily Dickinson: Woman Poet* (1990), Helen Shoobridge's '"Reverence for Each Other Being the Sweet Aim:" Dickinson Face to face with the Masculine' (2000), as well as Sielke (1997), to show how Dickinson's poetry can be seen as a radical articulation of the disruptive and subversive feminine body. The third section will then look at how the approach of feminist critics such as Bennett led to queering Dickinson, and how this opened a critical space for subsequent scholarship on gender fluid, non-binary and trans readings of Dickinson. It will provide an analysis of the critical 'queering' of Dickinson, in texts such as Bennett's, which centralizes her homoeroticism, and Mary E. Galvin's *Queer Poetics: Five Modernist Women Writers* (1999) which employs queer theory and locates Dickinson within a tradition of women writers, by focusing on her 'trickster' lesbian identity. It will also discuss texts which focus upon reading lesbian identity through Dickinson's letters and biography, such as Martha Nell Smith's key critical interventions on Dickinson and her 'textual and sexual priorities', as well as her important collaboration with Ellen Louise Hart in '*Open Me Carefully': Emily Dickinson's Intimate Letters to Susan Huntington Dickinson* (1998), which allowed readers to see Dickinson's intimate letters to Sue for themselves.[2] Lena Koski's exploration of the issues surrounding the identification of lesbian expression in Dickinson's work – 'Sexual Metaphors in Emily Dickinson's Letters to Susan Gilbert' (1996) – will also be discussed. Dickinson's increasing significance to LGBTQ+ readers and critics will be considered and the possibilities for self and identity to be found in gender fluid, non-binary and trans readings of Dickinson will be examined in texts such as Maggie Glover's essay 'I'm Ceded: Sexual, Social and Gender Role Rebellion in the Poems of Emily Dickinson' (2017) and Joy Ladin's book *Soldering the Abyss: Emily Dickinson and Modern American Poetry* (2010) and essay 'Supposed Persons: Emily Dickinson and "I"' (2013), respectively. The new paradigm for queer theory which is presented in Michael D. Snediker's *Queer Optimism: Lyric Personhood and Other Felicitous Persuasions* (2010) will also be considered. Landmark critical and archival interventions such as these have helped to amplify Dickinson's LGBTQ+ icon status within American popular culture as much as they have transformed the shape of Dickinson studies, and this is explored in the discussion of Marianne Noble's essay 'Emily Dickinson in the Twenty-First Century' (2021).

3.1 The female tradition

Many feminist critics of Dickinson read her work within the context of a female literary tradition and build upon the efforts of earlier scholars to uncover texts by women which have been lost and uncommented upon by literary critics. Indeed, one of the main projects of feminist criticism is to highlight, and in many instances unearth, a female tradition which has hitherto been overlooked and therefore unrecorded. Feminist critics of Dickinson have sought to highlight connections between Dickinson's work and that of other women writers, both contemporary and, in the case of Sabine Sielke, for example, with those from another era. Paula Bernat Bennett's work, namely, 'Emily Dickinson and Her American Women Poet Peers' (2002), is instructive in this area.[3] The task feminist critics of literature are faced with, in attempting not only to uncover a traceable female tradition in writing but also to uphold, define and defend a tradition which is itself made up of differences, is not without difficulty. Mary Loeffelholz makes this cautionary point very well in her book *Dickinson and the Boundaries of Feminist Theory* (1991), in which she traces the relationship between feminist criticism and psychoanalysis in readings of Dickinson alongside key exponents from Romantic and Transcendental tradition, such as Wordsworth and Emerson. She argues that in attempting to identify and consolidate a female tradition in writing, feminist critics must also recognize that 'interrelationship, connection, is not the same as full presence or the absence of difference' in women's texts.⁴ As we shall see in the following section, this is especially true of Dickinson criticism from the early 1990s, when feminist critics utilized what some would now regard as essentialist and self-limiting theoretical frameworks such as psychoanalytic theories of subject-formation as the basis for such enquiries into a female tradition of writing. Critics seeking to identify Dickinson's place within a female tradition must also allow for the integral differences her poetry and 'life' carry with them. That said, the effect of uncovering hitherto ignored connections between Dickinson and her contemporaries is to underscore a tradition of female writers who were not only influenced by each other but also 'speaking' to those before and after them. Highlighting the shape and elements of such a tradition goes some way to counter the various obstacles women have faced in getting their voices heard, and as such, continues the feminist project. In this, reading Dickinson's work through the context of a female tradition, we come to a fuller and more informed understanding of her unique voice.

To understand the many ways in which Dickinson's poetry speaks from within a female tradition, we must at first locate her poetic responses as adjacent to a literary (and religious) tradition which is predominantly masculine. Benjamin Lease's *Emily Dickinson's Reading of Men and Books* (1990) is pivotal in our understanding of Dickinson's reading, the predominantly masculine nature of this literary tradition, and the impact it had upon her poetry.⁵ Lease coherently puts together Dickinson's reading list as observed from what we know of her family's library (including that of her brother and sister-in-law), information gleaned from her letters, such as items she likely read at school, hymns and songs she sang, biblical passages she favoured and of course the books she borrowed from (or was given by) Susan Dickinson. Lease creates a picture for us of the ways in which her poetry was at once informed by, but also a reaction against, the literary and religious texts she encountered. In this way, she can be seen as engaging in a life of vision and 'deep involvement' by producing a large body of work which is in part a response to masculine tradition.⁶ It is this engagement and involvement which, when viewed against the literary works of her contemporaries, can be seen as a part of a tradition which is also born of female experience.

Cheryl Walker's *The Nightingale's Burden: Women Poets and American Culture Before 1900* (1982) places Dickinson within the context of a female literary tradition which is intrinsically bound up with the societies and literary histories which have silenced women.⁷ Walker discusses writers such as Anne Bradstreet, Phillis Wheatley, Lydia Sigourney, Frances Osgood, Julia Ward Howe, Margaret

Fuller, Ella Wheeler Wilcox and Louise Guiney alongside Dickinson and shows how the Philomela/Nightingale myth has served as a model for the paradoxical position of the women poet, being compelled to sing and also being silenced. Walker dedicates a chapter to Dickinson and Helen Hunt Jackson to explore the ways in which both writers negotiate the culturally prescribed versions of a female tradition of writers. She argues that Dickinson readily eschewed the various stylistic conventions of American women's poetry but embraced the 'poetess' persona promoted in literary society and popular culture. An element of this persona involved the notion of the reclusive female poet, which, she argues, other women contemporaries such as Lucy Larcom and Anne Lynch also adopted. The term 'recluse' was also readily applied to Lucretia Davidson by Catharine Sedgwick. This important point, that there was an established culture of the poetess 'recluse' in nineteenth-century America, has been lost in subsequent and more recent arguments about whether Dickinson's reclusive nature indicates separation from society and culture, especially a literary one.[8] The various tropes of nineteenth-century American female literary tradition should be frequently re-examined to fully appreciate Dickinson's uses of and departures from it.

The notion of a female tradition, as well as providing an outlet and model for women writers such as Dickinson, has also been to an extent an obstacle to overcome, or a set of stereotypes to react against. Elizabeth Petrino (1998) draws upon the conventions of nineteenth-century publication houses and their preferences for a particular kind of writing by women to analyse Dickinson's place within a group of female writers who engage with those conventions. She analyses the work of writers who were associated with the specific poetic genres and topics which were deemed as appropriate for women writers, and for which there would be a wide audience, such as the 'Child Elegy', the 'Culture of Mourning' and the 'Language of Flowers'. She focuses on Dickinson's American contemporaries, who, she argues, are not as often discussed as their British contemporaries.[9] Petrino's list ranges from Lydia Sigourney, the 'premiere infant elegist of nineteenth-century America', who was part of a 'wide-spread cult of death in nineteenth-century America', to Frances Sargent Osgood, 'who combines a floral dictionary, poetry, and botanical treatise in her book, *The Poetry of Flowers, and Flowers of Poetry* (1841)'.[10] The group of writers extends to Helen Hunt Jackson, whose novels and poems Dickinson admired, and who served as an important model of successful female authorship for her.[11] Petrino describes how Dickinson's poetry both engages with the prescribed course for women poets of her time and simultaneously subverts and overturns the very assumptions about female writers underpinning those editorial preferences.

Margaret Homans (1980) makes a compelling argument for Dickinson's place within a tradition of nineteenth-century women poets whose work and struggle for poetic identity were forged in the shadow of Romanticism and the gendering of nature inherent in the work of poets such as Wordsworth. Using British examples of Dorothy Wordsworth and Emily Bronte, but also significantly the American Emily Dickinson, Homans argues that 'Romantic tradition makes it difficult for any writer to separate sexual identity from writing'. Here the trans-Atlanticism of Dickinson's work lends itself to an argument about Romantic ideas on gender, and Dickinson is included once again in this.[12] Wendy Martin shows in *An American Triptych: Anne Bradstreet, Emily Dickinson and Adrienne Rich* (1984) that Dickinson speaks from within a tradition of American poetry by women and illuminates Dickinson's position with readings of Bradstreet before her and Rich after.[13]

Therefore, as we have seen, many critics seeking to locate Dickinson within a tradition of female writers ultimately position her as being at a remove from such a tradition whilst also speaking from within it, articulating a dual existence. Critics such as Joanne Dobson (1989), and Sharon Leder and Andrea Abbott (1987), have discussed this duality in terms of Dickinson's adoption of linguistic 'strategies', articulating the absences produced by a culture which does not represent the self as it is known and felt to be.[14] Such criticism as this focuses on female literary tradition within a particular period and, in the case of Dickinson, the nineteenth century. However, situating Dickinson within a female tradition which can be seen as speaking across the different historical periods has been seen by some critics as a progressive critical move. In 1976 poet, writer and feminist critic Adrienne Rich wrote a compelling essay on Dickinson, entitled 'Vesuvius at Home: The Power of Emily Dickinson', in which she argues that Dickinson's gender is a source of power and that it is her identity as a woman which informs her poetry, thus figuring the female tradition within literary culture as trans-historical.[15] Rich's prose is personal in tone as she takes the reader on her own present-moment journey towards Dickinson. Rich places herself as both reader and poet, blurring the distinctions between Dickinson's world and her own. The essay was deeply influential and shifted the critical landscape as far as it allowed feminist critics to declare an inheritance and cross-period connection with a great literary woman poet. The gender politics of Dickinson's work spoke to the gender politics of Rich's. Therefore, in addition to feminist critics who seek to place Dickinson within a context of a female literary tradition by analysing her work alongside that of her contemporaries, there are critics who have argued for an intertextual networking within women's writing which can be seen in the intimate recognition and appropriation of dominant cultural discourse which operates outside of period differences – as the recognition of Dickinson in Rich's text conveys.

Sabine Sielke argues in *Fashioning the Female Subject* (1997) that women writers have networked across the ages in their uses and positioning of subjectivity within literary texts. Dickinson 'appropriates dominant cultural rhetoric to invest it with new meanings'.[16] Sielke's study is concerned with illustrating the ways in which women poets connect with each other across time and space through their various articulations of subjectivity and how they become, in this, agents of history. She argues that Dickinson creates a female tradition in her work which is akin to that created by writers such as Adrienne Rich and Marianne Moore, despite their differences across time and cultures. Part of this creation comes with the acknowledgement that the reproduction of cultural contexts, and mimicry, when producing literary texts, is always inevitable. She sets up a 'dialogue' between Dickinson and Adrienne Rich in her comparison, where both poets are seen as self-referential and aware of their self-construction. Both Rich and Dickinson are aware of the fictional nature of their subject formation because of the extent to which it depends upon engagement with cultural rhetoric and versions of the self which are themselves unstable and constantly evolving. Rich's reading of Dickinson, and the incorporation of elements of Rich's own biography, in 'Vesuvius at Home' present for Sielke a moment during which the female subject can be seen as 'a process of present and past'.[17] Sielke finds in Rich an example of the female subject highlighting the female tradition by placing herself directly within it, in 'dialogue' with Dickinson, who, she argues, 'dismissed history and transcendence for the temporality of writing'.[18] Crucially, Sielke argues that Dickinson 'recognises subjectivity and history as constructs and rhetorical strategies, as ongoing and open-ended processes based upon appropriations and transformations of concepts'.[19] She concludes her study with a redefinition of female subjectivity within a tradition she identifies within the study, of which Dickinson, Moore, Rich, Kristeva, Irigaray, Cixous and herself are all a part, by describing it as 'a process that is never coherent and historically continuous but, rather, negotiates between deconstructive and (re)-constructive modes as well as between past and present discourses'.[20] The idea of a female tradition is therefore also being reconstructed in critical analysis of Dickinson's texts.

The problem of placing Dickinson within a female tradition and also of describing that tradition is explained in Vivian R. Pollak's book *Our Emily Dickinsons: American Women Poets and the Intimacies of Difference* (2017). Pollak takes gender and psychology as a centralizing focus in her study of Dickinson and her influence on other women poets, such as her contemporary, Helen Hunt

Jackson, and those who came after her, such as Marianne Moore, Elizabeth Bishop and Sylvia Plath. To explain the 'intimacies of difference' within this group of women poets she traces the critical reception of Dickinson contemporary to each poet, and also considers the personal agendas and situations which likely influenced their own responses to Dickinson's work. Pollak's aim is not to describe the direct influence of Dickinson on her contemporaries and subsequent fellow women poets, but to show how these women poets used Dickinson 'to clarify what is at stake in personal and professional battles of their own', asserting that:

> Dickinson represents the intimacies of difference: the sociability that draws us together and the profound self-absorption that keeps us apart.[21]

Pollak argues that Dickinson does not sit neatly within any category, and that is part of her unique style. We can therefore only describe the 'intimacies of difference' in her poetry which draws others to it. Pollak's study outlines such 'intimacies of difference' and suggests why these women poets were each so powerfully drawn in.

Finally, the notion of exceptionalism should be mentioned as it ties in with the feminist project of constructing a female tradition as well as upholding one. Many feminist critics of the twentieth century sought to forge a space for Dickinson within the Anglo-American canon of literature and as such emphasized her exceptionalism, her unique genius. More recently, twenty-first-century critics such as Michelle Kohler have sought to question this notion of exceptionalism in relation to Dickinson's genius, and there has been a critical move to effectively 'decentre' Dickinson. In the introduction to her edited collection of essays she argues that Dickinson is 'not necessarily exceptional' and that the essays in her volume present 'a radically decentred understanding of the networks, environments and temporalities that shape writing and reading – and to a decentring of Dickinson herself'.[22] The critical urge to place Dickinson within a centralizing literary canon as well as within a female tradition has also led perhaps in some cases to the privileging of critical perspectives and historical contexts over the work of the poet herself.

3.2 Writing the body

When feminist critics write about 'the body' either as a site of subversion in Dickinson's work or in reference to a collection of images associated with the body which are frequently scattered throughout her work, mostly they refer to the terms of psychoanalytic theory to discuss its position. Lacanian psychoanalytic theory informs the work of many feminist theorists to whom feminist Dickinson critics refer, such as Luce Irigaray, Julia Kristeva and Hélène Cixous. Indeed, Sabine Sielke reiterates the continuing relevance of the work of such theorists precisely because they recognize the centrality of the body and its role in subject formation.[23] The use of psychoanalytic terms in relation to the body in Dickinson's work by feminist scholars differs greatly from the use of psychoanalysis to explain Dickinson's *life*, as in biographies such as John Cody's *After Great Pain* (1971). Rather, Sielke is interested in the ways in which such theorists can help us to understand the presence of Dickinson's body (even when it is registered most by the absence of it and/or the speaker's separation from it) in her poems, and the ways in which this affects our reading of them. Furthermore, they provide a matrix for understanding the connections between the body and subjectivity which many of Dickinson's poems articulate. The pioneering work on gender, sexuality and the body discussed in this section has become paradigmatic for subsequent Dickinson scholars.

In *Emily Dickinson: Woman Poet* (1990) Paula Bennett examines what she sees as a sequence of genital imagery in Dickinson's work and makes a case for the strong connection between her sexuality and creativity. She places particular importance upon the representation of specifically female genital imagery, such as that which invokes the clitoris and vagina, such as 'references to crumbs, berries, peas, pearls and other small, round objects'.[24] Bennett argues that the female sexual metaphor provided Dickinson with a range of symbolism for female poetry and poetic power which was an alternative to a traditionally masculine and phallocentric one. She provides many examples of this, utilizing letters and poems to demonstrate Dickinson's use of such imagery. Bennett concludes by connecting Dickinson's use of such symbolism, her 'clitorocentrism' with Irigaray's articulation of a need for a 'new syntax', and a new language for female jouissance.[25] In the nineteenth century female sexuality may not have been as visible as male sexuality, but Bennett argues that Dickinson's use of female sexual imagery carries with it the notion that that which is smaller and hidden can be just as powerful. As will be discussed in the following section, Bennett takes the argument further to provide evidence not only for a poetics of smallness to emphasize female sexuality, but also for poetics which expresses another mode of relationship which is essentially lesbian and homoerotic. In this way, Bennett's work on gender, sexuality and the body can be seen as an important springboard for later scholarship on queering Dickinson. Bennett is discussed in relation to the homoeroticism of Dickinson's texts and the issue of lesbian identity in Section 3.3.

Sabine Sielke is interested in the ways Julia Kristeva's subject theory is transhistorical and allows us to map it onto writers across periods and uses it to carve out a convincing argument for intertextual networking between women writers of different periods. Kristeva's description of the semiotic chora (the origination of the articulation of the pre-linguistic other, aligned with maternal rather than paternal and symbolic language) as disruption to symbolic order is used by Sielke to analyse the doubleness, de-centredness, partial views and indefiniteness of the subject in Dickinson's work (and in a chapter dedicated to this subject alongside the work of Marianne Moore). Sielke sees subjectivity represented in Dickinson's work as unstable, non-unified and unlike the linearity and certainty provided by the symbolic order. She explains it thus:

> Constituted by dominant, syntactically structured discourse and by social institutions that inscribe paternal law and cultural constraints, the symbolic provides a kind of scaffolding for the subject. The semiotic, in contrast, consists of heterogeneous flow of pre-oedipal energies, drives, and rhythms, originating from what Kristeva termed the semiotic chora and from the dyadic phase, in which subject and maternal body are still united [...]. Due to this return of the body in language, the subject can no longer be understood as a fixed entity. It has turned into a subject-in-process and on trial.[26]

In line with Freudian theories of subject-formation, the subject which identifies with the maternal body cannot speak directly and is instead open to the disruption which characterizes the semiotic. Sielke makes connections between Kristeva's uses of the semiotic as a site of empowerment, and the semiotic qualities of Dickinson's work, which 'presents pieces of a puzzle, which never form a full picture'.[27] These qualities range from the rupturing of syntactical forms, ellipsis, deletions; non-linearity, emphasis on in-between states; non-standard uses of grammar and prosody; the representation of the self as divided, fragmented or disembodied; the emphasis on loss, lack and pain; as well as sound repetition pointing towards the physicality of language and the body, to the association of otherness with femininity. She describes Dickinson's use of regularized, nameless forms, such as the common hymn metre or ballad stanza to register the disruptive nature of her subjectivity and the 'disguise' of conformity this provided. Sielke offers many incisive readings to demonstrate her argument but also provides instances where connections between the theories and the poetry diverge. She asserts that whilst Kristeva's subject mourns the loss of the initial love object and ultimately retreats into a self-sufficient narcissism, Dickinson's speakers 'do not care for female origins', and, moreover, they are concerned not with what may be available in this life but always with what lies parallel to and beyond it.[28] Sielke's study is important because it is one of the best examples of criticism where such theories have been employed and used to go beyond a comparative analysis of features of the theory and of the poetry. Sielke demonstrates the usefulness of French feminist theory and the terms of psychoanalysis but explains that it also 'lacks […] a sense of the position of the female subject as an agent of history'.[29] Therefore, it is to the question of a female literary tradition and intertextual networking of female agents of history that she expertly turns her argument.

Helen Shoobridge uses psychoanalytic theories of difference and binary opposition as a basis to analyse Dickinson's relationship with the 'masculine' as exemplified by her so-called 'Master' letters and a few poems which appear to subvert gender stereotypes, such as those where the flower imagery is employed to challenge the traditional view of female subordination.[30] She identifies Dickinson's engagement with the biblical text of the *Song of Songs* as a discursive model in which to illustrate an 'ethical' meeting between the sexes and argues that Dickinson adopts a 'feminine discursive role in order to renegotiate her relegated position as the inferior other in the sexual binary'.[31] She argues that the 'discursive space of seduction' is a space in which women can speak back to men and address the imbalance of power.[32] She sees Dickinson employing the tactics of mimicry and excessive femininity in the 'Master' letters, as that recommended by Irigaray, in order *not* to be absorbed and defined by the limiting binaries and separate spheres ideology which traditionally confined nineteenth-century women. This excessive femininity, she argues, includes writing the feminine body rather than running away from and undermining it. Critics have been too keen, in Shoobridge's view, to see Dickinson doing the latter. Moreover, she sees Dickinson's engagement with the *Song of Songs* (as a text in which the feminine human voice speaks to both the masculine human and divine lover, where secular and divine discourse meet) as having parallels with Irigaray's description of an encounter with the divine other in language. Shoobridge attempts to recover Dickinson from the various readings of her 'Master' letters which see her adopting positions of lack, loss and female subjugation. The keen grasp of Irigarayan philosophy in this article will sustain enlightened readings of Dickinson's poems. Shoobridge's mapping of Irigaray's use of 'distance' (as well as the distance between the speaker and lover within the *Song of Songs*) onto the various 'deferrals' and 'delays' she identifies within the

'Master' letters is instructive. The concepts of distance and excessive femininity are extremely useful for reading Dickinson's poetic strategies, and the essay provides a helpful example of how theoretical concepts can be used to shed light upon the dynamics at work in Dickinson's poetry.

Nineteenth-century discourse on emancipation provides the context for another good example of analysis of Dickinson's poetics where the body and a notion of 'doubleness' are both centralized. Karen Sanchez-Eppler has written on the relationship between the body as it is represented in Dickinson's work and the language associated with the abolitionist cause. She is interested in the ways in which the rhetoric of abolitionism and feminism merges in nineteenth-century writing. In her book *Touching Liberty: Abolition, Feminism and the Politics of the Body* (1993) she includes a chapter on the political implications of Dickinson's depictions of the body, entitled 'At Home in the Body: The Internal Politics of Dickinson's Poetry'.[33] Rather than seeing Dickinson's relation to the body as a denial of place and history, and her poetry as being therefore 'non-referential' as other critics have, Sanchez-Eppler sees instead a paradox, perhaps as part of Dickinson's lyric mode, in which tensions and contradictions within this strategy arise. She sees Dickinson, in a comparable way to the African American writer Harriet Jacobs, as reclaiming the limitations of the gendered body as well as the domestic space of the home to assert a paradoxical sense of liberty. She argues that Dickinson's poetic depictions of the body as fragmented or absent echo the way images of the body were frequently employed in the political discourse of emancipation. The limitations of physical experience and ideas of confinement are reclaimed and reimagined in Dickinson's poetics of the body. Sanchez-Eppler shows how Dickinson's technique of asserting 'liberty in retreat' draws attention to the language of embodiment in abolitionism.[34] She highlights the paradox or doubleness in Dickinson's relation to the body, in that there is a desire to be bodiless, to transcend physical constraints, but also, simultaneously, to be 'at home' within that confined and limited space. She provides many examples from the poems to describe this flight from, and dualistic relation to, the body and argues that Dickinson's poems 'lay bare the paradoxical complicity between the ideal of liberty and the structures of bondage' and in 'revealing the instability of liberty, domesticity, sexuality, and identity, such a position is uncompromisingly radical'. Moreover, in doing so, Dickinson's poems illuminate the 'practices of appropriation and displacement by which reformers so often sought to deflect their anxieties about their own bodies, homes, and freedom'.[35]

Many twentieth-century critics interested in gender focused on the emancipation from bodily constraints, and the dramatization of this as a performance of various voices and identities within Dickinson's work. In this they highlighted the ways her poetry dramatizes the nineteenth-century woman writer's precarious relation to a largely masculine literary tradition. In their groundbreaking *The Madwoman in the Attic: The Woman Writer and the Nineteenth-Century Literary Imagination* (1979) Sandra M. Gilbert and Susan Gubar describe the performance of various identities in Dickinson's poetry and explain the 'masks' Dickinson utilizes to negotiate the limitations of cultural expectations for women. For example, the 'child mask' or 'Daisy' and 'Nobody' figures are employed to explore the dynamics of power relations. These 'diminutive' speakers in her poems are positioned alongside the 'master' or 'sun of Noon' figure who is paradoxically silent by comparison. At other times the speaker is 'Queen' or 'Empress' where the marriage is with the elements of self as opposed to a real other, conveying self-governance and autonomy.[36] Gilbert and Gubar's identification of the performance of multiple identities which rehearse gendered relational dynamics as well as the idea of a fully autonomous female self forcefully impacted upon future scholars' understanding of the ways in which her poems negotiate gender stereotypes. As will be discussed in Chapter 6, their work was also crucial for critics who became interested in the performative aspects of Dickinson's work and the ways in which her poetics are reader-oriented and beckon the reader to be complicit in their performances of identities and ideas.

In *Sexual Personae: Art and Decadence from Nerfertiti to Emily Dickinson* (1990) Camille Paglia sees Dickinson's performances of gender as part of her essential duality, where her work is in either a 'Wordsworthian' or a 'Sadean' mode in its treatment of the body and nature.[37] Paglia sees Dickinson's depictions of the body largely as a catalogue of abuses and restraints, something which, Paglia argues, also signals her connection to late decadent Romanticism. The book concludes with a chapter on Dickinson, entitled 'Amherst's Madame de Sade: Emily Dickinson'. Paglia's analysis focuses heavily upon Dickinson's depictions of the body and how she negotiates and subverts traditional British Romantic views of nature – as 'Mother Nature', and as feminine. Paglia finds a gratuitous violence in Dickinson's use of the body and argues that she has, therefore, more in common with a writer like the Marquis de Sade, than with Wordsworth or indeed Emerson:

> Dickinson, like Sade, draws the reader into ascending degrees of complicity, from eroticism to rape, mutilation, and murder [...]. Romanticism's overexpanded self requires artificial restraints. Dickinson finds these limitations in sadomasochistic nature and reproduces them in her dual style.[38]

If a primary element of Dickinson's style is its duality, as Paglia argues here, then criticism which focuses on Dickinson's uses for the body seems to be most successful in highlighting such duality. Paglia's compressed style is crammed with literary and cultural references and invokes the terms of psychoanalysis and its concept of subject formation frequently. For example, when it is asserted that Dickinson rids herself of the female within to create poetry, and as such attacks the body as a site of difference, Paglia argues that her poems require a 'separation from the mother'.[39] The female body here cannot match up with the spiritual and poetic 'I'. Bodily wounds and impalement (her 'sadomasochism') appear throughout her poetry as metaphors for mortality.[40] She concludes by declaring that 'this shy Victorian spinster was a male genius and visionary sadist, a fictive sexual persona of towering force'.[41] With the concluding idea of Dickinson's genius being masculine (albeit a performance of it) such criticism – which is careful to avoid a clearly feminist (or queer) trajectory – runs the risk of appearing to be constrained by the essentialist terms of its arguments. The duality Paglia finds in Dickinson's poetry is inevitably reproduced in her own arguments about sexual difference.

In Paglia's view the sentimental poems present undefended femininity, where femininity is artifice, and that Dickinson accepts femininity but denies femaleness, 'sweeping it out of her cosmos'. Femininity is a performance and is also characterized as a performance in some of these poems. Another representational mode is that of freezing, fracture and monumentality, what Paglia calls 'Titanic Dickinson'. This mode involves alienation from the female body, a 'Brontean swerve from gender' as she calls it. Her sadomasochistic metaphors are a 'technique of self-hermaphrodization' and are an 'emptying out of female internality'. Paglia observes Dickinson's performance of gender in her freely applied use of 'transexual titles', as discussed in the following section of this chapter, where the poem 'My Life had stood a Loaded Gun' (Fr 764/M 354) is described as 'one of Romanticism's great transsexual self-transformations'. Paglia also sees an 'eroticized religious exhibitionism' which 'belongs to the Italian and Spanish Baroque, not to American Protestantism' in poems such as 'I tend my flowers for thee –' (Fr 367/M 194) where 'My Cactus – splits her Beard / To show her throat'.[42]

Paglia's treatment of Dickinson is instructive in the way it illuminates the various performances of gender stereotypes that her poems enact and convey. Her work points towards the discussions to be had by contemporary critics interested in gender categories and especially gender fluid, non-binary identities. Paglia concludes the chapter on Dickinson with a comparison between Dickinson and Walt Whitman which describes a shared preoccupation with 'sexual all-inclusiveness'. It is conveyed in a deliberately provocative style, and Paglia's critical text is itself performative, perhaps speaking more readily to our own times than describing Dickinson's, where Dickinson still waits for her readers to know her, and the nature of her 'sexual all-inclusiveness':

> Both are self-ruling hermaphrodites who will not and cannot mate. Both are homosexual voyeurs gaming at sexual all-inclusiveness [...]. Dickinson in her ritualistic condolences and lubricious death-connoisseurship. Voyeurism, vampirism, necrophilia, lesbianism, sadomasochism, sexual surrealism: Amherst's Madame de Sade still waits for her readers to know her.[43]

Paglia's text sets up a framework in which two dominant representational modes are explored, and she maintains that readers are yet to fully understand and 'know' her. In other words, for Dickinson to be fully understood, and her uses of gender to be performed, then the reader must also allow these performances to be there within the poems.

The relationship between the reader and the poet is seen as a crucial element of the performance of gender in Dickinson – something Suzanne Juhasz and Cristanne Miller's essay 'Performances of Gender in Dickinson's Poetry' (2006) examines. They make use of performance and reader-response theories to support their argument that Dickinson's poetry and the reading of gender in Dickinson's poetry constitute intersecting performances beyond those usually ascribed to lyric poetry. They illustrate how Dickinson constructs alternatives to a fixed binary system for gender and opens a space in which the reader can perform alternative genderings. They argue that Dickinson's work demands engagement and participation from the reader in this. Importantly, Juhasz and Miller argue that it is the various performances of gender in Dickinson's work which are crucial to the general construction of her poetry.[44]

An interesting comparison can be made between Paglia's examination of Dickinson's relationship with Late Decadent Romanticism and Cynthia Griffin Wolff's treatment of Dickinson and the Romantic Grotesque, in her article '[Im]pertinent Constructions of Body and Self: Dickinson's Use of the Romantic Grotesque' (1993).[45] Where Paglia's examination focuses on Dickinson's uses for and descriptions of the body to construct an argument about her relationship with Romantic tradition, Wolff's analysis uses the notion of the Romantic Grotesque to consider the modes of bodily representation of 'self' in her work. Both critics focus on the body in Dickinson's work and how, in diverse ways, those representations of body and self connect with distinct aspects of the Romantic tradition. By highlighting Dickinson's interventions within a traditionally masculine literary tradition both critics demonstrate new ways to see Dickinson as well as the literary critical canon.

A major area of focus for critics interested in the ways Dickinson's poetry destabilizes the gendered body is her various depictions of the natural world. H. Jordan Landry's important article 'Animal/Insectual/Lesbian Sex: Dickinson's Queer Version of the Birds and the Bees' (2000) shows how Dickinson uses the natural world to destabilize our ideas about the gendered body. In work which is also important for critics concerned with 'queer' identity in Dickinson this study examines, amongst other imagery, the use of bee imagery as a 'system' which demonstrates the poet's lack of interest in fixed gendered (human) bodies and a desire to see gender as flexible.[46] Shira Wolosky's essay 'Emily Dickinson: Being in the Body' (2002) considers the body or, rather, the 'problem of embodiment' as a central site for identity in Dickinson's work and illuminates the ways we can see the cultural challenges and forces working upon that site in her poems.[47]

As we have seen in the instances above, approaches to examining Dickinson's relationship to the physical body are concerned primarily with the ways in which her texts negotiate gender and the ways in which gender impacts upon them. When discussing Dickinson's uses and depictions of the body, critics highlight a sense of paradox or quality of doubleness. Whether feminist psychoanalytic theory is employed, or as we have seen in the case of relating Dickinson's work within the context of discourses of emancipation, or in relation to a largely masculine literary tradition such as Romanticism, as Paglia and Wolff have shown, critics describe a doubleness which is essentially unresolved. Criticism which uses the terms of psychoanalytic theory relies upon a model of difference which ultimately re-inscribes the terms of patriarchy and separation under scrutiny. Critics utilizing feminist theorists such as Irigaray argue that we must engage with the binaries of sexual difference to change the symbolic order and that without this nothing will change for the status of women in society. Sexual difference is seen either as enabling or as something which needs to be transcended. By focusing on Dickinson's relationship to the body, critics highlight a paradox and tension inherent within feminist relation to language as well as within discourses on other forms of emancipation such as racial, spiritual, social and sexual freedom. In focusing on the body in this way and describing the ways in which Dickinson's poetry evades and frustrates the boundaries of many socially prescribed expectations regarding gender, these pioneering critics also paved the way for future work on queering Dickinson.

3.3 Queering Dickinson

Criticism which takes not only sexual politics but also sexuality and the nature of identity as its focus became a popular strand within the field of Dickinson studies in the 1990s when 'queer theory' was emerging from the work of feminist and gay liberationist critics. Queer theory asserts that literary texts, and in particular lyric poetry in which a version of 'self' is arguably most clearly constructed, are produced out of their respective political environments and can thus be seen as forms of political discourse.[48] Whilst sexuality has been discussed in the previous section in terms of Dickinson's uses for the body, and the employment or suppression of excessive femininity or 'jouissance' in order to subvert limiting sexual binaries, 'Queering Dickinson' in this section describes the critical mode of inquiry primarily concerned with LGBTQ+ readings of her work. This area of study incorporates an examination of the variety of sexualities, including those which are fluid and mobile, and the gendered, gender-fluid and non-gendered identities which many critics see articulated in Dickinson's poetry. This discussion includes the work of critics who assert and emphasize identities such as trans and non-binary selves and the role they play in reading Dickinson's work. It is also a way of describing the critical tools they use to do this. 'Queering' Dickinson therefore is not a way of reading lesbian identity in Dickinson exclusively but, rather, the fluid eroticism and spectrum of possibilities for identification in her poems which had previously been ignored or brushed over by scholars of her work in the past. This critical 'queering' mode of enquiry seeks to deconstruct the heteronormative assumptions which have been placed upon Dickinson's work and is a powerful theoretical framework through which to view the ways in which her poetry itself destabilizes those assumptions and structures. Whilst all the texts discussed in this section may not expressly employ 'queer theory' as a theoretical framework, they all seek in numerous ways to 'queer' Dickinson. By including recent critical interventions around sexual identity in this section, the aim is not to place lesbian, trans and non-binary readings of Dickinson together as somehow interchangeable positions, but rather to view these readings alongside each other as a way of usefully discussing the ways in which they each challenge the heteronormative assumptions of some of the earlier gender-critical perspectives on Dickinson.

Paula Bennett's *Emily Dickinson: Woman Poet* (1990) was the first book-length piece of work to bring together the issue of Dickinson's homoeroticism with close analysis of her poems and letters. For Bennett, Dickinson's homoeroticism was an overarching viewpoint, which permeated everything she wrote:

> Homoeroticism was not just a matter of sexuality for the poet. It was a point of view. And her love of women and things female affects everything she wrote.[49]

Dickinson's work and life was 'woman-centred'. She sees Dickinson as being both interested in, and part of, a nineteenth-century tradition of women poets (citing Elizabeth Barrett-Browning, George Eliot and Helen Hunt Jackson as a few of her many influences) whilst also presenting an entirely new model for female poetry of this period. Bennett's analysis begins with interrogation of the experiments she produced in both linguistic and intellectual terms, thus rejecting the phallocentric ordering of the Western tradition, and presenting a poetry which privileges both 'process' and 'incompletion'. What is underscored are metaphysical uncertainties and the rejection of a tradition which privileges certainty and completeness, in all religious, intellectual and linguistic forms. She argues that Dickinson's formal linguistic rejection of finite endings in her poems also expressed a rejection of the wider social, intellectual and spiritual knowledge which claimed to have final answers. Bennett sees Dickinson's commitment to incompletion as concomitant with her rejection of a transcendent (and therefore apparently masculine) version of God. Her analysis of Dickinson's nature poems focuses on what she sees as a 'woman-centred and materially-based alternative' to established religion. It is in this quest for an alternative to a transcendent God that Bennett sees Dickinson's use of natural and specifically female imagery. She then goes on to discuss Dickinson's 'psychological' poetry, which has a quality of 'indeterminacy' which, like incompleteness, presents a less fixed view of the self, countering societal categories of woman.[50] It is this quality of indeterminacy and doubt about a fixed identity which has parallels in queer theory, and it is interesting that Bennett's text emerges around the same time as Eve Kosofsky Sedgwick's *Epistemology of the Closet* (1990) which emphasizes the importance of non-binary thinking about sexual orientation and gender.

The book's final chapter focuses on the 'female-centred' eroticism which Bennett identifies in Dickinson's poetry. It is this homoeroticism and autoeroticism which Bennett sees as the driving force behind Dickinson's ability to see herself as, and to be, a forceful woman poet. Bennett asserts a few basic assumptions from the outset of her study, one of them being that it is the poet's relationship with, and love for, her sister-in-law Susan which informs her poetry the most, as she argues it was the 'central emotional experience' of her life.[51] In this way, she centralizes the homoeroticism in Dickinson's work. Bennett argues that critical attention to a masculine 'Master' has only served to obscure her homoeroticism. She shows Dickinson subverting literary and cultural binaries, and principles of opposition, to place herself in the traditionally masculine/active role, and, at other times, to reject it. She describes the flower imagery used by Dickinson in letters as sexual metaphors which evidence her homoeroticism and preference for 'woman-to-woman affection'.[52] She also cites the 'man of noon' letter written to Susan Dickinson, in which Dickinson appears to warn her of the dangers of love for men, and highlights the satisfaction gained between women. Bennett makes comment in the notes about lesbian objection to her use of the term 'smaller' when describing women's relationships with each other. However, she argues that in Dickinson's conceptualization of and preferences for the 'smaller' things over large and dominant ones, small may not necessarily be less and often pertains to a sense of abundance.[53] Moreover, Bennett asserts that treatment of Dickinson's relationship with an anonymous 'Master' misses the obvious conventionality at play in her work, which is striking. As Bennett and others have noted, this period and relationship is represented by Dickinson in terms of 'hierarchy, difference and domination'.[54] Thus, heterosexual relationship is expressed in terms of a struggle and is separate from, and in direct contrast to, the commitment to the values of process and incompleteness we see in much of her other output. Bennett states that heterosexuality was 'not a source of poetic or psychological strength' for Dickinson. She sees instead an emphasis on 'smallness, mutuality and nurturance' in poems addressed to and about women.[55] She identifies an intensely erotic attraction to the female body, and a delight in it which does not require explanation, in many of Dickinson's more well-known poems, such as 'Come slowly – Eden!' (Fr 205/M 121), to argue that homoeroticism is the dominant mode of expression in her work. Furthermore, Bennett argues that in the poem 'All the letters I can write' (Fr 380/M 202) Dickinson's 'sexual orientation in it seems clear'. She does go on to make the caveat that this desire was, however, probably confined to fantasy, and that Dickinson solves the problem of the taboo on penetrative relations by expressing this desire through a frame of doubt and 'imaginative rescripting'.[56] In this way, Dickinson projects an idea of what sexual relations and love could potentially be. In Bennett's readings, clitoral imagery is central to Dickinson's homoeroticism and her penchant for small imagery, such as pearls, berries and bees – her 'clitorocentrism' – is seen as being a conscious or unconscious alternative to phallocentric discourse, and the 'hierarchies that disempowered her as a woman and as a poet'. Bennett concludes her argument by reasserting the point that Dickinson's ability to question and challenge the phallocentric discourses inherent in religion, philosophy and literature and to create a poetic alternative to those discourses which delimited women was something 'directly rooted in her homoerotic and autoerotic commitment to women'.[57] As an addendum to this argument, Bennett uses Luce Irigaray and the concept of 'jouissance' from French feminist psychoanalytic theory to explain Dickinson's method and commitment to what she calls 'smallness'. The expression of clitorocentrism and imagery of smallness in Dickinson's poems is likened here to the idea of the requirement of an entirely new language, syntax or discourse for women to express themselves, being outside the symbolic order of the phallus in Freudian psychoanalytic theory of subject formation. Bennett ends the book by claiming Dickinson found a 'jouissance' of her own. Although psychoanalytic terminology has been rejected by some feminist scholars as another form of phallocentric discourse, this connection between clitorocentrism and the desire for a new language and mode of expression is a powerful one which influenced subsequent feminist readings of Dickinson. Bennett's book laid down an important framework for discussing homoeroticism in relation to Dickinson and paved the way for the 'queering' of her.

Mary Galvin's *Queer Poetics: Five Modernist Women Writers* (1999) places Dickinson at the forefront of a tradition of lesbian writers.[58] In the chapter entitled 'Poltergeist of Form: Emily Dickinson and the Re-appropriation of Language and Identity'[59] Galvin reviews and then dismisses the 'heterosexist myth' of Dickinson in favour of a view of her as a lesbian who wanted to 'disrupt the linguistic and epistemological structures of phallocentrism in order to speak her (queer) mind'. Galvin's reading places Dickinson 'on the continuum of lesbian existence'. With identity as the focus, Galvin sees Dickinson as a proto-Modernist who was able to resist the restraints of nineteenth-century culture and the traditionally prescribed gender roles because as a lesbian, she was able to understand identity itself as a socially constructed concept. She sees Dickinson and Whitman as 'sexual rebels', both being able to transcend such socially constructed norms of self because of their resistance to heterosexuality.[60] However, whilst Whitman, being male, was able to live in a robust and relatively free way, Galvin sees Dickinson's defiance in her construction of a life which appeared to be that of a traditional spinster, but allowed her intellectual and therefore poetic freedom, and in her radical uses of language. She provides readings of several poems which argue that Dickinson wrote about the socialization of women directly ('They shut me up in Prose', Fr 445/M 223) and of the 'civilizing' process of women and the suppression of their voices. The poem describes the requirement of keeping girls 'still' and therefore also silent. In recollection, the speaker likens the confining space of prose to the closet:

> They shut me up in Prose –
> As when a little Girl
> They put me in the Closet –
>
> (Fr 445, M 223)

Galvin sees the 'strategy of coded speech' in poems such as 'Tell all the Truth but tell it slant' (Fr 1263/M 563) as an expression of rebellion on both a personal and a political level. Poems such as 'I'm ceded – I've stopped being Theirs' (Fr 353/M 186) are read in terms of their resistance to the 'rituals of patriarchal religion'. Dickinson's uses of the hymnic common metre are discussed in terms of its disruption not only of metrical regularity but of 'regularity itself in regard to any epistemological stance'. Galvin argues that Dickinson inhabits poetry 'like a ghost', defying our expectations of forms, such as the hymn form, and changing its shape from within. She goes further to argue that the disruption of form visible in Dickinson's work is analogous to the disruption of the confines of heterosexuality also found in her work and accounts of her life. Dickinson 'lurks within the circumference of acceptability. I call it queer'. She sees an 'inversion of values' echoed within and signalled by Dickinson's uses and abuses of metre and cites 'Much madness is divinest Sense' (Fr 620/M 304) as an example of this. The commitment to ambiguity in many of Dickinson's poems Galvin sees as 'an indication of her "lesbian sensibility" or her "queer mind"' and is likened at the end of the chapter to the image of the 'trickster' who pokes fun at our desire for certainty and Truth.[61] This piece is decisive in its view of Dickinson's queer identity, and it maps that on to a method and meaning in her work.

Martha Nell Smith's groundbreaking study *Rowing in Eden: Rereading Emily Dickinson* (1992) seeks to assess and 'reread' the poet's 'textual and sexual priorities', making a persuasive case for Dickinson's relationship with her sister-in-law Susan Huntington Dickinson being romantic and erotically charged.[62] She argues that Susan was her closest critic and to cite but one example, she provides textual evidence for Susan's reading of (and collaboration on) the poem 'Safe in their Alabaster Chambers' (Fr 124/M 83/122).[63] Crucially, Smith argues that Dickinson's correspondences with Susan were 'dispersed' across and effectively buried throughout the various edited collections of letters, and as such her process of writing and matrix of influences have also been overlooked by critics.

She powerfully argues that Susan was not only her literary critic and mentor, lending her books and introducing her to the vast literary culture and society she was immersed in, but also that she was her muse, love object and confidante.[64] Moreover, Smith disagrees with critics who do not see lesbian desire in Dickinson (in this instance Karl Keller) and asserts that 'female bonding and a woman speaking her love for a woman repeatedly over the decades of her adulthood are in fact central to Dickinson's work'.[65] Smith's examination of Dickinson's poetic processes therefore has Susan at the centre, theirs being the 'primary relationship' in the poet's life.[66] Her reading of Dickinson's poems, life and letters through the lens of this central fact shaped the critical trajectory and highlighted the need for a collection of letters which placed their correspondences at the centre. As discussed in Chapter 1 of this guide, Smith's work shows how central Susan's input was to the poet's process of self-'publication'.

'Open Me Carefully': Emily Dickinson's Intimate Letters to Susan Huntington Dickinson (1998) is a collection of the correspondence, in the form of both letters and poems, between Dickinson and Susan Gilbert (Dickinson), edited by Martha Nell Smith and Ellen Louise Hart, which builds upon Smith's earlier work. The introduction states that Dickinson's relationship with Susan went beyond the traditionally accepted same-sex crush permitted to girls and young women in the nineteenth century. Smith argues that the expression in Dickinson's letters to Susan was both 'romantic and erotic', and that the poetry the women exchanged was 'infused with eroticism'.[67] Crucially, Hart and Smith are critical of the decades of editorial choices which have 'ignored' or 'suppressed' evidence of Susan's place in Dickinson's life and literary production.[68] As they note, 'there was simply no place in the official Dickinson biography for the revelation of an immediate confidante and audience for her poetry'.[69] Criticism of this collection lies in the editors' assertions of Dickinson's lesbianism, without providing what they see as any discernible, incontrovertible evidence.[70] Furthermore, the issue of Dickinson's lesbianism has invited a call for a re-clarification on the terms used by critics to discuss the 'queering' of Dickinson. For example, Lena Koski argues that Adrienne Rich's notion of a 'lesbian continuum' needs to be expanded in order to encompass the ways in which female relationships were spoken about in different periods in history.[71] She argues that Rich's notion of every woman existing on a 'lesbian continuum' is useful, but needs to be expanded because the expressions of woman-woman love and desire which were unthreatening to nineteenth-century society look very different to twentieth-century readers, claiming that 'the boundaries between romantic friendship and sexual lesbianism have changed during the past century'. She uses the categories of 'affectionate', 'erotic' and 'romantic' to explain the ways in which Dickinson's correspondences with Susan may have been misinterpreted due to cultural differences across a century. Ultimately, she calls for a 'wider definition of love between women' if we are to discuss Dickinson's relationship with Susan and the impact it had upon her work.[72]

The burgeoning area of studies concerned with trans and non-binary identities in Dickinson's work is beginning to inform the current critical trajectory, paving the way for further exploration. Critics such as Joy Ladin are concerned primarily with the ways in which Dickinson's work can be read as reflecting upon her as an allay for social justice. Ladin's monograph *Soldering the Abyss: Emily Dickinson and Modern American Poetry* (2010) argued for a reading of Dickinson's work as a nineteenth-century precursor to each of the qualities we assign to modern American poetry that are typically associated with Eliot, Pound, Stevens and as a type of poetry which illuminates the essential instability of American public discourse.[73] Dickinson's uses of pronouns is perhaps what best aligns her work with the instability of the dominant discourses of gender identity. Ladin's account of meeting trans identity in Dickinson's work is compelling, where her own journey of casting off an unsatisfactory ('male') binary identity is conveyed alongside discussion of the liberating force of Dickinson's poems which themselves evade or negotiate binaries. Although Ladin does not think Dickinson was herself transgender, she argues that her speakers occupy the margins in a comparable way to transgender people. Moreover, she powerfully concludes that Dickinson teaches us to reclaim the signifier 'I':

> I can 'state myself' by claiming and redefining terms and syntax that aren't intended to rep-resent selves like mine; that 'I' can signify 'Nobody' selves that don't fit the existing terms, roles, and hierarchies; that 'I' can mean, and enact, a sometimes sputtering, sometimes triumphant processes of becom-ing.[74]

Ladin's work has paved the way for other trans critical perspectives on Dickinson, and it illuminates the many ways in which readings of Dickinson's work are yet to be fully explored. Critics interested in trans readings of Dickinson should note Camille Paglia's analyses of Dickinson's 'transsexual titles' such as 'Boy', 'Czar' and 'Earl':

> Dickinson's sadomasochistic metaphors are a technique of self-hermaphrodization, for as externalizations of internal events, they are an emptying out of female internality. [...] Dickinson's royal titles are honorary degrees of extremity, marking advance into the afterlife. They are hermaphroditic because transcendental. Death makes woman an earl in the same way impersonality makes her an androgyne, by masculinizing her into abstraction.

In her transsexual leaps into eternity, Dickinson is like Swinburne's Sappho, who turns male at death by sloughing off her passive female body.[75]

Paglia labels Dickinson's poem 'My Life had stood a Loaded Gun' (Fr 764/M 354) as 'one of Romanticism's great transsexual self-transformations'.[76] The term 'transsexual' is used indiscriminately to describe the way Dickinson negotiates binary opposition and the socially constructed confines of her gender to achieve poetic and spiritual transcendence. In Paglia's formulation Dickinson therefore also becomes 'hermaphroditic' or 'male' when she discards her 'passive female body'. Paglia's use of such terms is problematized by the fact that they are placed within the argument as being interchangeable. Paglia, who identifies as transgender, has been heavily critiqued by students and trans allies for her position on transgender issues.[77]

Maggie Glover (2017) has foregrounded the ways in which Dickinson's poems challenge gender categories by voicing non-binary, non-gender specific narrators. Glover highlights Dickinson's 'gender role rebellion' and provides many examples of these 'non-gender specific' narrators. She argues that Dickinson's poems challenge the reader to 'establish a new identity apart from what is expected'.[78] She argues that Dickinson highlights the sensations within the body as opposed to the assignment of gender:

> In many of her poems, Dickinson fails to identify with a particular gender at all, suggesting that that which is important about our bodies is not whether they are assigned 'male' or 'female,' but how they affect us, the feelings they stir within us, the ability that they give us to physically experience.[79]

Glover uses one of Dickinson's best-known poems 'I'm Nobody! Who are you?' (Fr 260/M 128) to show how she prizes having no assigned, discernible gender:

> Here, the narrator is praising the state of being 'nobody,' the state of possessing no gender or recognizable features of identity. She does not identify whether or not the narrator or the subject is male or female – indeed, they are neither. Their consciousness grows from their physicality from sensation and thought, not from the ways in which society has characterized their bodies. She again cautions her subject to keep their 'state' a secret, as it is certainly unacceptable to identify with something that society condemns. The narrator goes on to point out the flaws of being 'somebody' and fitting into specific categories that society has pre-planned. By avoiding these categories, such as gender, they will not be able to be discriminated against. The only way to avoid prejudice and injustice is to abandon all signs of that which is subjected to injustice. Dickinson is stating that we can find our identity beyond the gender so why not abandon the target of social injustice that society has forced upon its members?[80]

Where other critics such Gilbert and Gubar have read Dickinson's 'I'm Nobody!' representation of self as another version of the 'invisible, inoffensive soul' she used to negotiate the binary opposition of gender and socially prescribed roles,[81] Glover argues that Dickinson's poem negates the need for gender altogether. In Glover's reading, the poem's speaker readily adopts an identity which is not socially prescribed, to become 'Nobody'. We can see how Dickinson invites the reader to consider this proposition directly, by asking:

> I'm nobody! Who are you?
> Are you – Nobody – too?
>
> (Fr 260. M 128)

Therefore, the struggle in this poem is not about overcoming binary oppositions of gender, of the masculine/active role, or a passive female self or masculine other, but how to fully confront and inhabit an identity which is not socially prescribed.

Various applications of queer theory have been used over the decades in critical readings of Dickinson's poems. This has meant that critical work on Dickinson has reflected the evolution of queer theory and its continuing development. Critics such as Suzanne Juhasz use the theoretical framework of queer theory to explore the connection between desire and identity and, in this case (2005), to explore the ways in which Dickinson's poetry articulates desire as transformational.[82] Juhasz's essay with Cristanne Miller 'Performances of Gender in Dickinson's Poetry' (2002) discusses the ways in which poet and reader 'perform' gender in Dickinson's poetry.[83]

More recently, interventions made within queer theory have produced works which include Dickinson as a key literary voice in their rethinking of the field. One such work is *Queer Optimism: Lyric Personhood and Other Felicitous Persuasions* (2010) by Michael D. Snediker. His work seeks to provide a new paradigm for queer theory, reimagining 'optimism' and the 'positive affect' as concepts which he finds more useful and instructive to the queer theorist rather than the more negative preoccupations of previous critics, such as melancholy, shame and the death drive. Snediker's reimagining of 'optimism' involves a reinterpretation of conventional ways of viewing it; for example, ideas about hope and futurity and their representations in literature come under intense scrutiny in his new vision for 'Queer Optimism'. His reading of Dickinson as a major part of this new paradigm for queer theory is also instructive for the area of Dickinson studies as it reclaims Dickinson's capacity to express a queer identity as well as a body of work which expresses joy, grace and ultimately a 'positive affect' and 'queer optimism'.[84]

Marianne Noble's essay 'Emily Dickinson in the Twenty-First Century' (2021) includes a section on 'Queer Revolution' which explains how the 'unprecedented visibility of and support for LGBTQ+ lives has rendered current readers receptive to and indeed enthusiastic about Dickinson's own queer expressions'.[85] She explains how twentieth-century critics ignored same-sex desire in Dickinson's work or wrote it off as child-like pathology. Tracing lesbian readings of Dickinson from Rebecca Patterson's *The Riddle of Emily Dickinson* (1951) through to Martha Nell Smith's *Rowing in Eden* (1992) she explains how archival research is converging with queer theory to enable us to see same-sex desire in Dickinson's work more clearly. Examples of this are Martha Nell Smith and Ellen Louise Hart's *Open Me Carefully: Emily Dickinson's Intimate Letters to Susan Huntington Dickinson* (1998) in which Smith claims Sue's name had been erased and scratched out in letters by editors (possibly Mabel Loomis Todd) and also Smith's presentation in 2012 of an 1859 daguerreotype of a woman who appears to be an adult Emily Dickinson with her arm around a woman who is likely Kate Scott Anthon, whom Dickinson knew and perhaps loved.[86] Noble then goes on to cite critics such as Henneberg (1995) who warn against definitely categorizing of Dickinson's eroticism, who suggest that to search for heterosexual or homosexual identities in her work is ultimately futile. Noble cites theorists such as Judith Butler who have encouraged readers to resist gender binaries and to see those as imposed structures to be resisted – something which Dickinson scholars have seen in her poetry. Henneberg (1995) sees Dickinson resisting such gender binaries and sees in her poetry 'eroticism which resists definition'.[87]

Crucially, viewing the 'queer' in Dickinson allows critics to access multiple possibilities for readings of her work, in the shape of her metaphors, references and ambitions for her poetic vision, together with the very personal elements of the processes by which such poetic vision comes into being and is presented to us as readers. The fluidity of Dickinson's eroticism and the possibilities for self and identity evident in her poems ('gender role rebellion') make her a poet of increasing significance to LGBTQ+ readers and critics. As will be discussed in Chapter 6, recent screen adaptations of Dickinson have helped to shape emerging scholarship which sees Dickinson as a queer ally and an LGBTQ+ icon.

This chapter has shown the ways in which ideas of the female tradition, gender, sexuality have shaped criticism on Dickinson and the reciprocal relationship between critical writing and those ideas. It is perhaps the awareness of the power of language to speak across time and to effect change which makes Dickinson's poetry so engaging to feminist and LGBTQ+ scholars and critics of her work. We have seen from the scope and range of critical work discussed in this chapter that Dickinson's poetry acts as a catalyst to writing creatively as well as critically. The next chapter looks at criticism which is concerned with Dickinson's work in its historical context and with Dickinson as a literary agent of social and structural change.

Notes

1. White refers to this period as 'The Feminist Revolution in Dickinson Studies' in *Approaching Emily Dickinson*, pp. 64–84.
2. Martha Nell Smith, *Rowing In Eden: Rereading Emily Dickinson* (Austin: University of Texas Press, 1992), p. 8. See also *'Open Me Carefully': Emily Dickinson's Intimate Letters to Susan Huntington Dickinson*, ed. by Martha Nell Smith and Ellen Louise Hart (Ashfield, MA: Paris Press, 1998).
3. See for example, Paula Bernat Bennett, 'Emily Dickinson and Her American Women Poet Peers', pp. 215–35, in *The Cambridge Companion to Emily Dickinson*, ed. by Wendy Martin (Cambridge: Cambridge University Press, 2002).
4. Mary Loeffelholz, *Dickinson and the Boundaries of Feminist Theory* (Urbana and Chicago: University of Illinois Press, 1991), pp. 170–1.
5. Benjamin Lease, *Emily Dickinson's Readings of Men and Books* (London: Macmillan, 1990).
6. Lease, *Emily Dickinson's Readings of Men and Books*, p. 58.
7. Cheryl Walker, *The Nightingale's Burden: Women Poets and American Culture before 1900* (Bloomington: Indiana University Press, 1982), pp. 15, 21–2.
8. Walker, *The Nightingale's Burden*, p. 87.
9. Elizabeth Petrino, *Emily Dickinson and Her Contemporaries: Women's Verse in America, 1820–1885* (Hanover and London: University Press of New England, 1998), p. 5.
10. Petrino, *Emily Dickinson and Her Contemporaries,* p. 54 and p. 129.
11. Petrino, p. 162.
12. Margaret Homans, *Women Writers and Poetic Identity: Dorothy Wordsworth, Emily Bronte and Emily Dickinson* (Princeton: Princeton University Press, 1980), p. 3.
13. Wendy Martin, *An American Triptych: Anne Bradstreet, Emily Dickinson, Adrienne Rich* (Chapel Hill: University of North Carolina Press, 1984).
14. See Joanne Dobson, *Dickinson and the Strategies of Reticence* (Bloomington: Indiana University Press, 1989); Sharon Leder and Andrea Abbott, *The Language*

of Exclusion: The Poetry of Emily Dickinson and Christina Rossetti (New York: Greenwood Press, 1987).
15 Adrienne Rich, '"Vesuvius at Home": The Power of Emily Dickinson', pp. 49–74 in *Parnassus*, 5 (1976).
16 Sielke, *Fashioning the Female Subject*, p. 17.
17 Sielke, p. 181.
18 Sielke, p. 217.
19 Sielke, pp. 16–17.
20 Sielke, p. 228.
21 Vivian R. Pollak, *Our Emily Dickinsons: American Women Poets and the Intimacies of Difference* (Philadelphia: University of Pennsylvania Press, 2017), pp. 6, 266.
22 Michelle Kohler, 'Introduction: Dickinson Dispersed', pp. 1–14 in *The New Emily Dickinson Studies*, ed. by Kohler, pp. 4, 12.
23 The work of Jacques Lacan draws upon that of Sigmund Freud and gendered subject formation. Lacanian psychoanalysis emphasizes the connection between the body and language where identification with either parent as gendered affects subject formation (and therefore relation to language and the symbolic order) in different ways for each of the sexes. For further discussion see, Maggie Humm, *A Reader's Guide to Contemporary Feminist Literary Criticism* (Oxford: Routledge, 2013). Sielke, p. 3: 'this work [of Kristeva, Irigaray and Cixous] continues to be important because it has acknowledged subjectivity as a position in language *and* recognizes the function of the material body in subject constitution.'
24 Paula Bennett, *Emily Dickinson: Woman Poet* (New York and London: Harvester Wheatsheaf, 1990), p. 154.
25 Bennett, *Emily Dickinson: Woman Poet*, pp. 183–4.
26 Sielke, p. 23.
27 Sielke, p. 25.
28 Sielke, pp. 42–5.
29 Sielke, p. 16.
30 Helen Shoobridge, '"Reverence for each Other Being the Sweet Aim": Dickinson Face to Face with the Masculine', *The Emily Dickinson Journal*, 9.1 (Spring 2000), 87–111.
31 Shoobridge, 'Reverence for each Other Being the Sweet Aim', p. 87. She notes Julia Kristeva's view of the *Song of Songs* as 'a first liberation of women' where woman speaks as an 'amorous loved one' (p. 90). She quotes Kristeva's *Tales of Love* (p. 99).
32 Shoobridge, p. 89.
33 Karen Sanchez-Eppler, *Touching Liberty: Abolition, Feminism and the Politics of the Body* (Berkeley: University of California Press, 1993), pp. 105–33. See Chapter 4, Section 4.3, for discussion of this text in relation to Dickinson and race.
34 Sanchez-Eppler, *Touching Liberty*, pp. 106–11.

35 Sanchez-Eppler, p. 130.
36 Sandra M. Gilbert and Susan Gubar, 'A Woman-White: Emily Dickinson's Yarn of Pearl', in Sandra M. Gilbert and Susan Gubar, *The Madwoman in the Attic: The Woman Writer and the Nineteenth Century Literary Imagination* (1979) rev. edn (New Haven: Yale University Press, 2000), pp. 581–650.
37 Camille Paglia, *Sexual Personae: Art and Decadence from Nerfertiti to Emily Dickinson* (London and New Haven: Yale University Press, 1990), p. 624.
38 Paglia, *Sexual Personae*, pp. 652–3.
39 Paglia, p. 658.
40 Paglia, pp. 624–32. Paglia cites many examples from the poems of Dickinson's 'Sadean mode' where pain is inflicted upon the body, and at turns brains, lungs, eyes and the heart each come under pressure – THJ: 556, 315, 1727, 280, 315, 565, 293, 474, 1031, 384, 263, 244, 479, 1729, 379, 1764, 512, 485, 327, 640, 414 (all with numbering from *The Poems of Emily Dickinson*, ed. by T. H. Johnson, 3 vols (Cambridge, MA: Harvard University Press, 1955).
41 Paglia, p. 673.
42 Paglia, pp. 639–42.
43 Paglia, p. 673.
44 Suzanne Juhasz, and Cristanne Miller, 'Performances of Gender in Dickinson's Poetry', in *The Cambridge Companion to Emily Dickinson*, ed. by Wendy Martin (Cambridge: Cambridge University Press, 2002), pp. 107–28.
45 Cynthia Griffin Wolff, '[Im]pertinent Constructions of Body and Self: Dickinson's Use of the Romantic Grotesque', *The Emily Dickinson Journal*, 2.2 (1993), 109–23.
46 H. Jordan Landry, 'Animal/Insectual/Lesbian Sex: Dickinson's Queer Version of the Birds and the Bees', *The Emily Dickinson Journal*, 9.2 (2000), 42–54.
47 Shira Wolosky, 'Emily Dickinson: Being in the Body' in *The Cambridge Companion to Emily Dickinson*, pp. 129–41 (p. 129).
48 For further information about queer theory, see Nikki Sullivan, *A Critical Introduction to Queer Theory* (Edinburgh: Edinburgh University Press, 2003). A key example of a text which emerged from and helped to shape 'queer theory' is Eve Kosofsky Sedgwick's *Epistemology of the Closet* (Berkeley: University of California Press, 1990) as well as feminist and gay liberationist texts such as Adrienne Rich, 'Compulsory Heterosexuality and Lesbian Existence', *Signs: Journal of Women, Culture and Society*, 5.4 (1980), 631–60.
49 Bennett, *Emily Dickinson: Woman Poet*, p. 22.
50 Bennett, p. 20.
51 Bennett, pp. 21–2.
52 Bennett, pp. 155–8 (p. 157).
53 Bennett, p. 207 (Note 6).

54 Bennett, p. 158.
55 Bennett, pp. 162–3.
56 Bennett, pp. 168–70 (p. 170).
57 Bennett, pp. 173–80.
58 Mary E. Galvin, *Queer Poetics: Five Modernist Women Writers* (Connecticut and London: Greenwood Press, 1999).
59 Galvin, *Queer Poetics*, pp. 11–20.
60 Galvin, pp. 11–12.
61 Galvin, pp. 14–19.
62 Smith, *Rowing in Eden*, p. 8.
63 Smith, *Rowing In Eden*, pp. 189–200, for discussion of this poem and Susan's place in Dickinson's poetic production.
64 Smith, pp. 3–4.
65 Smith, p. 167.
66 Smith, p. 220.
67 Smith and Hart, *'Open Me Carefully'*, p. XIV and p. XVIII.
68 Smith and Hart, p. XIII.
69 Smith and Hart, p. XV.
70 An example of this is Martha Ackmann's review of 'Open Me Carefully', *The Emily Dickinson Journal*, 8.2 (1999), 111–13.
71 Lena Koski 'Sexual Metaphors in Emily Dickinson's Letters to Susan Gilbert', in *The Emily Dickinson Journal*, 5.2 (1996), 26–31. Koski quotes Rich (1980: 648) (p. 27).
72 Koski, 'Sexual Metaphors in Emily Dickinson's Letters to Susan Gilbert', pp. 30–1.
73 Joy Ladin, *Soldering the Abyss: Emily Dickinson and Modern American Poetry* (VDM Verlag, Dr Muller, 2010).
74 Joy Ladin, 'Supposed Persons: Emily Dickinson and "I"', *The Emily Dickinson International Society Bulletin*, 25.1 (2013), 15–18, 24 (p. 24).
75 Paglia, pp. 640–1.
76 Paglia, p. 643.
77 See: www.theatlantic.com/ideas/archive/2019/05/camille-paglia-uarts-left-deplatform-587125/
78 Maggie Glover, 'I'm Ceded: Sexual, Social and Gender Role Rebellion in the Poems of Emily Dickinson', *Articulāte*, 10.2 (2017), 11–12.
79 Glover, 'I'm Ceded', p. 10.
80 Glover, p. 10.
81 Gilbert and Gubar, 'A Woman-White', p. 587.
82 Suzanne Juhasz, 'Amplitude of Queer Desire in Dickinson's Erotic Language', *The Emily Dickinson Journal*, 14.2 (2005), 24–33.
83 Suzanne Juhasz and Cristanne Miller, 'Performances of Gender in Dickinson's Poetry' in *The Cambridge Companion to Emily Dickinson*, pp. 107–28.

84 Michael D. Snediker, *Queer Optimism: Lyric Personhood and Other Felicitous Persuasions* (Minnesota: University of Minnesota Press, 2008).
85 Marianne Noble, 'Emily Dickinson in the Twenty-First Century', *American Literature*, 93.2 (2021), 282–305 (p. 285).
86 Noble, 'Emily Dickinson in the Twenty-First Century', p. 286.
87 Noble, p. 286. Cites Sylvia Henneberg, 'Neither Lesbian Nor Straight: Multiple Eroticisms in Emily Dickinson's Love Poetry', *The Emily Dickinson Journal*, 4.2 (2009), 1–19 (p. 4).

4

History, Civil War and race

4.1 Historicizing Dickinson	98
4.2 The US Civil War	108
4.3 Dickinson, ethnicity and race	116

The later-twentieth-century turn to historicist approaches to Dickinson's work will be examined in this chapter by surveying studies with a broadly historicist and/or cultural-political perspective. The more recent archival turn in Dickinson studies, which has meant a move away from theoretical historicism, towards material history, is represented by some of the latest criticism. In addition to its consideration of the discussions around historicizing Dickinson, this chapter focuses on critics engaged more directly with issues of ethnicity, race and class surrounding Dickinson's work and life. These approaches and issues, together with the question of Dickinson's engagement with abolition, coalesce in studies which analyse her responses to the most notable historical event of her lifetime – the US Civil War (1861–5). The act of placing Dickinson within a specific historical context will be examined with reference to Jane Donahue Eberwein's 'Dickinson's Local, Global and Cosmic Perspectives' (1998) and also the pioneering historical methodology of Jay Leyda's biography *The Years and Hours of Emily Dickinson* (1960), and also Betsy Erkkila's key essay 'Emily Dickinson and Class' (1992). The collection of critical debates in Vivian Pollak's *A Historical Guide to Emily Dickinson* (2004) will be assessed as important twenty-first-century directions on the question of what it means to study Dickinson within history; for example, to place Dickinson's work within the context of the Civil War and also alongside contemporary women writers of the period. Work which situates Dickinson within specific cultural and historical contexts, such as Judith Farr's studies – which take in nineteenth-century visual culture in *The Passion of Emily Dickinson* (1992) and the cultivation of plants in *The Gardens of Emily Dickinson* (2004), respectively – exemplifies the historical turn in placing Dickinson's work at the centre of very particular, and culturally specific, historical contexts. Similarly, Cristanne Miller's *Reading in Time: Emily Dickinson in the Nineteenth Century* (2012) is an example of criticism which situates Dickinson within the very specific context of nineteenth-century textual borrowings and literary influences, such as the use of the popular ballad stanza, whilst drawing out her engagements within historical moments. For example, Chapter Six of Miller's book, 'Reading and Writing the Civil War', deals with Dickinson's poetic innovation and engagements with the Civil War in particular. There are essential critical texts which seek to contextualize and historicize Dickinson through her reading, such as Benjamin Lease's *Emily Dickinson's Reading of Men and Books*, and more recently, Páraic Finnerty's *Emily Dickinson's Shakespeare* (2006). The extensive range of books, chapters and articles, each with varying critical perspectives, which are concerned with the Civil War in Dickinson's work and its related topics such as slavery and abolition, death and exile, will be examined closely here. Among the key texts covered will be Shira Wolosky's *Emily Dickinson: A Voice of War* (1984), Karen Sanchez-Eppler's *Touching Liberty: Abolition, Feminism, and the Politics of the Body* (1993) and essays such as Leigh-Anne Urbanowicz Marcellin's 'Emily Dickinson's Civil War Poetry' (1996) and Daneen Wardrop's '"That Minute Domingo": Emily Dickinson's Cooptation of Abolitionist Diction and Franklin's Variorum Edition' (1999). This chapter concludes with a consideration of critical treatments of issues of ethnicity and race in Dickinson's work. Although still a much understudied area within the field, ethnicity and race have been explored more directly by critics such as Paula Bennett, in the article '"The Negro Never Knew": Emily Dickinson and Racial Typology in the Nineteenth Century' (2002), and also by Vivian Pollak in 'Dickinson and the Poetics of Whiteness' (2000). A consideration of how different cultures affected Dickinson's poetry will be explored in twenty-first-century critical pieces such as Aífe Murray's *Maid as Muse: How Servants changed Emily Dickinson's Life and Language* (2010) and Hiroko Uno's essay 'Emily Dickinson's Encounter with the East: Chinese Museum in Boston' (2008).

4.1 Historicizing Dickinson

It is only relatively recently that assumptions about Dickinson's self-imposed isolation, mainly that it was shorthand for a lack of engagement with her own culture, have been corrected. There have been many critics throughout the decades of her reception who have been quick to make a connection between her apparent reclusiveness and a perceived lack of personal concern with the major issues of her day. How could a poet who stayed mostly in her bedroom, within the home of her parents, be seriously engaged with society at large and be deeply immersed in the political, cultural, social, artistic and religious climate in which she lived? Particularly when her poems seem to revel in that isolation, for example, poems such as 'The Soul selects her own society' (Fr 409 / M 218) suggest a turning away from society at large rather than embracing it. As we have seen in the early biographies of Dickinson in Chapter 1 and in the early critical reception of Dickinson's work explained in Chapter 2, often the mythology of Dickinson as a recluse got in the way of serious considerations of her poetic craft and the sheer scope and ambition of its reach. The historical turn in Dickinson studies, which began in the mid-1980s with the publication of two landmark texts, Shira Wolosky's *Emily Dickinson A Voice of War* (1984) and Barton Levi St. Armand's *Emily Dickinson and Her Culture: The Soul's Society* (1984), has continued up to the present day. Critics have continued to attend to the many different ways in which Dickinson's work can be read as evidence of her specific cultural engagement and how she produced poetry which was deeply rooted in, and shaped by, her experience of living in mid-nineteenth-century New England. Historicizing Dickinson and placing her work within a particular context is a necessary, but also somewhat precarious, endeavour.

Jane Donahue Eberwein's essay 'Dickinson's Local, Global and Cosmic Perspectives' (1998) understands 'placing' Dickinson as a reader and participator within her local network of relatives, friends and people of note, as an act which also requires a recognition of Dickinson's point of view as being itself intrinsically *enlarged*. By drawing out the many influences available to her in Amherst in the areas of religion, science and law for example, Eberwein shows how these significant intellectual and spiritual influences brought about an enlarged perspective in her work. Eberwein's essay warns the critic against the trap of imposing a false dichotomy between Dickinson's frequently 'cosmic' or otherworldly perspectives (such as her frequent focus on death and (im)mortality for example), and a false perception of a lack of concern with the immediate life around her. Rather, Eberwein sees that 'cosmic' perspective as arising out of the poet's direct engagement with the vicissitudes that her particular culture produced. Reframing Dickinson's speculative, meditative or 'cosmic' perspective as something which was enabled by the environment with which she engaged redresses assumptions about Dickinson's lack of engagement with her own immediate social milieu and culture. We can see in Dickinson's poetry her engagement with the culture of religious revivals in Amherst, for example, thus displaying the benefit of her education and the location of specific childhood experiences she gained in Amherst. Local, national and global environments, pressures and knowledges are readily on display in her work but are at the same time subsumed into a wider, more speculative and cosmic perspective:

> And, for all her awareness of local and global environments, her truest perspective remained more vertical than horizontal, more attuned to speculations on immortality (experienced even and now and promised hereafter) than on Amherst, America, or the wider world opened by friendships and reading.[1]

It is not the case that Dickinson cut herself off from knowledge of the rest of the world; rather, her acquired forms of knowledge produced in her a more 'vertical' perspective of questioning on a 'cosmic' level. Dickinson's 'speculations on immortality' were achieved precisely through her engagement with the cultural, social, political and religious environments specific to the network of people she knew and were the culmination of her intellectual, artistic and spiritual distillations of them. Eberwein's essay therefore provides an instructive and perhaps cautionary approach to the task of historicizing, and 'placing' Dickinson within a particular context where the 'local', 'global' and 'cosmic' perspectives should not necessarily be viewed as mutually exclusive. Tracing Dickinson's scope of reference to show a poet who is not only aware of the direct concerns of her local and national environments but is also producing work shaped by them has become a critical mainstay. More recently, Páraic Finnerty has written of the 'Global Dickinson' and traced references in her poems to countries and cultures other than her own, to show how her expansive vision can be plotted out specifically by such referents, underscoring the point that we do not need to see evidence of physical travelling to foreign lands to gain an understanding of the poet's knowledge of cultures other than her own immediate surroundings.[2] This point can also be broadened out by extension when thinking in this chapter about Dickinson's engagement with specific historical moments such as the Civil War and also political issues such as abolition and issues of race. The work she produced has been shaped by these things.

The collection of essays edited by Eliza Richards, entitled *Emily Dickinson in Context* (2013), showcases some of the main historical approaches within Dickinson studies and some of the most innovative research which has taken place. Taking three sections as a way of dividing the critical focus, the book explores within those sections the various historical contexts that shaped Dickinson's work. In her essay on critical history since 1955, Magdalena Zapedowska describes the gradual shift in critical perception of Dickinson which moves from a view of her as isolated and unconcerned with society at large, to one which sees her as radically engaged with the culture, views and events of her day. She takes the publication of Thomas H. Johnson's edition of *The Poems of Emily Dickinson* (1955) as a starting point, and this, as she rightly points out, is when the canonical status of Dickinson was first established. She usefully summarizes the shift in critical perception of Dickinson:

> The Dickinson of the 1960s was isolated from the world and indifferent to current events. She explored timeless metaphysical questions in a poetry that transcended her culture and did not develop. Albeit influenced by Calvinism and Transcendentalism, she wrote in a fragmented proto-modernist style, which made her difficult to situate in American literary history. By contrast, today's Dickinson engages with her historical, political, social, and cultural environments in ways that reflect her gender and class status, is deeply affected by the Civil War, draws strength from her relationships with other women, and absorbs the motifs, sentiments, and forms of nineteenth-century popular American poetry. Not only is she immersed in history, but her views, style and composition practices change over time. Her place in literary tradition is among other nineteenth-century genteel American women poets and, more broadly, within transatlantic poetic culture.[3]

Zapedowska's essay describes the shift from the perception of Dickinson as isolated, to the contemporary view of her as connected to her culture in different ways, indicating by extension how methods of literary criticism have changed over the decades. The dominance of the New Criticism of the 1920s–1960s meant that historical contexts were generally eschewed. However, perhaps the temporary critical paralysis we observe within the first half of the history of critical reception of her work can also be explained by her poetry's invitation of a multitude of perspectives; and that this quality, this in-built ambiguity, is part of Dickinson's poetic strategy. Dickinson's poetry urges the reader to make imaginative connections between what she presents, and what we think we might already be familiar with, or what we think we may already know about any given subject. Early reviewers who looked for simplicity and did not anticipate this level of complexity saw this quality (which requires a reader's engagement) as simplicity, awkwardness and naivety.

One of the strongest critical resistances to the creative-critical pull of Dickinson's work has been in the laying bare of the details, fragments and minutiae of her daily life for the purposes of 'mere' observation. Arguably the first to lead the way in resisting the urge to project onto Dickinson in this fashion was the film-maker and film historian Jay Leyda. As discussed in Chapter 1, his groundbreaking biography *The Years and Hours of Emily Dickinson* (1960) presents each document or evidence of her life without any accompanying critical interpretation or conjecture. The result of Leyda's biography was a shift in emphasis away from the interests of the critic, and the beginning of a critical wave which sought to historicize Dickinson, rather than romanticize or privilege a particular view or aspect of her life and work. In many ways this groundbreaking approach to presenting Dickinson's life offered future historicist critics and those interested in political theory a clearer way into her poetry which had previously been obscured by the thrust of critical conjecture. Both Vivian Pollak's *Historical Guide to Emily Dickinson* (2004) and Martha Nell Smith and Mary Loeffelholz's *Companion to Emily Dickinson* (2008) exemplify the commitment to a historical approach laid out in Leyda's biography. Only by getting to grips with the material history surrounding Dickinson can we appreciate her immersion within her own culture but also the radical ways in which her art departs from it. Both important volumes show how Dickinson's poetry is reached effectively through an understanding of the textures of her daily life, through an examination of the social, literary/cultural and political landscape in which she created her work. One important example of this can be seen in one of the key essays in Pollak's *Historical Guide to Emily Dickinson* (2004), 'Dickinson in Context: Nineteenth-Century American Women Poets', by Cheryl Walker.[4] In this essay Walker outlines some of the poetic themes and concerns of Dickinson's female contemporaries and how they may have influenced her work, either as a direct response to them, or as a reaction against culturally prescribed notions of the female poet which were commonplace during this period. Crucially, Walker uses detailed analysis of the poems to discuss recurring themes, common imagery and uses of form, to highlight the ways in which Dickinson's work shares similarities with her female contemporaries. Walker's essay is especially useful to feminist critics because it provides a summary of the debates within feminist criticism on Dickinson to show how our evolving views of gender have influenced our readings of her work within a feminist context. Walker's argument is that Dickinson's work needs to be understood 'as simultaneously inside and outside the realm of nineteenth-century American women's poetry, the beneficiary of its strengths as well as our most exemplary critic of its limitations'.[5] Walker traces the similarities between Dickinson's poetry and that of contemporary poets such as Maria White Lowell. Significantly, she also outlines the ways in which Dickinson's work diverges from those poets with whom she has most in common, such as Lowell. Dickinson's poems condense meanings, where three or more meanings can co-exist in a single phrase. This 'Dickinsonian strategy', she argues, is something extremely rare in other nineteenth-century women poets. Dickinson's poems do not conform to any prescribed sense of female literary decorum, and her 'volcanic lines are anything but reticent or ladylike'. Furthermore, Dickinson's poetic innovations and her frequent impulse towards self-reflexivity on the nature of poetry, her need to write poems *about* poetry, set her apart. In Walker's view, her work seems to anticipate both modernism and postmodernism unlike any of her nineteenth-century American contemporaries. Dickinson is seen here as a forerunner, sharing more with future twentieth-century American women poets such as Amy Lowell, H.D., Marianne Moore, Elizabeth Bishop and Sylvia Plath than with her nineteenth-century contemporaries. However, by looking at her work alongside that of contemporary female nineteenth-century American writers, Walker shows how these women's lives (and also their literary output) were equally affected by the challenges imposed by the construction of gender during the period. The feminist historical contextualizing of Dickinson serves to highlight the ways in which she was ultimately a nonconformist, and, in this, she is unlike her female *or* male contemporaries. Although she was in a league of her own, Dickinson's work does not arrive to us as if in a vacuum:

> She was both at home and at sea in her New England female context. The most accurate judgement we can make is that her work remembers others' poems even as it forgets them.[6]

The importance of historical context and also the turn to materiality in Dickinson studies was predicted by Suzanne Juhasz (1998) in the late twentieth century as a new direction for Dickinson studies.[7] With the advent of the full digitization of Dickinson's corpus being made available for all, work which focuses upon the materiality of the poems has continued well into this century.[8] Historical material such as this has been used by critics interested in cultural and political theory to emphasize the concomitant structures of power reflected in the poetry as, for example, in Betsy Erkkila's (1992) essay 'Emily Dickinson and Class' which locates Dickinson's work within a position of class privilege. Whilst acknowledging that Dickinson did not share her father's political (and public) Whig persuasion, Erkkila demonstrates Dickinson's espousal of his class-based values and social fears in response to a burgeoning democracy, such as the fear of the expansionist, pro-slavery, commercial impetus of the masses, including immigrants.[9] In a later essay, 'Dickinson and the Art of Politics', Erkkila argues forcefully that we must read Dickinson's 'interior' struggles within the context of the 'exterior' political struggles of her time if we are to fully comprehend the engagement with her culture evident in her poems. An important aspect of this study is the way in which Erkkila asks us to reconsider the frames of 'public' and 'private' which have, as she argues, 'too often structured past approaches to her work'.[10] Much of the work of historicizing Dickinson is done in negotiating this public/private dichotomy.

Domhnall Mitchell's work on Dickinson and class similarly prioritizes the need to read Dickinson's work within specific historical and cultural contexts. His argument positions Dickinson as speaking from the perspective of both the oppressed and the privileged, having a dual vantage point from which to formulate her own literary responses to society and culture, being both a woman and middle-class. His book *Dickinson: Monarch of Perception* (2000) provides sensitive readings of Dickinson's poems against the backdrop of their sociopolitical histories. He considers the mid-nineteenth-century concerns around the advent of the railroad and immigration, examines the nature of Dickinson's domesticity and explores her interest in horticulture in order to show how these historical and cultural contexts inform the language of her work. Crucially, Mitchell argues that Dickinson could 'occupy positions of oppression and privilege at the same time', being both female and middle class.[11] Similarly, in his chapter 'Dickinson and Class' in *The Cambridge Companion to Dickinson* (2002), he argues that Dickinson's relative silence on specific political events and the casual comedy she attaches to the lives of those considered be of a lower social status in her letters give voice to a classist and hierarchical mentality. However, he also suggests that these silences and hierarchical attitudes have more to do with Dickinson being a woman than her being middle class. The absences in her writing on various political subjects, for example, reveal to us not disinterestedness, but the outline of topics which may have been deemed as being beyond her scope as a woman to discuss. Moreover, Mitchell suggests that as the sister of an influential brother who was viewed by the family and their social circles to be the authority on these matters and who also inherited his father's prominent place within their society, Dickinson perhaps remained silent to give precedence to his voice. Mitchell re-states what perhaps bears repeating: the status of women in nineteenth-century American society is also a historical context through which to view Dickinson's work. Therefore, Dickinson's writing 'can simultaneously be seen as a site of political resistance and reaction'.[12] Historical contexts matter in Mitchell's assessments of Dickinson, not only in the way they impart indispensable meaning to our understanding of particular poems but also in the way we can use them to interpret her responses and in some cases her silences around specific historical events or cultural attitudes. Mitchell argues that Dickinson went to great lengths to not include contextual information in her writing, to leave no trace of what she saw as the 'contamination of the contemporary'.[13] Whilst many critics would take issue with this, Mitchell's point is that the indirectness, and thus flexibility, of the poems lead us back towards meanings which hover on the margins of her text. Her sophisticated and oblique use of language generates meaning and interpretation without having to name specific topics, or historical events, directly. In this way, her poems contain what Mitchell describes as the 'magnificent architecture of surmise'.[14]

Another important way in which Dickinson's work can be seen historically is by tracing the many influences, artistic, literary and spiritual, to which Dickinson was exposed, through her reading. Benjamin Lease's book *Emily Dickinson's Reading of Men and Books* (1990) was pivotal in this area, perhaps leading the way in research which sought to position Dickinson as a wide and vividly engaged reader and to highlight the ways in which such reading showed up in the poetry, either obliquely or directly. Much has been done on Dickinson's engagement with individual writers from Renaissance to eighteenth-century writing, on the influence of British Romantic and Victorian literature, on Dickinson's literary predecessors and contemporaries in the United States, as well as on the transatlantic exchange between women writers during the mid-nineteenth century.[15] Critics have sought to historicize Dickinson through her reading practices, preferences and habits. The historical turn has moved critics to draw from a broad spectrum of arenas within nineteenth-century culture, such as hymnody, visual art and horticulture, and to produce book-length studies such as Judith Farr's *The Gardens of Emily Dickinson* (2004). Meanwhile, Cristanne Miller's *Reading in Time* (2012) contextualizes Dickinson's work within specific nineteenth-century literary modes and practices.

What it means to read Dickinson in the twenty-first century is something upon which Martha Nell Smith focuses in her essay 'Forever Young: Rereading Emily Dickinson in the Twenty-First Century' (2015), where the central question she asks is, 'What is it like to read this?'[16] Smith rehearses the widely held critical views of the past, such as Dickinson being reclusive and reluctant to publish, and counters them with evidence from more recent scholarship to bring scholars of Dickinson up to speed and to locate her work within current critical thinking. For example, she reminds readers that Dickinson's method of distributing poems in letters and binding them together into forty fascicles or manuscript books is now accepted as a form of scribal or manuscript publication, whereas earlier critics saw her lack of traditional publication as fitting with her reclusive persona and as evidence of her 'refusal' to publish. Digitized access to Dickinson's poems in the twenty-first century, including the 'scraps' of paper she wrote on, such as the backs of envelopes, has increased our understanding of the ways in which she worked and the shape and scope of her corpus. Smith shows how such technology enables us to have a greater understanding of the traces of Dickinson's audiences, the ways in which the poems were handled, folded, pinned, stained, returned to, read aloud and lived with. Far from being the reclusive virgin Thomas Wentworth Higginson would have us believe she was, she is known to have entertained visitors at the Evergreens and the Homestead, sometimes playing piano, well into her thirties. Crucially, Smith explains how the critical past has informed the current thinking on Dickinson in the twenty-first century, and in turn how twenty-first-century technology has enabled us to learn more about nineteenth-century reading.[17]

Meanwhile, in her essay 'Overcoming Oneself as Subject in Dickinson's Poetry: Adorno and Heidegger' (2015), Colleen Shu-Ching Wu considers what might be lost by the drive to historicize Dickinson. Prioritizing a philosophical model of interpretation over historicism, she argues that the tension between Dickinson's poetic self and the external world can be seen more clearly through the theory of dialectical relation put forward by Theodor W. Adorno. In dialectical relation, the self is in resistance to social context. Bringing the work of Adorno and philosopher Martin Heidegger together to show how each challenges the other, providing an example of what she sees as a more genuine dialectical relation, Shu-Ching Wu uses this model to show how Dickinson's lyrical self overcomes herself as a subject. She argues that there is a 'confined self – a self confined in poetry, not in social context. It is an "I" mediated within poetry that contends with an "I" mediated by social context'.[18] She provides a critique of the 'dominant historicism' in Dickinson studies, and the way in which 'ahistoricism' has been perceived as a weakness in criticism of Dickinson's work.[19] She argues that Dickinson's poetic 'I' is already mediated through poetry in various ways, such as through memory, so that the mediated 'I' in her poetry is in tension with the 'I' which is mediated through social context. She finds in Dickinson's work a notion of self which competes with the philosophy of Adorno and Heidegger, thus providing a thoughtful consideration of the ways in which we may encounter a philosophical blind spot when viewing other critical approaches against historical studies of Dickinson's work.

And yet, what *is* at stake if we attempt to read Dickinson's lyric 'I' in isolation from history? That is to say, what if we do not read Dickinson alongside her contemporaries and the concomitant historical events and literary and political culture in which she lived, but see her instead as a special case, a lone genius, removed from the society and the time in which she lived? Part of the problem of this rather polarized view of Dickinson's engagement with culture may lie in our perception of lyric poetry itself, and of our practices in reading lyric poetry. Virginia Jackson's book *Dickinson's Misery: A Theory of Lyric Reading* (2005) addresses this very problem. She shows how the editing, organization, printing and circulation of Dickinson's work ('the heterogeneous materials of her practice') echo the story of the lyric genre as a way of interpreting literature, arguing that 'the circulation of Dickinson's work as poetry chronicles rather exactly the emergence of the lyric genre as a modern mode of literary interpretation'.[20] Jackson shows how Dickinson's work strays beyond and evades the parameters of our version of the lyric genre and therefore also beyond our own perceptions of what reading lyric poetry should be like. Many different literary forms were subsumed under the title of the lyric in the nineteenth century, such as the ode, song, elegy and valentine. Jackson argues that Dickinson has been represented by her various editors as a lyric poet and that these editorial processes have sidelined the individual material contexts of each poem as well as an understanding of the lyric as a diverse and eclectic literary genre. Dickinson the lyric poet, as presented to the reader, is also a product of a narrow twentieth-century interpretation of the lyric as enclosed and contextless.

Wu's (2015) philosophical model via Heidegger and Adorno, that the lyric 'I' in Dickinson's work is in tension with a mediated social self which positions each lyric 'I' in a kind of isolated state, is to be at a remove or at least in a poetical safe harbour from the tidal pull of society and the events of history which shape it. As Paula Bennett (2002) argues, where Dickinson fails to deliver on writing overtly about racial inequality, many of her female contemporaries were able to provide this easily and unambiguously. As with other (albeit usually male) 'canonical' poets, the cult of the genius thrives in a discourse which sees the poet in isolation. Bennett argues that Dickinson's limitations, that is to say, her comparative ambiguity about the political issues of her day, and in particular then also her '"racism," such as it was', must be acknowledged alongside her undisputed genius.[21] The extent to which Dickinson's work engages with the social issues and main historical events of her time, such as the American Civil War, is something which occupies a large critical space within Dickinson studies. To some extent this appears as much a reaction to the 'lone genius' model as it is to the question of Dickinson's racism. In Bennett's view, the 'undisputed genius' of Dickinson can, and must, co-exist with the limitations and ambiguity she sees in her work.

4.2 The US Civil War

A major theme to emerge from the historical turn in Dickinson studies is the extent of her engagement with the Civil War (1861–5), and the scale and nature of her creative output during this time. Much of her work, including her most iconic poetry, was produced during the Civil War years. Early critical views maintained that Dickinson was largely unaffected by the effects of the American Civil War. These views were routinely reproduced up until the twentieth century, when scholars began to reassess her poems of this period. Dandurand's (1984) important work on Dickinson and the publication history of a few of her poems during the Civil War period imparts information about 'four newly discovered texts' which had come to light to show how Dickinson was deeply moved by and engaged with the effects of the Civil War. Moreover, she argues that Dickinson's published poems were 'her contribution to the Union cause' and crucially that 'more poems would have been published had she offered them'. This article goes some way to dispel the original view that Dickinson was uninterested in the events of the American Civil War and that her poems were routinely rejected by editors or that she was uninterested in publication.[22] Dandurand's article forged a concrete case for Dickinson's engagement with the Civil War by employing a combination of vigorous archival research and alertness to the echoes of war in her poems. Dickinson's references to, and concern with, the Civil War is something which is now taken as given by most scholars. Vivian Pollak writes in her introduction to the *A Historical Guide to Emily Dickinson* (2004) that it was (then):

> an emerging consensus that Dickinson wrote most powerfully during the Civil War, and that she participated in a larger national debate about the meaning of life itself when pressured by death. As a poet of the inner civil war, she used images of death and dying to clarify her own experience, and she frequently psychologized military tropes.[23]

This 'consensus' of Dickinson being the most productive during the Civil War years has been consolidated by nearly two decades of scholarship in this area. Shira Wolosky has continued to lead the way, a field of enquiry which began with her major work *Emily Dickinson: A Voice of War* (1984) which sought to illuminate to the reader the various ways in which Dickinson was engaged with the political upheavals of the Civil War and how this showed up very forcefully in her poetic landscape.[24] Wolosky's was one of the first full-length studies to powerfully argue against the notion of Dickinson as a poet of privacy and introspection, and as someone who remained relatively silent on contemporary events and about the Civil War in particular. The view of Dickinson as being largely unaffected by the political climate of her day had hitherto been espoused by critics such as Richard Sewell, Karl Keller and David Porter. In her groundbreaking study, Wolosky shows how the war prompted a crisis within her poetics and argues forcefully that Dickinson questions the Calvinist-inflected rhetoric of the war as well as the linguistic foundations for human discourse on the divine in her Civil War–era poems. One of the major contributions the book makes to Dickinson studies is to re-cast the dynamic of the masculine public sphere and feminine domestic self and to resituate Dickinson within it. Wolosky is at pains to show how the details of Dickinson's life argue against the idea that she could be anything but socially and politically engaged. The rich political and cultural environment of her own household, as well as her circle of correspondence, and her consumption of newspapers and magazines, meant that she was not only fully informed of key events, but that her poems and letters are inflected with their detail. One of the main reasons for Dickinson's 'crisis' during this period is brought on by the theological justification for war. Wolosky reads Dickinson's poetry working through this central concern and compares her responses with the wartime writings of Herman Melville, Ralph Waldo Emerson and Nathaniel Hawthorne. More recently, Wolosky has underscored these arguments, namely in a chapter of *A Historical Guide to Emily Dickinson*, edited by Vivian Pollak, entitled 'Public and Private in Dickinson's War Poetry' (2004). In this, she emphasizes the connection between the political crisis in American culture and the metaphysical crisis of representing the self which is evident in Dickinson's writing of the Civil War period. She writes that

> Dickinson's texts are battlefields between contesting claims of self and community, private and public interest, event and design, metaphysics and history, with each asserted, often against each other.

Wolosky concludes with an assertion that Dickinson's war poetry is never 'only about a specific historical event. They always reach into figural spaces beyond any immediate referent'. And:

> In the context of war, her poetry emerges as scenes not only of personal conflict but also confronting the most imperative concerns of her – and our – culture, in a poetics of contest and strain and concealment, but also of address and courage and revelation.[25]

Wolosky's argument about how we view the connection between different aspects of Dickinson's poems of the Civil War coalesces into a completely realized view of her 'relational aesthetics' in her chapter 'War and the Art of Writing: Emily

Dickinson's Relational Aesthetics' (2015). In it, she describes Dickinson's poetry as a 'paradigm lyric' which offers the reader a 'map of critical history'. However, whilst Dickinson's poetry appears to every kind of critic to exemplify their own modus operandi, what makes Dickinson's work so enduring is that it also 'challenges these methodological divisions, pointing instead to a revision of aesthetics as *relational theory*. Art, rather than being defined in terms of any one of these parameters, emerges as exactly the ongoing inter-conjunction and trajectory of multiple engagements'.[26] Wolosky sees it necessary to amplify the aesthetic elements of her poetic responses to the Civil War amidst the wealth of material-historical approaches which the subject has engendered in recent debates.

Leigh-Anne Urbanowicz Marcellin's essay on Dickinson's Civil War poetry '"Singing off the Charnel Steps": Soldiers and Mourners in Dickinson's War Poetry' (2000) develops the thematic groupings of these poems as identified by Shira Wolosky in *Emily Dickinson: A Voice of War* (1984) and argues that Dickinson's war poetry can be separated out into three distinct groups.[27] The first is a group of poems in which Dickinson questions the value of war and whether peace is achievable. The second is more spiritually probing, where she considers the relationship between God, Nature and War and we see her struggling to conceive of war in any divine plan. The final group, which Marcellin identifies and focuses on in this essay, comprises the lyrical, elegiac and dramatic modes in which Dickinson considers the deaths of the soldiers and the experiences of their mourners. However, citing poems such as 'He gave away his Life' (Fr 530 / M 291), 'He scanned it – Staggered' (Fr 994 / M 456) and 'My Portion is Defeat – today – ' (Fr 704 / M 342), Marcellin shows how Dickinson's attention to detail of the grim realities of war demonstrates a bleakness and sentiment which is ultimately anti-romantic. The soldier who, at the moment of despair, 'gropes' for God and is without human affection as he:

Caressed a Trigger absently
And wandered out of Life –

(Fr 994, M 456)

'Caressed' is ironic and has the effect of shifting focus to the reality of the trigger, which is easily activated during such moments of abject isolation. Dickinson shows us how the realities of war disrupt the confines of poetry. In these poems dramatic monologues are interrupted and, crucially, the meaninglessness of war is left unresolved:

How different Victory
To Him who has it – and the One

> Who to have had it, would have been
> Contenteder – to die –
>
> (Fr 704, M 342)

In Dickinson's evocation of war, concepts such as 'victory' which are upheld during wartime are not romanticized but scrutinized for their validity.

Faith Barrett's chapter 'Slavery and the Civil War' in *Emily Dickinson in Context* (2013) reconsiders the notion that Dickinson's poems of the Civil War show only an internalized response. She challenges the perception of Dickinson's 'inner Civil War', which sees her 'personal crisis' of 1862 as related to the Civil War era only insofar as she was able to borrow metaphorical language of suffering and apply it to her own mental state. Barrett sees in Dickinson's Civil War poetry a reflection of the ambiguity felt by many Americans during that time, where opposing thought, and a reversal of thought, are retained within a single poem. Focus is given to poems which denote the toll of the war and the use of 'battlefield' imagery, such as Fr 465 / M 233, in which Dickinson connects the colours of autumn with words suggestive of violence, such as 'blood' and 'artery', and to poems which seem to question the validity of those not on the battlefield remaining alive:

> It feels a shame to be Alive –
> When Men so brave – are dead –
> One envies the Distinguished dust –
> Permitted – such a Head –
>
> (Fr 524, M 257)

Barrett argues that Dickinson's Civil War poems are experimental, where she tries out 'opposing ideological positions, sometimes skeptically questioning wartime ideologies and sometimes endorsing them', and it is within poetry that Dickinson is able to find the possibilities for 'equivocation, ambivalence, and reversal'.[28] Arguing that we should 'resituate' Dickinson within the context of the American Civil War to discover the extent of her innovation and political awareness, Barrett charts what is a sophisticated development in her poetic responses to war, death and suffering. Of particular note is her comparative reading of the treatment of slavery, ethnicity and race in two Civil War–era poems: Fr 788 / M 386 and Fr 836 / M 412. The first poem likens the auctionable slave to the writer proffering her work (and soul) for publication, and, as Barrett argues, she 'perversely appropriates abolitionist rhetoric'. The second poem sees Dickinson presenting an opposite stance, without any equivocation, where all hierarchies are 'erased in the grave'. As Barrett notes, 'central to "Colour – Caste – Denomination" (Fr 836 / M 412) is the image of the mass grave in which the blood of different races is mingled.'[29] The poem envisages the 'democratic fingers' of death, seeming to erase all markers of difference:

> As in sleep – all Hue forgotten –
> Tenets – put behind –
> Death's large – Democratic fingers
> Rub away the Brand –
>
> (Fr 836, M 412)

Barrett's essay shows how 'resituating' Dickinson's Civil War–era poems within their historical context and observing the ways in which her poetry allowed her to 'test out' opposing ideologies enable us to see the divided responses of American society at that time and beyond:

> In her divided responses to the war, Dickinson explores the divided perspectives of Americans – both Northern and Southern – who celebrated fallen soldiers as Christian martyrs, mourned the meaninglessness of wartime deaths, lamented the rising human and financial costs of the conflict, reasserted arguments about white racial superiority, or dared to imagine a nation undivided by differences of race, class and creed.[30]

Far from being disengaged with the political climate of her day, Dickinson's poems provide us with a more rounded vista of its various viewpoints and, at the same time, echo the disorienting effects of the Civil War period.

Dickinson's poetry of the Civil War is featured in Eliza Richards's *Battle Lines: Poetry and Mass Media in the U.S Civil War* (2019). This study is interested in the relationship between mass media and poetry during the war and how the war 'generated a powerful sense of single-minded collectivity in readers and writers, which altered the terms of poetic expression'. Using Dickinson's poem 'How News must feel when travelling' (Fr 1379 / M 521; written a decade after the end of the Civil War) to open her introduction, Richards argues that poets, whose work often featured in newspapers and magazines, had to step up to the increasing power of the news during war time and to make their work instantly and recognizably relevant to the events of the day and to anticipate and frame the thoughts and feelings of readers. Moreover, 'Poetry's compressed forms traveled more easily than stories, novels or essays through ephemeral print media, allowing it to move alongside and rapidly respond to news reports.' It is no coincidence then that Richards finds the perfectly distilled form of Dickinson's words to open her book on this subject:

> If News have any Heart
> Alighting at the Dwelling
> 'Twill enter like a Dart!
>
> (Fr 1379, M 521)³¹

Dickinson's poem conveys the immediacy of news which has 'heart', and has the power to explain details with instant accuracy – as the 'dart' contained within Dickinson's poetry itself.

In Chapter Two, which is entitled 'The "Ghastly Harvest"', Dickinson's work is set alongside that of John James Piatt and Walt Whitman to show how war alters their terms of poetic expression. Here it is specifically the 'autumnal traditions' found in poetry of a pastoral kind such as those typified by Keats which are being adapted. Richards argues that each poet offers 'meditations on how to adapt autumnal traditions to account for mass death' and that they 'mark dissatisfaction and a sense of tragic discontinuity between pastoral traditions and present conditions, peace and wartime'. Furthermore, she argues that

> none of the poems fully accept the limitations of poetic traditions in addressing critical aspects of the war. None of them offer the pastoral as a kind of solace or refuge. Noting the stark difference between the autumn tranquility surrounding Northern civilians and the bloody autumn of war, these poets challenge themselves and their readers to make war at a distance real enough to disrupt comfort and safety at home. They conclude that reading about the war in newspapers and meditating on the experience of war from a remote position can't overcome the gap.[32]

What is refreshing about Richards's approach is that her argument does not get caught up in what Dickinson's involvement in the war may or may not have been – but rather her focus on the alterations to poetic expression during the Civil War (poetic engagement with the pastoral genre or with emerging knowledge about photography) is flexible enough to speak for itself and to accommodate multiple ideological viewpoints, thus also allowing for a more flexible view of Dickinson's work. Richards shows how Dickinson's poems 'explore the immediate effects of mediacy', where hearing about a battle remotely, and of those who have died on your behalf, suggests a type of death conferred upon the unsuspecting reader by proxy. She draws parallels between Dickinson's treatment of the war and the emerging interest in photography and the subject of mediated viewing – that is to say, the gap between the viewer and the viewed.[33] The frame of Richards's argument – that the terms of poetic expression are collectively altered during the Civil War and are synchronized with the emergence of mass media – is brilliantly conceived because it shows how the pressures of war are inevitably within the poem's expression. It also shows how the effects of the war were present in her work long after the war had ended. This work successfully delineates an entire genre of Civil War poetry and places Dickinson's work firmly within it.

Critics have read Dickinson's work through the lens of the abolitionist movement. Karen Sanchez-Eppler's pioneering work on Dickinson and abolitionist rhetoric, *Touching Liberty: Abolition, Feminism, and the Politics of the Body* (1993), paved the way for new directions in scholarship in the 1990s. Using the body, and bodily difference, as a focus in her analysis of the political and literary expression of the period from the early 1830s to the Civil War era, Sanchez-Eppler reads lyric poetry and sentimental anti-slavery fiction alongside slave narratives to show how they produced a new model of personhood, where boundaries between public and private become blurred. The constricted body of the slave becomes analogous to the domestically circumscribed body of the woman, where race and sex are equally distinctive. Therefore, Sanchez-Eppler sees in Dickinson's work a flexibility between traditionally opposite notions such as 'freedom' and 'bondage', when such opposing notions were frequently upheld in abolitionist writing of the period. She works through notable literary examples such as Walt Whitman and Harriet Jacobs to show how gender and race intersect in Antebellum-era literary expression. In Dickinson's work she sees an internalized version of the social and historical meanings which in the work of her contemporaries was more overtly public and political. Crucially, she also sees exploitation of the black body in this cultural appropriation, of which Dickinson's work is a part.

Following on from Sanchez-Eppler, Daneen Wardrop's work on Dickinson, '"That Minute Domingo": Emily Dickinson's Cooptation of Abolitionist Diction and Franklin's Variorum Edition' (1999), seeks to uncover the ways in which she was actively engaged with the energies of abolitionism and democracy. She states that 'abolitionist inflections can provide a basis for the designation of ontological states in some of her poems'.[34] She uses Franklin's Variorum edition of the poems (1998), then hot off the press, to show how all the exhaustive versions of a given text weigh in on meaning and our readings of her. She focuses on three poems closely, which she sees as exemplifying the inflections of abolition: 'One of the ones that Midas touched' (Fr 1488 / M 617), 'Civilization spurns the leopard!' (Fr 276 / M 529) and 'A dying tiger moaned for drink' (Fr 529 / M 290). She brilliantly contrasts the editorial choices made by Johnson in presenting the poem 'One of the ones that Midas touched' (THJ 1466 / Fr 1488 / M 617), with Franklin's variorum edition which lays bare each version plus a fragment. In Johnson's version the first stanza of the poem is from a variant, which includes the subject of a 'confiding Prodigal', whereas Franklin's variorum edition provides the alternative version, featuring 'that minute domingo':

> One of the ones that Midas touched
> Who failed to touch us all,
> Was that minute domingo
> The blissful oriole
>
> (Fr 1488, B.1)

Interestingly, Miller's version (M 617) also retains the 'confiding Prodigal'. Wardrop cites Folsom and Price's 'Dickinson, Slavery and the San Domingo Moment' (1997) to show that Dickinson's use of the word 'Domingo' is particularly resonant, and a 'vortex' word, which to the reader would immediately evoke the violent San Domingo slave revolts of the early nineteenth century in the same way that Viet Nam would evoke war to the later-twentieth-century generation.[35] She sees Franklin's organization of Dickinson's variants and his description of where each poem is placed within a fascicle as crucial to our understanding of how Dickinson's poems 'express furtive Africanist concerns'.[36] For example, she traces Dickinson's concentrated thought from one poem to the next in fascicle twenty-eight, where the poem 'A dying tiger moaned for drink' (Fr 529 / M 290-291) appears alongside 'One anguish in a crowd' (Fr 527 / M 290). In this latter poem Dickinson employs the image of the hound being chased, imagery common in slave narratives such as those written by Frederick Douglass and Harriet Jacobs, and also in anti-slavery fiction such as Harriet Beecher Stowe's *Uncle Tom's Cabin*, to describe the experience of the fugitive slave. Wardrop shows us how the presence of this poem in the same fascicle as poem (Fr 529 / M 290-291), which is evocative of the slave, suggests a direct correlation between the use of the hound in slave narratives and Dickinson's use of it in the poem. The word 'hound', as the word 'Domingo', would have been immediately synonymous with the cause of abolition. Wardrop's work shows how Franklin's variorum edition enabled a new way of reading her work and of tracing thematic continuity across the fascicles as well as highlighting the editorial choices which had obscured these themes from the reader. Importantly, by uncovering such thematic continuity Wardrop highlights the ways in which Dickinson's texts speak to the themes and motifs in slave narratives and the Africanist concerns of her time.

The issues of how Dickinson conceived of herself as a poet during the Civil War era and how she viewed the publishing market, and also of how we view her work from this period, as considered by Dandurand (1984), are worth closer examination. Benjamin Friedlander (2009) argues that Dickinson's inclusion in anthologies of American War poetry, two of which consist of American Civil War poetry, specifically is something that confirms Dickinson's place within the canon of American Civil War Poets.[37] In his article 'Emily Dickinson and the Battle of Ball's Bluff' he makes a convincing argument that Dickinson's engagement with Civil War stories and themes shows an astute awareness of the publishing market and of what the public wanted to read about. He shows how her response to the Battle of Ball's Bluff is remodelled in the poem 'When I was small, a Woman died' (Fr 518 / M 253) to highlight local heroism (Amherst's first fatally wounded soldier) and to glorify death in a way to make it a more palatable version of events from the war for a newspaper readership. Arguing that because two poems which were a response to this event were published in the local newspaper, her remodelled version for Amherst readers was a serious bid for publication on her part. Comparing Dickinson's responses to events with the sombre war poetry of Melville, for example, shows how Dickinson's joyous mode was somewhat uncharacteristic, and, therefore, a calculated attempt at publication and popularity. These local interest themes and stories were something from which Dickinson later distanced herself:

> Conceivably, in writing about 'The Battle of Ball's Bluff', Dickinson gave herself over entirely to the needs of publication, to what it takes to 'get in the books', rejecting or even recoiling from the final result. Such recoiling is now a familiar story; the willingness that occasionally preceded it still needs to be told.[38]

Therefore, the Civil War period gave Dickinson an opportunity to engage with the popular literature of her day, and with public expression of private grief, which included hymns as well as the poetry she read in magazines and periodicals. As we shall see in the following chapter, Dickinson's engagement with hymns and hymn culture during the Civil War period is perhaps something which binds her most closely to history.

4.3 Dickinson, ethnicity and race

The direct discussion of ethnicity and race is a relatively recent development within the long history of Dickinson's critical reception. There have been excellent twenty-first-century critical interventions on Dickinson and the issue of ethnicity and race, but frequently they have formed part of a broader discussion on the intersection of class and politics, and there is therefore much more work to be done.[39] One of the earliest interventions in this area is Betsy Erkkila's (1992) essay 'Emily Dickinson and Class', in which she surveys the hierarchy of ethnic, racial and class difference which influences Dickinson's poems. For example, she sees in 'Mine – by the Right of the White Election!' (Fr 411 / M 219) language which 'cannot finally be separated from nineteenth-century debates about the racial hegemony of the white race and of New Englanders in particular'. Moreover, she maintains that 'Dickinson's elitism is evident in her almost complete silence on the major social issues of her time' and goes on to describe a 'xenophobia' and an 'assumption of a natural order of class and race' as evidenced in detail from her letters and poetry. Using 'Color – Caste – Denomination –' (Fr 836 / M 412) and 'The Malay – took the Pearl' (Fr 451 / M 226) Erkkila argues that Dickinson's poems reproduce an 'unchangeable social order of race and class difference and subordination'.[40]

Erkkila's work asks that we reconsider the 'public' and 'private' frames of seeing Dickinson's work as she sees this as being crucial to our understanding of the representation of ethnicity and race in Dickinson. Whilst many of her poems may seem personal, 'interior', and not to refer to current events directly, she argues that their interiors are 'full of "public" attitude about the political, social, religious, sexual, racial, scientific, and economic contests that marked her time'.[41] Erkkila's discussion of 'Dickinson's language of white precedence' understands an entire 'perdurable racist *mentality*' and 'psychology of whiteness' reflected in Dickinson's work:

> Although Dickinson's language of white precedence is grounded in biblical and Judeo-Christian symbolism, her poems suggest the ways religious symbolism joins with racial ideology and Western aestheticism to create a perdurable racist *mentality* – a psychology of whiteness – that remains intact despite the legal passage of constitutional amendments that abolished slavery, declared black men citizens, and provided for black male suffrage in the post-Civil War period.[42]

Similarly, Paula Bennett's discussion of the racial stereotyping Dickinson would have seen reproduced in journals such as the *Springfield Republican* finds this stereotyping replicated in the poet's work, also reading her poem 'The Malay – took the Pearl' within this context. Bennett's essay explores how 'the failure to acknowledge Dickinson's racism speaks to the reading of her generally' and by this she means that the view of her as a lone genius needs to be deconstructed somewhat in order to view her as 'one more nineteenth-century poet and a woman of her time and place' – not to see past or through the racism but to allow it to be there in the poems. Bennett argues that other women poets of the nineteenth century wrote about ethnicity, race and class in an effective way, and by studying those other poets we can see precisely what Dickinson did *not* do in her verse. She argues that we must not continue to exploit Dickinson's ambiguity in order to find in her work values and experiences that we can find in the work of other poets contemporary with Dickinson more readily.[43]

Alternatively, Vivian Pollak sees the racial stereotyping evident in Dickinson's poems as her 'use of race as a politically subversive form of self-definition'.[44] In her discussion of 'The Malay – took the Pearl' (Fr 451 / M 226), whilst recognizing the poem is not without its 'own kind of racism', she argues that we need to distinguish between 'the racial stereotypes the poem absorbs, its ambivalent critique of imperialism and the larger vision it projects'. This 'larger vision' can be seen in this poem, for example, in the ways Dickinson is 'figuring whiteness as a burden' and then also 'opens up a space to dwell in possibility'.[45] Pollak argues that this 'larger project' is one which 'depended on validating desire as it pushed against cultural stereotypes'. Furthermore, that Dickinson through her writing 'sought to transcend "Color – Caste – Denomination," by […] producing those intermittent and self-contradictory elegies for whiteness'. Most striking here is Pollak's conception of Dickinson's efforts in language to be within the realm of a war effort of her own, a 'war of words':

> This woman's war critiques the racial exclusions on which her own class privilege also depended.[46]

Domnhall Mitchell's work on ethnicity, class and culture in Dickinson's poetry has also focused on the uses for, and significance of, colour, and particularly 'whiteness', as it appears in her poetry in different ways. He argues that Dickinson's uses for colour, and especially white, are antagonistic, as it symbolizes a desire to be abstracted from societal definitions of identity, to be at a remove from history, but also, at the same time, cannot be fully dissociated from it. Her uses of colour and whiteness cannot be removed, ultimately, from mid-nineteenth-century discussions around racial stereotyping, notions of an elect society and the association of white with ideas of purity.[47]

Erica Fretwell's work on Dickinson takes depictions of sensory experience as its focus to interrogate her interactions with nineteenth-century ideas of race. Her innovative book *Sensory Experiments: Psychophysics, Race, and the Aesthetics of Feeling* (2020) examines mid-nineteenth-century American psychophysics (the study of sensory experience) to show how it served to racialize aesthetics. She provides a historical approach and framework to understand the far-reaching nineteenth-century drive to regulate and 'civilize' the senses by historicizing the points at which nineteenth-century conceptions of materiality, race and aesthetic experience converge. She considers nineteenth-century literature as well as contemporary literature to demonstrate the effects of mid-nineteenth-century American psychophysics. The book's chapters are organized according to the hierarchy of each of the five senses established by psychophysics, where sight and sound are 'higher' and more refined than the 'lower' more embodied senses of smell, taste and touch. Chapter Four considers the sense of taste and the idea of sweetness, which, Fretwell argues, is racialized not only by psychophysical discourses but by the material realities of plantation slavery as well. Molasses and sugar occupied different positions within the hierarchies of taste and race. In this chapter she examines Dickinson's poems and recipes to show how her various explorations in an imagined sensuous indulgence in blackness reflect this hierarchical organization.[48]

In her essay on 'Dickinson in Domingo' (2013) Fretwell analyses Dickinson's uses of 'Domingo' by examining them alongside nineteenth-century debates about race, food and poetics. Fretwell utilizes the recovered culinary prose of freewoman Malinda Russell's *A Domestic Cookbook* (1866) in order to interrogate the ways in which taste is racialized in Dickinson's work. She identifies a shift in Dickinson's poetry which occurs after the Civil War period and argues that readers had previously used taste to racialize Dickinson's poetics. However, Fretwell argues by reading Dickinson's work through 'Domingo' we can see sensory and aesthetic taste as a synthesis of racial, gustatory and literary influences.[49] Dickinson references 'Domingo' in a letter to T. W. Higginson in 1862 in which she replies to his opinion on her poetic style:

> Dear Friend, Your letter gave no Drunkenness, because I tasted Rum before – Domingo comes but once [...] You think my gait 'spasmodic' ... You think me 'uncontrolled' – I have no Tribunal.[50]

Fretwell shows how Dickinson's connection between Domingo and poetic style in this letter references both lawlessness and Black emancipation:

> Referenced in the midst of war and reprinted at the height of the 'Negro Problem,' Domingo names a stylistic taste that is 'uncontrolled' – and a sweet taste that indexes black emancipation.[51]

Dickinson uses 'Domingo', which had become at the time shorthand for successful slave revolution (Haiti had regained independence in 1804), and employs the word metaphorically in this letter to equate with her own literary and stylistic rebellion – and at the same time fully exploiting concurrent anxieties about the prospect of black revolutionary power.

Páraic Finnerty's essay '"We Think of Others Possessing You with the Throes of Othello": Dickinson Playing Othello, Race, and Tommaso Salvini' (2002) takes mid-nineteenth-century American reception and production of Shakespeare's *Othello*, one of Emily Dickinson's favourite plays, as its focus for a greater understanding of the poet's identification with the play's protagonist. This includes the performance of *Othello* by Italian actor Tommaso Salvini.[52] *Othello* was one of the most popular Shakespeare plays in mid-nineteenth-century America, reflecting the fact that race was such a central and controversial subject of the time. Finnerty shows how the play's theme of an interracial relationship, and Othello's character drew both contempt and sympathy from audiences, according to contemporary reviews of productions of the play. The popularity of the play led to burlesques, travesties and parodies, where Othello's 'blackness' was 'constantly mentioned and exaggerated as a source of humour and amusement' and was 'hyperbolically performed'.[53] In order to ascertain what type of Othello Dickinson may have encountered he assesses contemporary views on *Othello* held by key nineteenth-century American figures of influence such as former US president John Quincy Adams, and notable American critics Richard Grant White and Mary Preston, in which a central concern with Othello's skin colour determined how each read and responded to the play. With varying viewpoints available to her, Finnerty concludes that 'for a reader like Dickinson Othello was a complex figure, both a noble and dignified Moor and a morally dangerous black man'. He explains how the 'tawny figure' became the most acceptable version in nineteenth-century American theatre:

> Othello's nobility and power made it inconceivable for many, like Preston, White and Kean, that he was black. Thus, they introduced the idea of a tawny figure, a noble Moor to underplay Othello's blackness or at least differentiate it from the 'blackness' of contemporary African Americans. Yet for others like John Quincy Adams and those who watched the Othello burlesques or performed in them, Othello was definitely black and this fact was an integral part of what Adams regarded as the moral lesson of the play and what the burlesques appropriated for humorous effect.[54]

Finnerty draws out the complex way in which Dickinson identifies with the character of Othello by utilizing evidence from her letters and poems. Her references to Othello are undoubtedly unconventional as well as controversial; a white woman addressing another white woman whilst inhabiting the identity of a figure who not only personifies intense jealousy and possessiveness, but also danger, sophistication, nobility and lawlessness at the same time. Through her use of quotations from Othello, as well as other Shakespeare plays, Finnerty argues that Dickinson demonstrates her familiar knowledge of Shakespeare as well as that of contemporary Shakespeare productions, including the one seen by her brother Austin featuring Tommaso Salvini as Othello. Dickinson's knowledge of Salvini came also from articles she read and cut out in the literary magazines such as *The Century* and *the Atlantic Monthly*. A critic for the former, Emma Lazarus's thoughts on Othello can be heard echoed within Dickinson's allusions to the play. Henry James's article on Salvini in *the Atlantic Monthly* supports Dickinson's view of Othello as a complex character. Finnerty shows how Dickinson's uses of the Othello figure in her letters and poems manage to draw out the different connotations and critical views of Othello simultaneously. Crucially, Finnerty posits the idea that Dickinson's posturing as a possessive Black man to her female friends in letters allowed her to 'go hyperbolically beyond contemporary ideals of femininity' and to use 'an extreme symbol of "otherness" that represented that which her culture thought should not be found in herself'.[55]

Aífe Murray's book *Maid as Muse: How Servants Changed Emily Dickinson's Life and Language* (2009) examines the cultural exchange between the poet and the Irish working-class and African American servants and labourers employed by the Dickinsons. Murray utilizes a wealth of archival material as well as interviews with the descendants of the servants to construct a convincing argument that this rich cultural exchange she encountered whilst living and working alongside these servants significantly influenced her work. This cross-cultural impact can be seen poetically and linguistically, for example, in Dickinson's use of Irish and African American vernacular. Further to this, Murray argues that Margaret Maher, Dickinson's Irish immigrant maid, played a key role in the preservation of the Dickinson manuscript poems. Murray's argument begins by asking the fundamental question of how Dickinson's writing came into being with so much labour involved in the day-to-day running of the Dickinson household. The baking alone would involve much more labour and effort than we know of today:

> For her to write so much and so well, someone had to relieve her of a portion of the unrelenting household tasks that proscribed nineteenth-century lives. Otherwise the spark may have died inside her; what Tillie Olsen describes so well in her book, *Silences*. Given that Emily's voice was dependent on someone, I knew it came at the price of the other's silence. My project, explored in writing and mixed media, became an investigation of 'silence and voice' in all its manifestations and interdependencies.[56]

Following on from Dickinson biographer Jay Leyda's insistence that the working people in the Dickinson household should be remembered and their stories documented, rather than ignored by biographers and critics, Murray's exploration of Dickinson's relationship to her servants is rigorous and addresses these critical gaps within Dickinson studies. The critical blind spot surrounding the working people in the Dickinson household served also to silence the ethnically and racially diverse voices in the story of the poet and the creation of her work. Murray's book illuminates the 'interdependencies' of her working environment – one which crucially enabled her to write her poetry, organize it into fascicles and preserve it for posterity– and invites the reader to hear the Irish and African American voices of the Dickinson servants both within her work and within narratives of Dickinson's creative processes.

Hiroko Uno's essay 'Emily Dickinson's Encounter with the East: Chinese Museum in Boston' (2008) explores her understanding of Chinese culture, how the East was perceived and the ways these conceptions influenced her work.[57] Li-Hsin Hsu's essay 'Emily Dickinson's Asian Consumption' (2013) examines depictions of Asia in Dickinson's work, along with evidence from her letters of her knowledge of Asia and of her encounters with Chinese people. Hsu shows the ways in which her poems, and therefore also her 'consumption' of Asia, both illuminate and problematize nineteenth-century control of Orientalist discourse on the racial other.[58]

Whilst scholarship on Dickinson, race, ethnicity and the racial other has focused largely upon Dickinson's engagement with African, African American, Haitian, Malay, Chinese and Irish identities, there is still a lot of work to be done. By examining Dickinson's encounters with race, ethnicity and the racial other in this way critics continue to shed important light upon Dickinson's understanding of race as well as the racism within her culture.

Notes

1   Jane Donahue Eberwein, 'Dickinson's Local, Global, and Cosmic Perspectives' in *The Emily Dickinson Handbook*, ed. by Grabher, Hagenbuchle and Miller, pp. 27–43 (p. 42).
2   Páraic Finnerty, 'Global Dickinson' in *The New Emily Dickinson Studies*, ed. by Kohler, pp. 187–203.

3   Magdalena Zapedowska, 'Critical History II: 1955 to the Present' in *Emily Dickinson in Context*, ed. by Eliza Richards (Cambridge: Cambridge University Press, 2013), pp. 321–31 (p. 321).
4   Cheryl Walker, 'Dickinson in Context: Nineteenth-Century American Women Poets' in *A Historical Guide to Emily Dickinson*, ed. by Vivian Pollak (Oxford: Oxford University Press, 2004), pp. 175–200.
5   Walker, 'Dickinson in Context', p. 176.
6   Walker, pp. 195–7.
7   Susan Juhasz, 'Materiality and the Poet' in *The Emily Dickinson Handbook*, ed. by Grabher, Hagenbuchle and Miller, pp. 427–39.
8   As Juhasz says in the above essay, materiality can take many forms, the most primary of these being work which focuses on the physical aspects of the poem as material artefact, such as Jen Bervin, Marta Werner and Susan Howe, *The Gorgeous Nothings: Emily Dickinson's Envelope Poems* (New York: New Directions, 2013).
9   Betsy Erkkila, 'Emily Dickinson and Class' *American Literary History*, 4.1 (1992), 1–27.
10 Betsy Erkkila, 'Emily Dickinson and the Art of Politics' in *A Historical Guide to Emily Dickinson*, ed. by Pollak, pp. 133–74 (p. 166).
11 Domhnall Mitchell, *Emily Dickinson: Monarch of Perception* (Amherst: University of Massachusetts Press, 2000), p. 162.
12 Domhnall Mitchell, 'Emily Dickinson and Class' in *The Cambridge Companion to Emily Dickinson*, ed. by Wendy Martin (Cambridge: Cambridge University Press, 2002), pp. 191–214 (p. 195).
13 Mitchell, 'Emily Dickinson and Class', p. 209.
14 Mitchell, p. 209.
15 See *Emily Dickinson in Context*, ed. by Richards. Part II of the book examines Dickinson's literary influences and intertextual engagement (pp. 69–147).
16 Martha Nell Smith, 'Forever Young: Rereading Emily Dickinson in the Twenty-First Century' in *The Cambridge Companion to American Poets* (Cambridge: Cambridge University Press, 2015), ed. by Mark Richardson, pp. 119–35.
17 Smith, 'Forever Young', pp. 119–35.
18 Colleen Shu-Ching Wu, 'Overcoming Oneself as Subject in Dickinson's Poetry: Adorno and Heidegger', *Style: A Quarterly Journal of Aesthetics, Poetics, Stylistics, and Literary Criticism*, 49.3 (2015), 334–53 (p. 337).
19 Shu-Ching Wu, 'Overcoming Oneself as Subject in Dickinson's Poetry', p. 336. She quotes Melanie Hubbard's review in *The Emily Dickinson Journal*, 18.1 (2009), of Jed Deppman's work *Trying to Think with Emily Dickinson* (Amherst, MA: University of Massachusetts Press, 2008).
20 Virginia Jackson, *Dickinson's Misery: A Theory of Lyric Reading* (Princeton: Princeton University Press, 2005), p. 1 and p. 6.

21 Paula Bennett, '"The Negro Never Knew": Emily Dickinson and Racial Typology in the Post-Bellum Period', *Legacy: A Journal of American Women Writers*, 19.1 (2002), 53–61 (p. 53 and p. 60).
22 Karen Dandurand, 'New Dickinson Civil War Publications', *American Literature*, 56.1 (1984), 17–27 (p. 17).
23 Pollak, ed., *A Historical Guide to Emily Dickinson*, p. 3.
24 Shira Wolosky, *Emily Dickinson: A Voice of War* (New Haven: Yale University Press, 1984).
25 Shira Wolosky, 'Public and Private in Dickinson's War Poetry', in Pollak, ed., *A Historical Guide to Emily Dickinson*, pp. 103–31 (pp. 127–8).
26 Shira Wolosky, 'War and the Art of Writing: Emily Dickinson's Relational Aesthetics', in Coleman Hutchison, ed., *A History of American Civil War Literature* (Cambridge: Cambridge University Press, 2015), pp. 195–210 (p. 195).
27 Leigh-Anne Urbanowicz Marcellin, '"Singing off the Charnel Steps": Soldiers and Mourners in Emily Dickinson's War Poetry', *The Emily Dickinson Journal*, 9.2 (2000), 64–74.
28 Faith Barrett, 'Slavery and the Civil War', in Richards, ed., *Emily Dickinson in Context*, pp. 206–15 (p. 207). For Barrett's work in this area, see also Faith Barrett, *To Fight Aloud Is Very Brave: American Poetry and the Civil War* (Amherst: University of Massachusetts Press, 2012) and 'Public Selves and Private Spheres: Studies of Emily Dickinson and the Civil War, 1984–2007', *The Emily Dickinson Journal*, 16.1 (2007), 92–104. The latter is an excellent overview of scholarly work on the topic of Dickinson and the Civil War.
29 Barrett, 'Slavery and the Civil War', pp. 213–14.
30 Barrett, p. 215.
31 Eliza Richards, *Battle Lines: Poetry and Mass Media in the U.S Civil War* (Philadelphia: University of Pennsylvania Press, 2019), pp. 1–2.
32 Richards, *Battle Lines*, pp. 55–91 (p. 70).
33 Richards, pp. 79–89.
34 Daneen Wardrop, '"That Minute Domingo": Emily Dickinson's Co-optation of Abolitionist Diction and Franklin's Variorum Edition', *The Emily Dickinson Journal*, 8.2 (1999), 72–86 (p. 72).
35 Wardrop, 'That Minute Domingo', pp. 73–4. Wardrop refers to Ed Folsom and Kenneth Price's website 'Dickinson, Slavery and the San Domingo Moment' which was set up in 1997.
36 Wardrop, p. 82.
37 Benjamin Friedlander, 'Emily Dickinson and the Battle of Ball's Bluff', *PMLA*, 124.5 (2009), 1582–99. He cites the following war poetry anthologies as evidence of the growing recognition of Dickinson as an American Civil War poet: Faith Barrett and Cristanne Miller, eds., *'Words for the Hour': A New Anthology of American Civil War Poetry* (Amherst: University of Massachusetts Press, 2005), Lorrie

Goldensohn, ed., *American War Poetry* (New York: Columbia University Press, 2006); and J. D. McClatchy, ed., *Poets of the Civil War* (New York: American Poets Project; Library of America, 2005).
38 Friedlander, 'Emily Dickinson and the Battle of Ball's Bluff', p. 1597.
39 See Kohler, ed., *The New Emily Dickinson Studies* for further reading on Dickinson and race.
40 Erkkila, 'Dickinson and Class', pp. 9–12.
41 Erkkila, 'Dickinson and the Art of Politics', p. 151.
42 Erkkila, p. 152.
43 Bennett, 'The Negro Never Knew', pp. 53, 60.
44 Vivian Pollak, 'Dickinson and the Poetics of Whiteness', *The Emily Dickinson Journal*, 9.2 (2000), 84–95 (p. 90).
45 Pollak, 'Dickinson and the Poetics of Whiteness', p. 90.
46 Pollak, p. 92.
47 Domhnall Mitchell, 'Northern Lights: Class, Color, Culture and Emily Dickinson', *The Emily Dickinson Journal*, 9.2 (2000), 75–83.
48 Erica Fretwell, *Sensory Experiments: Psychophysics, Race, and the Aesthetics of Feeling* (Durham, N. C.: Duke University Press, 2020). Chapter four: 'Taste: Scripts for Sweetness, Measures of Pleasure' (pp. 174–212).
49 Erica Fretwell, 'Emily Dickinson in Domingo', *J19: The Journal of Nineteenth-Century Americanists*, 1.1 (2013), 71–96.
50 *Emily Dickinson: Selected Letters*, ed. by Thomas H. Johnson, eleventh printing (Cambridge, MA: The Belknap Press of Harvard University Press, 2002), p. 174, letter #265.
51 Fretwell, 'Emily Dickinson in Domingo', p. 71.
52 Páraic Finnerty, '"We Think of Others Possessing You with the Throes of Othello": Dickinson Playing Othello, Race and Tommaso Salvini', *The Emily Dickinson Journal*, 11.1 (2002), 81–90.
53 Finnerty, 'We Think of Others Possessing You with the Throes of Othello', p. 82. Finnerty references Joyce Green Macdonald, 'Acting Black: Othello, Othello Burlesques and the Performance of Blackness', *Theatre Survey*, 46 (1994), 233–46.
54 Finnerty, p. 83.
55 Finnerty, p. 87.
56 Aífe Murray, *Maid as Muse: How Emily Dickinson's Servants Changed Her Life and Language* (Hanover and London: University Press of New England, 2009), pp. 3–4.
57 Hiroko Uno, 'Emily Dickinson's Encounter with the East: Chinese Museum in Boston', *The Emily Dickinson Journal*, 17.1 (2008), 43–67.
58 Li-Hsin Hsu, 'Emily Dickinson's Asian Consumption', *The Emily Dickinson Journal*, 22.2 (2013), 1–25.

5

Religion and hymn culture

5.1	Rejecting orthodoxy	131
5.2	Religion and aesthetics	134
5.3	Dickinson and hymnody	140

Dickinson's relation to the religious culture of her day is a topic which has gathered momentum on its course from the critical texts of the twentieth century to the present. The formal aspects of Protestant hymnody, and Dickinson's use of biblical imagery, are both often referred to by critics to describe the ways her poems engage with religious culture, and with culturally enshrined notions of the divine. Much twentieth-century criticism on Dickinson and the religious background to her poetry produced a broadly polarized view constructed around the central question of whether she possessed religious faith or continuously rallied against the religious impulses of her culture and its Puritan heritage. Francis J. Molson's essay 'Emily Dickinson's Rejection of the Heavenly Father' (1978) exemplifies the preoccupation with attempting to answer this central question.[1] More recently, W. Clark Gilpin's *Religion around Emily Dickinson* (2014) is an entire study based around the 'seeming paradox' that Dickinson's spiritually challenging poems were produced out of an apparent shunning of orthodox religion.[2] Although the question of Dickinson's faith or lack thereof undoubtedly remains, pervading the arguments of most aspects of critical enquiry on Dickinson, the variety of approaches critics take in discussing the historical, cultural, literary and theological background to this essentially unknowable question has become much more nuanced in recent years. The view of Dickinson's response to the religious drive of the second Great Awakening in New England as being primarily antagonistic, such as in Alfred Habegger's essay 'Evangelicalism and Its Discontents: Hannah Porter versus Emily Dickinson' (1997),[3] can be contrasted with texts which take a more positive view of her engagement with the religious culture of her day. For example, Jane Donahue Eberwein's essay '"Is Immortality True?" Salvaging Faith in an Age of Upheavals' (2004) charts the religious and civil upheavals affecting nineteenth-century New England and explains how the oscillations of Dickinson's spiritual life mirror those of others in her community and even that of the church:

> In part because Dickinson focused her imaginative energy on that 'Flood Subject' rather than dogmas or practices directly challenged by these cultural upheavals, she managed to cope and even to take some pleasure in the nimble balancing act she sustained between belief and doubt. Churches coped also. Although wounded by romanticism, Darwin, the Higher Criticism, and the Civil War, they enjoyed a period of renewed vigor with considerably increased membership.[4]

Eberwein sees Dickinson's 'balancing act ... between belief and doubt' as being part of her spiritual resilience during and after the Civil War, where doubt and belief become part of the necessities of cultural and political upheaval. She draws an interesting parallel between what she sees as Dickinson's coping mechanisms and those of the church, which, although it had to endure many opponents and challenges, continued in its business of opening to the community. It is this resilience and hope that Eberwein sees in Dickinson's poetry of doubt and questioning:

> Even while questioning, Emily Dickinson continued to hope for immortality, especially as death's depredations struck closer and closer. Though she could not know for sure where the dead went, she still trusted in their journey. When her mother died in 1882, she wrote, 'I believe we shall in some manner be cherished by our Maker – that the One who gave us this remarkable earth has the power still farther to surprise that which He has caused. Beyond that all is silence.' (L 785) Like amputation, abdication requires an agent. One must set aside whatever is being abdicated by an effort of will, and Dickinson never abdicated hope. [...] Even if the right arm Christians had earlier relied on for salvation had been amputated, the left one somehow pulled the sluice to release the flow of grace that sustained Emily Dickinson in 'the Balm of that Religion/That doubts – as fervently as it believes.'
>
> (Fr 1449/M 718)[5]

Eberwein paraphrases an oft-cited Dickinson poem which considers the 'abdication' of belief and references the 'amputation' of God's right hand, where the elect is typically seated:

> That Hand is amputated now
> And God cannot be found –
>
> (Fr 1581, M 638)

However, in the paragraphs which conclude her historical survey of Dickinson's religious culture, Eberwein chooses to stress the religious apparatus which sustained Dickinson, such as 'hope' and 'grace', despite the fluctuations in the political and religious climate of her day.

Many critics characterize Dickinson's work in terms which relate to religion and a religious life despite the polarized debates around her religious affiliation. Texts which focused on Dickinson's reading, such as *Emily Dickinson's Readings of Men and Books: Sacred Soundings* (1990) by Benjamin Lease, served to fan the flame of enquiry into Dickinson's own religious views via an examination of the modes of expression she assimilated from her extensive reading. Lease focuses on the literary and devotional texts which influenced her poetry – the King James Bible, the hymns of Isaac Watts, seventeenth-century poetry and prose, also on her correspondence with men who may have inflected her views on religion and poetry such as Charles Wadsworth, Thomas Wentworth Higginson and Edward Hitchcock. A large part of Lease's examination is underpinned by the idea of Dickinson's life and work as a religious and spiritual pursuit, asserting that Dickinson's final letters were 'the culmination of a lifelong religious quest', and that her poetry 'reflected her involvement with the language and imagery of the occult'.[6] Lease laid out Dickinson's reading and correspondence to delineate the spiritual aspect of her poetry, and his work served to set the tone for future critics wanting to engage with Dickinson's reading, her engagement with spiritual themes, as well as those interested in her reformulation of theological perspectives. Moreover, the self-conscious connection between 'men' and 'books' in Lease's title was an invitation for future feminist-historicist studies such as Victoria N. Morgan's *Emily Dickinson and Hymn Culture: Tradition and Experience* (2010) which examines Dickinson's education, reading, correspondence, familial and social conceptions of the sacred, to locate an alternative, female-oriented sphere of influence and tradition of hymn culture in her work.

Critics discussing Dickinson's relation to religion have shown in diverse ways the creative stimulus that religious culture afforded her, whether it was drawn from her immediate religious settings or not. Benjamin Goluboff's essay '"If Madonna Be": Emily Dickinson and Roman Catholicism' (2000) counters previous assertions that she was unfamiliar with this branch of the Christian faith, arguing that Roman Catholicism was 'at the centre of a pervasive cultural discourse with which Dickinson was certainly conversant'.[7] Dickinson's use of Catholic imagery does not convince the reader of any allegiance to Catholicism, but rather

> Dickinson's Catholic poems are undertaken in the spirit of exercise; they are experiments in voice and image [...] her Catholic poetry plays on the discourse over the 'foreign faith' widespread in her New England culture.⁸

Goluboff argues that Dickinson's incorporation of Catholic imagery as the subject of her sceptical and agnostic poetics serves to illuminate her culture's own preoccupation with the foreign Catholics as part of that scepticism.⁹ The fact of Dickinson's own personal allegiance to a particular faith remains in some senses a moot point, as critics such as Goluboff have shown. Dickinson utilizes the imagery and attitudes of religious discourse to broaden her experiments in poetry.

One of the influential earlier critical texts to be considered as representative of those which are concerned with the positive influence religious culture had on Dickinson's creative process is Martha Winburn England and John Sparrow's *Hymns Unbidden: Donne, Herbert, Blake, Emily Dickinson and the Hymnographers* (1966). England places Dickinson within a tradition of poet hymn writers, responding individually within a collective form, and considers her position and Puritan attitude in relation to religious orthodoxy and what she calls 'the Establishment'.¹⁰ More recently the arguments and points of view about Dickinson and her religious life have been much less polarized. Modern contemporary critics seem far more at ease with fluidity and contradiction (and indeed with the co-existence of faith and doubt) on these issues than they appeared to be in the twentieth and late nineteenth centuries. The more recent turn in criticism which examines religious imagery as a powerful aesthetic in Dickinson's poetry and the important contributions to the historical turn in Dickinson studies around Dickinson and religion exemplifies this new critical permissiveness. Increasingly, critics are allowing the difficulties and contradictions which exist in Dickinson's attitude to religion to speak. The body of criticism which deals with Dickinson's relation to religion through her serious engagement with the hymns of her day will be traced and examined as an example of this historical turn. Early key essays such as Shira Wolosky's 'Rhetoric or Not: Hymnal Tropes in Emily Dickinson and Isaac Watts' (1988) will be discussed alongside the work of twenty-first-century critics such as Morgan (2010), who examines the relevance of an entire hymn 'culture' – which Morgan sees as encompassing the practices of writing, editing, disseminating and singing hymns, as well as the devotional purpose of hymns to assert doctrine and theological perspectives. Morgan's book considers the theological implications of hymnody written by women in this period and views Dickinson's engagement with orthodox religion as a creative process, which similarly re-envisions theological ideas. Discussion of Roger Lundin's edited special forum in the journal *Religion and Literature*, entitled 'Dickinson and Religion', will summarize some of the more recent debates in this wide-reaching area within Dickinson studies. This forum is indicative of the relatively recent expansion of interest in Dickinson and religion specifically, whereas previous treatments were embedded within discussions of gender, for example. Collections of essays which point to key critical themes within the field at the time of their publication, such as *The Emily Dickinson Handbook* (1998), edited by Gudrun Grabher, Roland Hagenbüchle and Cristanne Miller, and *Emily Dickinson in Context* (2013), edited by Eliza Richards, differ in their treatment of religion as a subject in itself.[11] None of the essay titles in *The Emily Dickinson Handbook* reference religious culture directly despite the pervasive nature of this subject within Dickinson studies, whereas Richards, fifteen years later, places essays titled 'New England Puritan Heritage', 'The Bible' and 'Religion' within the first three sections of the volume. Debates about the ways in which Dickinson's poetic imagination engages creatively with theology and with ideas of the divine have come to the fore in more recent times and continue to be a key critical focal point.

5.1 Rejecting orthodoxy

Analysis of Dickinson's relationship with religion and the question of how much she embraced and/or openly rejected religious orthodoxy is one of the largest areas of criticism within the field. A considerable proportion of it takes her apparent rejection of orthodoxy as its focus, and this is especially true of criticism produced in the 1990s. Much of the politicized criticism of the 1990s had an investment in viewing Dickinson's rejection of various kinds of orthodoxy, including that of religion. Alfred Habegger's essay 'Evangelicalism and Its Discontents: Hannah Porter versus Emily Dickinson' (1997) positions Dickinson as antagonistic to the religious drive of the second Great Awakening. He sees her response to the women of this evangelical climate, namely Hannah Porter and those who taught her at Mount Holyoke and aimed to convert her, as a 'silent, a non-act, a turning away'.[12] In Habegger's view Porter represented to Dickinson an 'invasive community of devout women' whom Dickinson had to 'stand-off'.[13] Habegger furthers this perspective of Dickinson's relation to the religious culture of her day in his hugely influential biography *My Wars Are Laid Away in Books: The Life of Emily Dickinson* (2001). Here he sees the 'maternal inheritance' of the religious women in Dickinson's social milieu as setting up 'pressures and expectations' which the poet rejected.[14] Religious women in Dickinson's personal sphere included her maternal grandmother, Betsy (née Fay) Norcross, who belonged to the female praying circle in Monson, as did the popular hymnist Phoebe Hinsdale Brown. As discussed further on in this chapter, Dickinson's manipulation of hymnal metrics and modes of expression particular to the popular hymnody of her day has been seen by critics as a rejection of religious orthodoxy, whilst, at the same time, a co-optation of elements of that very culture.

Wendy Martin's section on Dickinson's 'unorthodox' use of biblical imagery, 'Blasphemous Devotion: Biblical Allusion in the Poems and Letters', in her volume *The Cambridge Introduction to Emily Dickinson* (2007), introduces the ways in which Dickinson can be seen as utilizing religious discourse in what she sees as an unorthodox and provocative way. Martin lays the argument about whether she possessed religious faith aside (albeit momentarily) to assert that Dickinson does not use the bible in a 'traditionally devotional way':

> She uses biblical allusion to reverse the expected object of religious devotion from God to earth/nature/friend, to reverse the relationship of creature and creator, and thus to reverse the existing hierarchy of authority. This is not to say that Dickinson had no 'faith,' but that whatever 'faith' she might have had she often chose to express in non-traditional terms. While scholars can argue incessantly about whether or not Emily Dickinson was a 'Christian,' it is obvious from the poems and letters themselves that Dickinson does not use the Bible in a traditionally devotional way. [...] Not only does Dickinson tend to undermine the traditional authority of the Bible by referencing it playfully and ironically, she uses these references to exalt what would normally be considered earthly (and thus secondary) relationships to a religious level.[15]

Martin sees in Dickinson a 'transfer of devotion from God to friends' and is clear that 'Dickinson's faith and devotion then are not directed to God'. She illustrates how Dickinson's love for God is also transferred to the natural world. Like many other critics, Martin gets caught up in explaining the ways that Dickinson's verse is 'devotional' but not in the 'traditional sense', and attempts to impose a separation between world and 'God' in her work:

> Dickinson was not interested in being a religious or devotional poet in the traditional sense. She was devotional; but her devotion, though expressed in biblical language, was often transferred to this world – to her friends and to nature. Inverting the normal arc of devotional poetry, Dickinson directed her thoughts downward to the earth and the present life, discovering in it things

worthy of true attention and adoration. For Dickinson, the Bible merely provided the vocabulary with which she could express her own devotion to the treasures this world has to offer.[16]

Other critics have emphasized the dualistic nature of Dickinson's engagement with religious culture, and the complex mixture of elements within her poetry which are able to rest with contradiction, and the unknown, in relation to the divine. It is this quality of her poetry which is perhaps most challenging in its relation to all forms of orthodoxy, religious and otherwise. The turn towards charting the nature of Dickinson's dualistic and often contradictory relation to religion and the divine can be seen in James McIntosh's *Nimble Believing: Dickinson and the Unknown* (2004) which shows how Dickinson's uses for religion within her poems serve her own purposes of supporting the private experiences she articulates and privileges over doctrinal assertions. Explaining the title of his book, a quotation which is taken from a letter of Dickinson to Judge Otis Phillips Lord, he writes:

> 'Nimble believing,' that is believing for intense moments in a spiritual life without permanently subscribing to any received system of belief, is a key experience, an obsessive subject, and a stimulus to expression for Dickinson.

McIntosh sees Dickinson within the tradition of other American writers of the period such as Emerson, Thoreau and Melville – as a poet who 'makes poetic use of her vacillations between doubt and faith'.[17] Tensions between faith and doubt provide Dickinson with creative palette for her poetic imagination. Roger Lundin's groundbreaking work on Dickinson and religion, and particularly his biographical study *Emily Dickinson and the Art of Belief* (1998), did much to lay down the necessary arguments for future Dickinson scholars wishing to reassess her relationship with religion and the Protestantism which permeated her society. *Emily Dickinson and the Art of Belief* is a tour de force in charting the development of Dickinson's spiritual journey and in describing her poetic and creative engagement with religion. Crucially, Lundin sees Dickinson, not only as the greatest of all American poets, but also 'one of the most brilliantly enigmatic religious thinkers this country has ever known'.[18] It is perhaps Lundin's perspective on Dickinson as a 'religious thinker' which has made his work so influential to other Dickinson scholars who are interested in her engagement with religion. Due to its popularity, the second edition of the book was printed in 2004, with Lundin's Preface explaining the inclusion of an expanded account of the religious and intellectual background to Dickinson's life as well as more extensive discussions of the poetry. His thorough scholarship and close examination of the poems offer fresh insight into how Christianity plays a pivotal role in shaping Dickinson's art. He shows how she was interested in the 'drama' of the Christian story and illuminates its influence in many ways including, for example, the traces of Trinitarian theology which can be seen in her poetry. Lundin's approach to the 'art of belief' in Dickinson's poetry is carefully balanced, and he is keen to highlight her uses for orthodoxy as much as her many challenges to it, as the following caveat about the 'primacy of personal experience' exemplifies:

> To claim the abiding influence of Trinitarian theology in Dickinson's life and work is not to argue that she somehow remained consistently orthodox in belief or practice. Her poetry, after all, provided as many challenges to the Christian faith as it did assurances of that faith's efficacy [...] her poetry clearly acknowledged the primacy of personal experience over doctrinal beliefs and liturgical practices.[19]

Therefore, to critics such as McIntosh and Lundin, Dickinson's shifting experience of Christianity and faith is a given. What is clear is that the nature of her challenges to orthodoxy does not depend upon statements of faith or non-belief. Rather, her challenges to orthodoxy lie in the unique ways in which her poems use the language and forms of Christian theology, biblical imagery and hymns, to articulate and assert a personal experience of the divine. Lundin's work shows us how closely poetic and religious thought is enmeshed for Dickinson. His championing of Dickinson as a key religious thinker illuminates, and prioritizes, her religious imagination. It is perhaps not in her rejection of religious orthodoxy per se, but of the polarized thinking it encourages, that Dickinson's religious imagination was able to fully assert itself.

5.2 Religion and aesthetics

What does Emily Dickinson's religious imagination look like, and what are the ideas about spirituality it gives voice to? Lundin's biographical study shows how Dickinson's imagination engages with religious orthodoxy to produce poetry which represents her own religious imagination, showing her engaging with the aesthetics of religion to think seriously about theology and the nature of her own position in relation to religious orthodoxy. Importantly, the turn to aesthetics around Dickinson and religion shows, in varying different degrees, the ways in which Dickinson's uses of religious aesthetics reassert a reconfigured and radical theological enquiry. What might this reconfigured and radical theological enquiry look like? Some of the critics outlined here have attempted to describe what they see, and the numerous ways of seeing, this aspect of Dickinson's work.

Leading on from Lundin and McIntosh, Linda Freedman's book *Emily Dickinson's Religious Imagination* (2011) explores what she calls Dickinson's 'equivocal appreciation of religion'.[20] She shows how Dickinson's reading of religious texts, and her knowledge and experience of religion, provided her with a 'religious imagination' which both enabled and delimited her own poetic expression. Freedman traces examples and echoes of biblical imagery in Dickinson's work and focuses on the story of the Gospels, baptism, quest narratives, Calvary, crucifixion and sacrifice, incarnation, transfiguration and associated imagery of light, and the colour white. Freedman shows how Dickinson brings this subject into the realm of her contemporaries, with a more liberal humanistic view of the incarnation, breaking with the Puritan's emphasis on God's condescension to become flesh. Drawing upon the work of twentieth-century theologian Jürgen Moltmann to explore theological and poetic interpretations of Christ's death, Freedman crucially connects the body in Pauline scripture with the body of Dickinson's poetry showing how she resists finite endings in a form which might 'live' again, that is to say, within the ultimate 'incorruptible body' of poetry.[21] Perhaps another important precursor to Freedman is Dorothy Huff Oberhaus's essay "Tender Pioneer': Emily Dickinson's Poems on the Life of Christ' (1987), which suggests ways in which Dickinson's reading of scripture could inform our understanding of her religious feeling but also her theological enquiry.[22] Many critics such as Roxanne Harde (2004) and Anne West Ramirez (1998, 2002) have gone on to construct feminist readings around Dickinson's use of biblical imagery and the aesthetics of her theological enquiries. Harde sees Dickinson's 'Christology of embodiment' as another version of the feminization of religion of the nineteenth-century period. She views Dickinson's depictions of Jesus as evidence of her part in the tradition of women poets identifying with Christ, and, in the process, reshaping traditional perspectives on the figure of Jesus.[23] Ramirez's analysis of Dickinson's use of religious aesthetics identifies a construction of a 'prophet persona' – 'a female prophet, a remarkably Christlike figure who speaks with sublime authority'.[24] Elsewhere, she identifies a female tradition of reformulating religious aesthetics with an examination of Harriet Beecher-Stowe's novel, *The Minister's Wooing* (1859), as an important example of Christian feminism for Dickinson.[25]

Siobhan Phillips's essay '"Loved Philology": Emily Dickinson's Trinitarian Word' (2005) interrogates religious aesthetics to forge a greater understanding of Dickinson's uses of religious discourse. Phillips enhances our understanding of Dickinson's religious aesthetics by showing us how the power of language was connected more forcefully with the Trinity in her day, through both the interrogation of biblical language, and of the relationship between religious authority and language. She focuses on Dickinson's use of Trinitarian imagery and shows how detailed attention to religious discourse augments feminist, symbolist or deconstructive approaches to her engagement with religion. Phillips outlines these broad critical approaches which, she argues, are not necessarily mutually exclusive, and in fact 'often combine in common support':

> The first is a broadly feminist analysis that finds in Dickinson's revision or rejection of patriarchal religion a suspicion in hierarchy in general, and a self-empowering endorsement of feminine mutuality. The second, a symbolist or deconstructive reading, argues that Dickinson believes language to constitute within itself a world to which it reflexively points, thereby replacing the paradox of Christological Incarnation with the paradox of the poet's own Word – a replacement that might lead to the disintegration or obfuscation of reference.[26]

Phillips argues that whilst approaches such as these have not ignored the spiritual language of Dickinson's poems, a closer detailed approach to their specifically religious elements can provide important qualification of our understanding of Dickinson's relation to religion and use of religious discourse. By taking the Trinity as a central aesthetic, and the Trinitarian language and tripartite metaphors in the poem 'A word made Flesh' as an example, Phillips skilfully demonstrates how, in Dickinson's poetry, 'a word's internal divisions' are part of its power:

> Dickinson, in 'A word made Flesh,' does not contrast an exclusively feminine consensual ideal to a patriarchal religious one; she assumes into her version of a single human word the qualities of a Trinitarian divinity. And through these qualities, a word's internal divisions become part of its divine and creative power rather than a symptom of danger or obfuscation.[27]

Phillips cites Habegger (2001) to show how aesthetic practice was given religious validation through the theologian Horace Bushnell and his book *God in Christ* (1849), of which Dickinson's clergy friends would have been familiar. She shows how Dickinson's uses of Trinitarian imagery have its origins in the Trinitarian theology of Jonathan Edwards, and in his concept of 'consent' specifically. Edwardsian consent sees God as excellent and needing consent and allowing eternal self-consenting and as therefore tripartite. All things are connected in the world by this consent. Divinity for Edwards is not unified and oppositional but multiple and inter-relational. The Edwardsian textual subject is therefore experiential and related, as opposed to Emersonian individualism and self-reliance.[28] Phillips's central argument is that this version of the trinity through Edwards's notion of 'consent' is crucial to Dickinson's descriptions and uses of language. Bushnell, following Edwards, argued that language must be multiple to reflect God, but Dickinson's language is:

> multiple, indeterminate, infinite, triune – no mimesis but itself potentially divine ... language is not metaphor for divinity, as essence or immanence, but itself both essence and immanence at once.[29]

Phillips shows us through a reconsideration of Dickinson's use of religious aesthetics how language can enact its 'godlike possibilit[ies]', stating that 'the heroism of her poetic undertaking lies in bearing the risks of such overwhelming power while daring to imagine its best, most godlike possibility'.[30] The connection Dickinson makes between possibility and poetry can be seen also in her notion of prayer. Dorothy Huff Oberhaus's essay 'Engine against th'Almightie': Emily Dickinson and Prayer' (1986)[31] places the notion of prayer at the centre of Dickinson's poetic power and shows how this affords her the ability to change voice and adopt different personas within it, much in the style of the Metaphysical devotional tradition. Citing evidence available at the time, Oberhaus illustrates Dickinson's familiarity with the Metaphysical poets and offers a useful precis of criticism which seeks to draw parallels between Dickinson and seventeenth-century metaphysical poets such as Herbert, Donne and Vaughan as well as the writing of Sir Thomas Browne. Focusing on a single thematic group of poems in which Dickinson offers a definition of prayer or refers to it, Oberhaus argues that they can be illuminated when viewed alongside the poetic tradition of devotion of the seventeenth century. Her remarkable knowledge of Dickinson's work, and particularly of the structure of the fascicles, comes to the fore as she describes how the various contradictions and contradictory voices or personae as they appear, and vary, even within a single fascicle. This flexibility of voice, she argues, is akin to that seen in the meditative and metaphysical tradition. Writing of Herbert and Dickinson's attitude to prayer, she states that 'both emphasize the human effort essential to successful prayer'[32] and it is this effort which can be seen in the various attempts the speakers in Dickinson's (and Herbert's) work make, to get God to listen:

> The diverse forms of these poems, echoing those of Herbert and other devotional poets, include meditations, protests for requests denied, laments spoken during

the dark night of the soul, prayers for and about forgiveness, and a retrospective narrative and colloquy with God, in which the sudden experience of God's felt presence causes the speaker to turn from prayer to praise. The tones of these poems vary as widely as their speakers and forms, but many mix playfulness with reverence, recalling the witty and colloquial metaphysical style.[33]

Oberhaus's examination of a cluster of Dickinson's 'prayer' poems through the lens of the Metaphysical devotional tradition is instructive in that it highlights prayer as a central aesthetic in Dickinson's poetry. The various aspects of prayer witnessed in Metaphysical poetry provided Dickinson with a model and focus for the expression of contradiction within her own spiritual life. Discounting any causal connection between Dickinson's disregard for church services and her ongoing spiritual struggles, Oberhaus concludes that:

> The figure that emerges when the prayer poems are read together is not one who disbelieves or blasphemes, but one who explores the many aspects of religious experience in a series of colloquies with God and with herself about her 'supposed person's' successful and unsuccessful attempts to reach God's ear.[34]

Therefore, this model of prayer provides Dickinson's speakers an opportunity to voice their experience to God, and to question theological problems, such as the nature of our relationship with God, directly.

Engagement with the aesthetics of traditional religious discourse, as well as the production of new aesthetics, can signal the emergence of a new spiritual schema. Dickinson's work has been viewed by some as delineating a new devotional paradigm or re-visioned theological perspective. Recently, studies have appeared which come from theological perspectives firmly rooted within religious practices and tradition, and these examine the ways in which Dickinson's work both reflects and enables such practices. An essential aspect of these studies is that they highlight the need, particularly for women writers of Dickinson's period, to reject orthodoxy to produce something new which speaks to their own experience within traditional religious settings. For example, *Mystical Prayer: The Poetic Example of Emily Dickinson* (2019) by Catholic theologian Charles M. Murphy uses the notion of mystical prayer through which to read Dickinson's poems. He sees Dickinson's work as being within the mystical tradition and as sharing features with the writings and lives of other mystics, and with St. Teresa of Ávila in particular. This tradition of mystical writers provides a precedent for the paradox of God being felt as an absence, a darkness or as a space. Murphy places Dickinson within this tradition and identifies her condition of 'believing unbelief' as being akin to this paradox.[35] Endemic to the mystic's position is the ability to turn away from orthodoxy, and from the prescribed notions of religious life which are contrary to those directed by inner resources. Murphy sees this kind of mysticism visible in Dickinson's mode of poetry, calling the situation of believing unbelief:

> the instinctive rejection, despite the cost, of religious conceptions that do not do justice to what we know to be the truth: that heaven is not supposed to hurt and humiliate.

Murphy describes St. Teresa of Ávila's new vision for the Carmelite monastery in similar terms.[36] Importantly, by mapping out the conditions for mystical prayer and showing how some of Dickinson's poems correlate with these conditions, Murphy sets out a case for Dickinson's verse to be read, not just as poetry, or even as sacred verse, but as mystical prayers for God:

> In this book I reintroduce Emily Dickinson's poems as examples of mystical prayer in the light of Christian tradition, and of St. Teresa of Ávila in particular. Those who discovered them at her death took them to be independent lyric poems, but I believe they were much more than that. She wrote them for herself – and for God.[37]

Theologically oriented studies such as this are useful in bringing to bear information around lived religious practices and experience. Murphy outlines the terms for mystical prayer and the conditions for it, unravelling the layers of the mystical tradition with the benefit of wide reading, biblical knowledge and a clear, experiential as well as intellectual understanding of the subject. He makes easy reference to a range of mystical writers, from St. Teresa of Ávila, to St. Therese of Lisieux, St. Augustine, St. John of the Cross and St. Teresa of Calcutta. Arguing that Dickinson is articulating mystical prayer in her poems, Murphy describes her challenges to religious orthodoxy, the articulation of pain and separation from God, as well as the ecstatic commune with the natural world as being in line with a tradition of mystical writers. Ultimately, he sees Dickinson's spiritual outpourings as her 'seeking to overcome the theologically artificial and unsupportable separation of God from the world that she inherited from her Puritan heritage' and as an 'authoritative interpreter of the world'.[38] His approach to Dickinson's poems is almost utilitarian, referencing them to illustrate the experience of mystical prayer he explains, providing what appears as a manual to mystical prayer with Dickinson as explicator. In this way, Murphy's work offers a unique approach within the subject of Dickinson and religion.

5.3 Dickinson and hymnody

Dickinson's formal revision of the hymns of the eighteenth-century hymnodist Isaac Watts (1674–1748) fast became a staple element of discussions around her engagement with the religious culture of her day. Critics often allude briefly to her experiments with the metrical regularity of Watts as shorthand for her challenges to the supposed religious certainties of Watts and of her time. This demonstrates the critical sway of twentieth-century research which sought to analyse her metrical experiments and musical borrowings within the context of her knowledge and experience of hymns. Key early critical interventions in this area such as Martha Winburn England's chapter on Dickinson – 'Emily Dickinson and Isaac Watts' in Martha Winburn England and John Sparrow's *Hymns Unbidden: Donne, Herbert, Blake, Emily Dickinson and the Hymnographers* (1966) helped to solidify the connection between Watts and our understanding of Dickinson's poetic sophistication.[39] However, England views Dickinson's uses of Watts as being more than mere parody. She is clear that Dickinson's use of the hymn form and her parody of Watts incorporate 'more or less serious intent':

> The method is parody in the usual sense: the imitation of an art form that handles any element of art so as to criticize the original form with more or less serious intent [and] frustrates the expectations raised by some familiar verse form and turns the reader from lyric mood to critical evaluation of statements commonly associated with the original form. Emily Dickinson handled various elements of words and music so as to comment on statements commonly associated with the hymn form.[40]

A point which has often been missed in descriptions of the connection between Dickinson and Watts is this 'more or less serious content' which England identifies. England sees Dickinson's work as explicitly commenting upon 'statements commonly associated with the hymn form'. This observation of a wider concern about the 'statements' (and by implication, the assertion of theological perspectives) associated with the hymn form is crucial to our understanding of the ways Dickinson's engagement with hymns goes beyond the formal concerns of metre and prosody. England is interested in Dickinson's relation to Watts as a Dissenter and a Puritan:

> She was a Puritan with a Puritan's attitude toward the Establishment, which is by definition a desire to purify it and recall it to the right ways. In her life, Watts had pre-empted control of the Establishment, and she saw a great deal that seemed wrong with Watts.[41]

Ultimately, England sees Dickinson's use of Watts as way for her to define her unconventionality in poetic as well as religious expression, seeing Watts's 'uprightness to define her angle of variation'.[42] England's chapter on Dickinson and Watts paved the way for critics interested in her engagement with traditional hymnody, Puritanism and religious culture. Ultimately, she sees Dickinson's echoing of Watts's hymns as a series of challenges to his rigid Puritan vision, and that he represented to her an example of 'how she would never write'.[43] England sees Dickinson as rebelling against the moral didacticism she heard in Watts's hymns and in his famous poem for children 'How doth the busy bee'. Importantly, she identifies the bee as a recurring image in Dickinson's poetry which she argues is used to parody Watts and the Puritan emphasis on salvation through work. She provides many examples of poems where the bee (and the figure of Moses) is used to parody Wattsian certainty of salvation. However, England's view of Puritanism colours her view of Watts to such an extent that she does not consider the ways in which Dickinson may have been influenced by Watts which were not based upon an outright rejection of his vision and modes of expression.

Shira Wolosky's essay on rhetoric and biblical/hymnal tropes in Dickinson's poetry, 'Rhetoric or Not: Hymnal Tropes in Emily Dickinson and Isaac Watts' (1988), similarly takes the influence of Watts's seeming regularity, and the apparent plainness of his Puritanism, as its starting point. Wolosky shows how Dickinson employs phrases and formulations which echo those used by Watts in order to undermine the apparent simplicity of his expressions of faith. She pays particular attention to Dickinson's challenging use of rhetoric, such as synecdoche, which, she argues, is dissociated from its doctrinal framework of symbolizing a part (individual) and whole (God) in co-existence.[44] Wolosky argues that Dickinson's interaction with the work of Watts goes beyond the formal conventions of metre, rhyme, punctuation, grammar and imagery. One of the main ways she sees Dickinson most engaged with Watts is in the tension she makes explicit between figuration, and its role in conveying Christian truth. Wolosky explains that Watts's excision of Jewish figures and his use of poetic language were justification for his own rewriting of the Psalms. As Christian figures are both diversionary and vehicles for truth in the Bible, this tension is therefore repressed in Watts, but exploited in Dickinson:

> She exploits and at times explodes tensions between the diversionary attractions of figures and their status as vehicles for doctrinal truths, a tension inherent but repressed in Watts's hymnody. In this, Watts mediates between figures common to all Christian rhetoric and Dickinson's treatments of them. For in Watts the

question of the role of figuration in conveying Christian truth becomes an issue that Dickinson in turn makes explicit.[45]

In addition to a discussion on the role of figuration in Watts, and Dickinson's subversion of it, Wolosky recognizes that Dickinson 'manipulates unique phrases, openings, and idioms' in his hymns, and offers a comparative analysis of what she calls the 'direct parallels' in Dickinson's poems.[46] For example, she cites the following Dickinson poem (as it appears in the Johnson edition) to compare it with lines by Watts:

> Go slow, my soul, to feed thyself
> Upon his rare approach –
>
> (THJ 1297, Fr 1322, M 578)

> Stand up my soul, shake off thy
>   fears,
> And gird thy gospel armour
>   on.
>
> [2:77][47]

In this poem Wolosky sees Dickinson responding to Watts – where his soul moves assuredly forward, toward Heaven – the progress of the soul in Dickinson's poem is much less certain. In Watts's hymn the soul goes towards a 'Heavenly gate', and in Dickinson's poem, the soul 'receives redemption only through a "Judas" Kiss'.[48] Another example is taken from 'A Pit – but Heaven over it – (THJ 1712):

> To look would be to drop –
> To dream – to sap the Prop
> That holds my chances up.
>
> (THJ 1712, Fr 508, M 249)

Which is compared with these lines from Watts:

> How can I sink with such a
>   prop,
> As my eternal God, –
> Who bears the earth's huge
>   pillars up
> And spreads the heavens
>   abroad?
>
> [2:116]

Wolosky sees that both Dickinson and Watts depict the heavens 'as supported by the prop of faith', but it is Dickinson who is 'terrified' that the prop is 'on the verge of collapse'.[49] Wolosky's examination of figurative language and rhetoric concludes, ultimately, with an uncertainty about Dickinson's apparent subversion of the doctrinal assertions in Watts. She sees in Dickinson's engagements with Watts a 'self-subversion', or 'double-negative', in which 'positive affirmations' emerge, almost as a by-product of her self-reflexive poetics:

> Dickinson restructures hymnal modes and tropes she borrows from Watts, clearly intending to subvert his doctrinal assertions. She then, however, often proceeds to subvert her own subversions, as she does here. Thus, traces from Watts are neither fully assimilated nor absolutely displaced as Dickinson struggles to deny doctrine and then to deny her denials. What results is a self-subversion that approaches a double-negative. Positive affirmations may then emerge but only despite themselves. Ultimately, however, Dickinson's art fails to close the gap between faith and figure, even when she attempts to turn against her own rhetoricity.[50]

Wolosky's description of Dickinson's process of 'self-subversion' suggests that Dickinson's interaction with doctrine, and her inability to 'close the gap' between faith and figure, are far more complex than a subversive use of rhetoric and hymnal tropes might account for. The 'positive affirmations' of a relation to the divine which Wolosky views as emerging within Dickinson's texts, 'despite themselves', are worthy of further consideration:

> That the objects of faith hold no certainty is precisely why faith is required. To believe is not to know; indeed, because one does not know, one is called on to believe. Thus, in a manner radically different from Watts's, Dickinson's poem finally affirms faith – if only out of fear of relinquishing it. The hymnal mode continues in this sense to serve a devotional purpose.[51]

What can be extracted from Wolosky's examination of hymnal modes and tropes in Dickinson is that the devotional purpose of the hymn cannot finally be relinquished, despite Dickinson's textual and spiritual engagement with the doctrinal assertions she draws out in Watts's hymns. Wolosky's essay brilliantly describes the tension that the hymn's presence creates in Dickinson's work, and the many ways in which it permeates her poetics.

Much of the work which had been done on the metrical experiments Dickinson executed poetically, such as Cristanne Miller's *Emily Dickinson: A Poet's Grammar* (1987), paved the way for critics interested more specifically in hymns and the scope and nature of her engagement with them. In *A Poet's*

Grammar, Miller sees Dickinson's interest in Watts as an example of how to break the rules – of grammar, prosody, as well as of literary and religious expression.[52] Judy Jo Small's book *Positive as Sound: Dickinson and Rhyme* (1990) includes discussion of the influence of Watts's hymns as part of a larger examination of Dickinson's style and the role of sound in Dickinson's work. Small focuses on the sounds which appear in her poetry and how they relate to elements of her life, such as her love of music, piano playing and birdsong. She is sceptical about overstating the influence of Watts on Dickinson's prosody:

> Isaac Watts is the predecessor who is ordinarily assumed to be the greatest influence on Dickinson's prosody. Though Watts indeed wrote hymns with deviant rhymes, the narrow linking of her forms with his is erroneous. […] All in all, the influence of the hymn form on her prosody has been greatly exaggerated.[53]

Small provides an especially useful overview of the critical discussions of the influence of Watts on Dickinson's work up to the point of her book's publication and concludes that the 'stanzaic patterns' in Dickinson's poems 'are by no means exclusive to hymnody'.[54] Miller's analysis of the variety of forms Dickinson employs in *Reading in Time* (2012), and particularly her discussion of Dickinson's use of the ballad stanza, support the view that the stanzaic patterns she uses are not from hymnody exclusively. Miller describes how the sounds of Dickinson's poems rely on her memory of hymns, and her poetic experiments take in other forms and an idea of 'song' which prioritizes aurality:

> While there is ample evidence that Dickinson wrote with the rhythms of hymns in her ears, several aspects of her verse suggest that a more accurate formulation would be that she wrote in relation to song. Song, in this context, includes hymns and ballads she sang, the poems she read, and the popular music she played on the piano.

Miller's notion of Dickinson's aurality, which takes in the influence of the popular tunes, ballads and hymns she knew and were often sung communally, is distinct from the idea that Dickinson meant her poems to be sung. Instead, she describes an aurality which has a secondary, 'written orality' in a similar manner to the poetry of Robert Browning and Walt Whitman, which

> creates the fiction of a speaking presence with great attention to inflections and rhythms of speech, but speech that she assumes will be known primarily through the page.[55]

Miller argues that although the influence of hymns is clear in Dickinson's rhythms, her aurality and the way she conveys a 'speaking presence' in her poems do not depend entirely upon the hymns she knew.

Attention to the prosody, and musicality, in Dickinson's work has led to discussion of its 'diacritical' mode – and the important ways her use of prosody makes meaning as well as sound. Christine Ross (2001) explores this in her key essay 'Uncommon Measures: Emily Dickinson's Subversive Prosody', which also raises the question about the centrality of Watts in Dickinson's engagement with hymns. She views Dickinson's use of prosody, her creation of 'metrical-rhythmic designs' as that which makes her work 'meta-critical' and 'an interpretative process':

> Dickinson used a Latin-English hybrid prosody, widely available in nineteenth-century textbooks, to create distinctive metrical-rhythmic designs. While a strictly romantic fusion of meter and accent promoted a reversal of metrical values, the appearance of expressivity acquiring the metaphysical weight that had accrued to the rational regularity of Augustan metrics, Dickinson's fusion privileges neither rhythm nor meter. Her imitations of spoken rhythms are too regulated to count as natural expression; her metrical designs, while highly patterned, are too irregular to count as reason. Indeed, her musical art is meta-critical, because it routinely exposes the illusion of representivity that both expressive and rationalist theories assume. Her subversive fusion of meter and rhythm is not only lyrical but metacritical. Through such a prosody, the music of the poetry 'means' as well as 'sounds,' prosodic design part of the signifying, symbolic force of the poetry and a diacritical art that is integral to the critique of immediacy that the poetry performs. Dickinson's uncommon measures are therefore open to an interpretive process as opposed to standard scansion only. While Dickinson knew and used stanzaic patterns inherited from hymnal and literary tradition, it is unlikely that she left those forms entirely unmarked by her projects, where she so clearly arranged everything else in the poetry to suit her distinctive aesthetic.[56]

Ross examines Dickinson's experiments in prosody to account for that uniqueness in her work – the privileging of 'interpretive process' as opposed to 'standard scansion only'. She provides detailed readings of Dickinson's poems and utilizes the nineteenth-century textbooks which informed Dickinson's ideas about prosody – thus illuminating the historically specific, literary prosody which influences the poems:

> In many respects, the poem is a *tour de force* of sonorous form that is integral to its overall poetic logic, unfolding at a point of intersection between grammar and rhetoric, language and experience. The assumption made by Wimsatt and Beardsley, of a fixed difference between meter and rhythm, suggests that it is possible to tell the difference between the rhetorical dancer and the *a priori* measures of the dance. Dickinson's poem employs virtually every formal feature

of the language to produce an integration of meter and rhythm, that, like metaphor, cannot be definitively parsed.[57]

Although Ross's focus is not on hymns, she is keen to assert that Dickinson's experience of hymns did go beyond that of Isaac Watts, citing other hymnals and anthologies in the family collection:

> The shift to romantic, expressive metrics was negotiated, in part, through analogies to music (Fussell 109–11), hymns being one source of Dickinson's knowledge of music. But it is inaccurate to say that Isaac Watts is the exclusive, or even the primary, source of Dickinson's knowledge. Dickinson knew several nineteenth-century anthologies of hymns.[58]

Hitherto, critics had focused almost exclusively upon the inflections and echoes of the work of Isaac Watts to be found scattered in Dickinson's poems and letters. Critics such as Ross began to shift the discussion away from Watts as being central to her musicality.

Victoria N. Morgan takes up the question of how Dickinson's knowledge and experience of hymns went beyond Isaac Watts in her book *Emily Dickinson and Hymn Culture* (2010), which seeks to explore the broad and far-reaching nature of the influence of hymnody on Dickinson's poetry. The book's detailed chapter on Dickinson's relation to Watts as a model for dissent includes examples of her dialogue with Watts, her adoption of Wattsian modes of expression, and of his challenges to tradition. It offers a comparative analysis of 'Some keep the Sabbath going to Church' (Fr 236/M115) and Watts's 'Heaven is my home, and I must use my wings'. Dickinson's poem states:

> Some keep the Sabbath in Surplice –
> I, just wear my Wings –
>
> (Fr 236. M 115)

And Watts:

> Heaven is my home, and I must use my wings;
> Sublime above the globe my flight aspires:
> […]
> I have a soul was made for infinite desires.[59]

Morgan's analysis highlights the inheritance of Wattsian dissent, where Dickinson's wing-wearing speaker articulates freedom from the surplice, and the physical and spiritual restriction it denotes:

Such inclination to non-decoration in worship echoes the Wattsian, Dissenter's distrust of obfuscation [...]. In these poems, true communion and victory lies in being able to overcome not only opposition and difficulty, but also the outward, worldly (artificial) ciphers of salvation and spiritual life.[60]

Whilst maintaining that arguments about Dickinson's adoption of Wattsian modes of expression are often accompanied by statements on her rejection of religion per se, and are made without full consideration of the Dissenting tradition, Morgan's book reassesses Dickinson's connection to hymnody in relation to her female hymnist forbears and the poet's reformulation of 'hymnic space'. Crucially, Morgan makes a special case for the hymn as a form which enabled Dickinson to invoke ideas of community and relation, both of which, she argues, are incorporated into a re-envisioned version of the divine in Dickinson's work. Unlike other forms, which are not expressly devotional, the hymn and its symbolic value enable Dickinson to critically engage with the theological perspectives of the hymnists she had internalized from childhood and carried into adulthood. The hymns of Isaac Watts are undoubtedly included in this, but the work of Antebellum women hymnists such as Phoebe Hinsdale Brown (1783–1861) and Eliza Lee Follen (1787–1860) should be considered as important to Dickinson's experience of hymn culture, not least, because of a connection with her matrilineal heritage, but also for the alternatives to traditional hymn address that they offer her.

Morgan's examination of the hymns of Brown (a founding member of the Praying Circle that Dickinson's maternal grandmother Betsey Fay also attended) and Follen breaks new ground by illuminating how their hymns, like Dickinson's poems, inscribe a 'fluid relationality' and 'anti-teleological narrative' which offers a model for a reconfigured speaker-God relation, and negotiates the hierarchical, 'I-Thou' model of address found in traditional hymns. For example, the imagery of flight employed in hymns by Brown and Follen provides Dickinson with non-linear models of hymn address, and non-static metaphors for the divine. Morgan sees Dickinson's use of flight imagery as an example of how such non-linear poetics anticipate the ideas of feminist theologians, who privilege community over hierarchy:

> Instead of replicating the linear movement upwards to a fixed God-head, Dickinson's poems restore the centrifugal aspect of hymn address and forge a multiple and diverse relation which is connoted by flight imagery and non-static metaphors.[61]

In this way, Morgan's work contributes to feminist criticism which seeks to analyse the diverse ways Dickinson's poems deconstruct a paternalized world governed by logic, logos and established devotional expression.[62] Morgan's work also highlights how the editorial processes which governed the publication of Brown and Follen's hymns echo those imposed, posthumously, upon Dickinson's work to obfuscate elements of dissent.[63]

Morgan's readings of Dickinson's extensive uses of bee imagery delineate a trajectory for a devotional schema – in line with critics who see Dickinson creating her own spiritual aesthetic. Expanding upon England's observation that Dickinson's bee is a 'defiant counter-emblem' to Wattsian bee of industry,[64] Morgan's work shows us how the recurring image of the bee is effective in its repetition, and its shifting nature, and is most emblematic of the poet, and of Dickinson herself. Dickinson uses the motifs of hymn culture to manipulate the space between concept and experience:

> The emblematic but repositioning shape of Dickinson's bee imagery enters directly into the conflicts created by the orthodox religious culture she had grown up within, as against her own spiritual experiences as she felt them. [...] The bee presents Dickinson with a paradigm for her own predicament; [...] a metaphor for the divine which is both emblematic *and* multivalent, both changing *and* unchanging. Bee imagery serves Dickinson to articulate the reconciliation of impossibilities, and therefore also, to trace the trajectory of the divine.[65]

Morgan argues that in forging connections between autonomy and community, and between the role of the poet and the Protestant work ethic, Dickinson's bee imagery delineates a 'heterologous space' in which she is able to express her own version of the divine.[66] Further, her use of bee imagery conveys a 'multivalent relationality', as a counter to the 'I-Thou' model of relation in traditional hymnody, which, Morgan argues, is 'only one version of relation'.[67] Morgan makes comparisons between the imagery and devotional expression in Watts, Antebellum women hymnists like Brown and Follen, and Dickinson's 'antiteleological' poetics, to show how her engagement with hymn culture produces a reformulated theological perspective:

> the product of Dickinson's experience of and engagement with the tradition of hymn culture does not merely offer a parody of the modes of expression and metrics of the popular hymnody of her day; it actively shapes a new kind of theology.[68]

In this way, Morgan's work broadens our understanding of Dickinson's use of hymns and illuminates her 'hymn culture' for the reader. Morgan, along with

Wolosky and England, sees Dickinson's style of poetics as being explicitly related to her critical engagement with religious culture, and to Protestantism specifically.

The subject of Dickinson and religion, and the place of hymns within this area of study, continues to hold critics' attention. Recently, Emma M. Duncan returned to the question of why critics read Dickinson's relation to religious discourse, and to hymns, in a polarizing way. In her essay 'Defamiliarizing Faith: Emily Dickinson's Use of Hymns, Scripture and Prayer' (2021) she argues that Dickinson's poems are rather 'projects in critical thought' and that Dickinson 'regularly employs a method of defamiliarization concerning the topic of faith'.[69]

Roger Lundin's special forum on 'Dickinson and Religion' (2014), in the journal *Religion and Literature*, highlights the past, present and future topics of interest and critical perspectives within the area. Bringing together innovative and influential scholarship on Dickinson and religion, this forum showcases work which examines religious aspects of Dickinson's poems; the religious experiences they instigate and the thoughts they inspire. These essays revise and/or challenge the various understandings we have of the historical and biographical contexts of Dickinson's religious beliefs. They also suggest new possibilities for reading 'Dickinson and Religion' in a pluralist world or post-secular climate, and alongside developments in contemporary theology. With the editor's acknowledgement of the 'shape-shifting' and 'protean' nature of its subject, the collection of eight essays (plus Lundin's introduction) are arranged around a reading of Dickinson's religious experience, where the 'centre' holds her affirmed religiosity and the 'circumference' opens out the definitions of her uses for and engagement with religion and religious experience. The essays largely oscillate between these two positions, some fixing more solidly to either the centre point or to the circumference's edges.

The forum is an important indication of critical movements in this specific area, bringing together established scholars as well as 'dynamic new voices'.[70] For example, James McIntosh argues for a reconsideration of Dickinson's 'kinetic' religious imagination in which she embraces adventure and escape from the confines of religious convention but never abandons the religious training of her childhood and its language. Lundin's brilliantly incisive essay sees Dickinson's interrogation of the elements of the Trinity as anticipating the revival of Christology in twentieth-century theology. In it, he bemoans critics who 'arrest the motion of her thought and fix it to the pole of unbelief' and demonstrates how readings of God, Christ and the Spirit are more complex than the various readings of her depictions suggest. Rather, Lundin shows how

Dickinson's constant re-examination of the Trinity imbues her poetry with a shifting and creative engagement which has perhaps evaded critics who seek to define her descriptions of it.[71] Both Lundin and McIntosh place Dickinson's spiritual questioning within the context of her early religious training at school and church and the ways in which that provided her with supportive apparatus as much as modes of thinking to move away from. Moreover, they both show in different ways how the oft-cited strict Puritanism and 'dour' Calvinism of her day was in fact by then modulated through Whig republicanism and evangelical moralism.[72] Victoria N. Morgan's essay on the social and gendered aspect of Dickinson's religious experience, '"When Bells Stop Ringing:" Tracing Dickinson's "Circumference" through the Tradition of the Praying Circle' (2014), shows how Dickinson's anti-teleological metaphors for the divine were shaped by the Praying Circle tradition of her matrilineal heritage.[73]

Essays in the second half of the forum point towards the various futures for studying Dickinson and religion. Miho Nonaka provides a reception history through a study of Dickinson's legacy in modern Japanese culture. She considers how powerfully resonating terms such as 'grace', 'crucifixion' and 'eternity' can be placed within a cultural setting with a complete absence of Christian categories such as these. Nonaka illustrates how Dickinson's depictions of seasonal imagery, spiritual austerity and solitude resonate with themes with a rich history in Japanese poetry, culture and religion, demonstrating Dickinson's relevance in twenty-first-century Japan.[74] Indeed, the subject of Dickinson and religion is often a barometer of how her work is received in contemporary cultures around the world and the ways in which her work is received within the popular imagination.

Notes

1 Francis J. Molson, 'Emily Dickinson's Rejection of the Heavenly Father', *The New England Quarterly*, 47.3 (1974), 404–26.

2 W. Clark Gilpin, *Religion around Emily Dickinson* (University Park, Pennsylvania: Pennsylvania State University Press, 2014).

3 Alfred Habegger, 'Evangelicalism and Its Discontents: Hannah Porter versus Emily Dickinson', *The New England Quarterly*, 70.3 (1997), 386–414.

4 Jane Donahue Eberwein, '"Is Immortality True?" Salvaging Faith in an Age of Upheavals' in *A Historical Guide to Emily Dickinson*, ed. by Vivian Pollak, pp. 67–102 (p. 95).

5   Eberwein, 'Is Immortality True?', p. 96.
6   Benjamin Lease, *Emily Dickinson's Reading of Men and Books: Sacred Soundings* (Houndmills: Macmillan, 1990), p. 38 and p. xii.
7   Benjamin Goluboff, '"If Madonna Be": Emily Dickinson and Roman Catholicism', *The New England Quarterly*, 73.3 (2000), 355–85 (p. 355).
8   Goluboff, 'If Madonna Be', p. 357.
9   Goluboff, pp. 384–5.
10 Martha Winburn England and John Sparrow, *Hymns Unbidden: Donne, Herbert, Blake, Emily Dickinson and the Hymnographers* (New York: New York Public Library, 1966), p. 120.
11 Grabher, Hagenbuchle and Miller, eds., *The Emily Dickinson Handbook,* and Richards, ed., *Emily Dickinson in Context*.
12 Habegger, 'Evangelicalism and Its Discontents' (1997), 386–7.
13 Habegger, p. 414.
14 As discussed in the section on biographies in Chapter 1. See Habegger: *My Wars Are Laid Away in Books: The Life of Emily Dickinson*, p. 28.
15 Wendy Martin, *The Cambridge Introduction to Emily Dickinson* (Cambridge: Cambridge University Press, 2007), pp. 58–9.
16 Martin, pp. 65–70 (p. 70).
17 James McIntosh, *Nimble Believing: Dickinson and the Unknown* (Ann Arbor: The University of Michigan Press, 2004), p. 1.
18 Roger Lundin, *Emily Dickinson and the Art of Belief* (Michigan: Eerdmans, 1998; repr. 2004).
19 Lundin, *Emily Dickinson and the Art of Belief*, p. 178.
20 Linda Freedman, *Emily Dickinson's Religious Imagination* (Cambridge: Cambridge University Press, 2011), p. 1.
21 Freedman, *Emily Dickinson's Religious Imagination*, Chapter 6.
22 Dorothy Huff Oberhaus, '"Tender Pioneer": Emily Dickinson's Poems on the Life of Christ', *American Literature*, 59 (1987), 341–58.
23 Roxanne Harde, '"Some—Are Like My Own—": Emily Dickinson's Christology of Embodiment', *Christianity and Literature*, 53.3 (2004), 315–36 (p. 320).
24 Anne West Ramirez, 'The Art to Save: Emily Dickinson's Vocation as Female Prophet', *Christianity and Literature*, 47.4 (1998), 387–401 (p. 387).
25 Harde, 'Some—Are Like My Own—', pp. 315–36, Ramirez, 'The Art to Save', pp. 387–401; and Anne West Ramirez, 'Harriet Beecher Stowe's Christian Feminism in "The Minister's Wooing": A Precedent for Emily Dickinson', *Christianity and Literature*, 51.3 (2002), 407–24.
26 Siobhan Phillips, '"Loved Philology": Emily Dickinson's Trinitarian Word', *ESQ: A Journal of the American Renaissance*, 51.4 (2005), 250–75 (p. 252).
27 Phillips, 'Loved Philology', p. 252.

28 Phillips, pp. 255–63. Phillips cites Horace Bushnell's *God In Christ* (1849) which explicates a theory of theological language. Although Dickinson never met Bushnell, the Clergy she knew would have known his work well. See Habegger (2001), pp. 310–11. Jonathan Edwards's Trinitarian theory was not published in its complete form until 1903, but his ideas on the Trinity were available in Dickinson's time – his 'Treatise on Grace' and 'Miscellanies' (p. 263).
29 Phillips, p. 262.
30 Phillips, p. 268.
31 Dorothy Huff Oberhaus, 'Engine against th'Almightie': Emily Dickinson and Prayer', *ESQ: A Journal of Nineteenth-Century American Literature and Culture*; 32.3 (1986), 153–72.
32 Oberhaus, 'Engine against th'Almightie', p. 156.
33 Oberhaus, p. 157.
34 Oberhaus, p. 169.
35 Charles M. Murphy, *Mystical Prayer: The Poetic Example of Emily Dickinson* (Collegeville, Minnesota: Liturgical Press, 2019), p. 16.
36 Murphy, *Mystical Prayer*, p. 16.
37 Murphy, p. 17.
38 Murphy, pp. 114–15.
39 Martha Winburn England, 'Emily Dickinson and Isaac Watts' in England and Sparrow, *Hymns Unbidden*, pp. 113–47. Another version of this essay, entitled 'Emily Dickinson and Isaac Watts: Puritan Hymnodists', appears in Paul J. Ferlazzo, *Critical Essays on Emily Dickinson* (Boston, MA: G. K. Hall, 1984).
40 England, 'Emily Dickinson and Isaac Watts', p. 121.
41 England, p. 120.
42 England, p. 121.
43 England, p. 120.
44 Shira Wolosky, 'Rhetoric or Not: Hymnal Tropes in Emily Dickinson and Isaac Watts', *The New England Quarterly*, 61 (1988), 214–32 (p. 232).
45 Wolosky, 'Rhetoric or Not', p. 216.
46 Wolosky, pp. 216–17.
47 Wolosky cites Watts's hymn by book and hymn number, from: Isaac Watts, *Psalms, Hymns, and Spiritual Songs*, 3 bks. in 1 vol. (Boston: James Loring and Lincoln & Edmunds, 1832).
48 Wolosky, p. 217.
49 Wolosky, pp. 217–18.
50 Wolosky, p. 232.
51 Wolosky, pp. 220–1.
52 Cristanne Miller, *Emily Dickinson: A Poet's Grammar* (Cambridge, MA: Harvard University Press, 1987), p. 142.

53 Judy Jo Small, *Positive as Sound: Emily Dickinson's Rhyme* (Georgia: University of Georgia Press, 1990), pp. 41–2.
54 Small, *Positive as Sound*, p. 44.
55 See Miller, *Reading in Time*, pp. 49–81 (p. 49).
56 Christine Ross, 'Uncommon Measures: Emily Dickinson's Subversive Prosody', *The Emily Dickinson Journal*, 10.1 (2001), 70–98 (pp. 91–2).
57 Ross, 'Uncommon Measures', pp. 84–5.
58 Ross, p. 72.
59 Isaac Watts, 'Heaven Is My Home', from *Horae Lyricae* (1706) in *The Poetical Works of Isaac Watts, with a Memoir* (Boston: Little, Brown and Company, 1866) part 1, p. 50.
60 Morgan, *Emily Dickinson and Hymn Culture: Tradition and Experience*, p. 111.
61 Morgan, p. 47.
62 Morgan, pp. 71–9, 213–18. Morgan uses Irigaray's notion of 'airy space' and Michel de Certeau's notion of 'heterologies' to show how Dickinson's poetic 'non-linearity' has the effect of destabilizing the linguistic and patriarchal 'certainties' of logocentric and religious discourse.
63 Morgan, p. 149.
64 England, p. 122.
65 Morgan, p. 160.
66 Morgan, pp. 154, 149.
67 Morgan, p. 54.
68 Morgan, p. 218.
69 Emma M. Duncan, 'Defamiliarizing Faith: Emily Dickinson's Use of Hymns, Scripture, and Prayer', *Women's Studies*, 50.2 (2021), 157–74.
70 Roger Lundin, ed., Introduction to Forum 'Dickinson and Religion', *Religion and Literature*, 46.1 (2014), 137–203 (p. 138).
71 Roger Lundin, 'The Tender Pioneer in the Prairies of the Air: Dickinson and the Differences of God', *Religion and Literature*, 46.1 (2014), 149–56 (p. 152). Lundin cites Helen Vendler's *Dickinson: Selected Poems and Commentaries* (2010) (pp. 16–17) as a case in point.
72 Lundin, 'The Tender Pioneer in the Prairies of the Air', p. 150.
73 Victoria N. Morgan, '"When Bells Stop Ringing": Tracing Dickinson's "Circumference" through the Tradition of the Praying Circle', *Religion and Literature*, 46.1 (2014), 172–9.
74 Miho Nonaka, 'Season of Eternity: The Resonance of Dickinson's Poems in Japanese', *Religion and Literature*, 46.1 (2014), 187–95.

6

Performance and reception

6.1 Performance in Dickinson's poetry	157
6.2 Dickinson and popular culture	160
6.3 Digital Dickinson and international reception	172

This chapter discusses the role of performance in Dickinson studies and the reception of her work both within the field and in our own popular culture. It is concerned with performance as an element in Dickinson's work, her reader-oriented poetics and aesthetics, and how her poems' ambiguities invite readers to 'perform' them, as well as the way Dickinson's work includes within it a performance of identities and ideas. It also considers performance as an important aspect of Dickinson's place in popular culture and the various creative outputs, through different media, that her work has inspired. The area of performance, which incorporates the role of popular culture, will be explored as a current critical wave. As an introduction to performance in Dickinson, key twentieth-century texts such as Sandra M. Gilbert and Susan Gubar's *The Madwoman in the Attic: The Woman Writer and the Nineteenth-Century Literary Imagination* (1979) will be discussed. Their identification of the various 'personae' and 'masks' Dickinson's speakers adopt was an important foundation for scholarship such as Elizabeth Phillips's *Emily Dickinson: Personae and Performance* (1988), Camille Paglia's chapter on Dickinson in *Sexual Personae: Art and Decadence from Nerfertiti to Emily Dickinson* (1990) and, more recently, Jessica Jessee's essay '"An Orator of Feather unto an Audience of Fuzz": Performance as Subject and Setting in Emily Dickinson's Poems' (2014). This discussion of performance in Dickinson's poetry then takes into consideration the ways it has been expanded by critics such as Paul Crumbley, in his essay 'Dickinson's Dialogic Voice' (1998), to describe a reader-oriented poetics and account for the wide appeal of her poetry.

Performance is a quality to be considered within Dickinson's poetry, but we can also scrutinize the 'performance' of Dickinson in popular culture. One of the reasons for Dickinson's position in our own popular culture and for the extent to which her work has been incorporated within many different forms of media is, it has been suggested, because of her own engagement with the popular culture of her day. Therefore, essays which are concerned with Dickinson's engagement with the popular culture of her day, such as David S. Reynolds's 'Emily Dickinson and Popular Culture' (2002) and Sandra Runzo's book *'Theatricals of Day': Emily Dickinson and Nineteenth-Century American Popular Culture* (2019), will be explored, followed by essays such as Jonnie Guerra's 'Dickinson Adaptations in the Arts and the Theater' (1998) which analyse the performance of Dickinson, the role of media and her place within contemporary popular culture. Crucially, in the twenty-first century, the Apple TV television series *Dickinson*, which first aired in 2019, and the Terence Davies film *A Quiet Passion* (2016), starring Cynthia Nixon, have both made Dickinson a much more prominent figure within popular culture. As a barometer for measuring the pervasive nature of Dickinson within American popular culture in recent times, her name could be seen blazoned across an advertising billboard in Time Square, NYC, in 2019 as part of the Apple TV series advertising campaign. Initial critical responses to this recent injection of Dickinson in popular culture will be explored in essays such as '"You'll Be the Only Dickinson They Talk about in Two Hundred Years": Queer Celebrity, Thomas Wentworth Higginson, *A Quiet Passion*, *Wild Nights with Emily*, and Apple TV+'s *Dickinson*' (2022) by Páraic Finnerty, which assesses the relationship between Dickinson's attitude towards celebrity culture and the representations of Dickinson in recent screen adaptations which have contributed to her LGBTQ+ icon status.

Perhaps the most significant aspect of the wider dissemination of the world and work of Emily Dickinson is technological. Essays which explore the impact of latest developments in technology, such as the digitization of Dickinson archive material, will be explored. The recent digitization of Dickinson's music binder has led to work on performance, theatricality and musicality specifically.[1] Recently George Boziwick's book *Emily Dickinson's Music Book: A Musical Life of a Poet* (2022) has made a significant contribution to the field by presenting the first in-depth, book-length study of her music book. The critical impact of the relatively recent (2013) public access release of the Dickinson digital archive will be explored. Finally, the chapter will conclude with a survey of work which has been done concerning the international reception of Dickinson's work and will highlight work by international scholars and translators of Dickinson, suggesting new possibilities for reading Dickinson in the twenty-first century.

6.1 Performance in Dickinson's poetry

Dickinson's life and work were imbued with a sense of the theatrical, and a willingness to evade a fixed identity. For example, she refers to herself in a variety of ways when signing off at the end of letters, including poetical variants of her name such as 'Emilie', and the various associations she had to the recipients, such as 'Your Scholar', 'cousin', 'friend', but also more overt subversions of identity such as 'Judah'.[2] The content of some of her letters has her characterized in various ways, for example, as 'Daisy' in the 'master' letter of 1862.[3] Her friend and literary mentor, Thomas Wentworth Higginson, describes a meeting with her which seems to have been stage-managed down to the hand-held lilies. Recently, critics have been keen to identify the elements of performance in her poetry, and some, such as Jessee (2014), see performance as a subject in Dickinson's poetry itself.[4] However, as discussed in Chapter 3, earlier critics focused on performance to draw wider conclusions about the ways in which her work subverts the notion of fixed identity, and, by extension, that of gender.

Gilbert and Gubar (1979) emphasize the elements of performance in Dickinson's work, as we have seen, with their description of the various 'masks' Dickinson invents for her multiple and varied speakers. They argue that Dickinson adopts such masks, such as the child-mask, in order to negotiate the binary organization of poetic imagination and nature that nineteenth-century women writers inherited from a literary tradition built upon patriarchal ideology. Poems such as 'I'm Nobody! Who are you?' and the suggestion of choosing privacy over status signal to Gilbert and Gubar a version of such masking:

How dreary – to be – Somebody!

(Fr 260, M 128)

The speaker does not wish to become an assertive 'Somebody', and the apparent absence of a public-facing self allows the speaker to avoid the dreariness of being commonplace or known, even. Significantly, this 'nobody' mask also delays self-definition and the 'naming' process. In their view this allows Dickinson the freedom to articulate her own voice within an inherently patriarchal and binary conception of literary creation which positions imagination as masculine and nature as feminine. Dickinson adopts self-diminutive voices and positions, to the point of self-abnegation, in their view, to negotiate the opposing forces of the female self and the masculine other which Romantic theory of poetic imagination dictates to the nineteenth-century woman writer.[5]

Gilbert and Gubar also illustrate Dickinson's performance of the poet figure, both in life and in her work, by focusing on the motif of whiteness in the poems, and emphasizing the fact that she is reputed to have worn white in later years:

> Where George Eliot and Christina Rossetti wrote about angels of destruction and renunciation, Emily Dickinson herself became such an angel. Where Charlotte Brontë projected her anxieties into images of orphan children, Emily Dickinson herself enacted the part of a child. Where almost all late eighteenth- and nineteenth-century women writers from Maria Edgeworth in *Castle Rackrent* to Charlotte Brontë in *Jane Eyre*, Emily Brontë in *Wuthering Heights*, and George Eliot in *Middlemarch*, secreted bitter self-portraits of madwomen in the attics of their novels, Emily Dickinson herself became a madwoman – became ... both ironically a madwoman (a deliberate impersonation of a madwoman) and truly a madwoman (a helpless agoraphobic, trapped in a room in her father's house).[6]

Although their estimation of Dickinson as 'truly a madwoman' would be questioned by many twenty-first-century readers, as would the emphasis they place upon her apparent agoraphobia, the connection they make between Dickinson's performances in both art and life compared with the work of her female forbears and contemporaries was a key critical intervention which has had lasting effects upon the field. Dickinson, in their view, was a nineteenth-century woman poet who produced great work because of her own removal from society and from the socially prescribed expectations for women. Her adoption of the white dress symbolized both her status as a poet and, in their view, her own dramatization of the 'madness' of the female psyche other nineteenth-century women writers 'secreted' into their novels.[7]

It is with emphasis upon the dramatization of the self and the nature of performance in Dickinson's poetry that critics writing after Gilbert and Gubar turned. In her book *Personae and Performance* (1988), Elizabeth Phillips is keen to show how Dickinson's poems were not autobiographical, but were, rather, self-conscious literary performances.[8] As discussed in Chapter 3 in relation to the performance of gender in Dickinson's poetry, Camille Paglia sees Dickinson's poetry as performing two representational modes, the Sadean and the Wordsworthian, in *Sexual Personae: Art and Decadence from Nerfertiti to Emily Dickinson* (1990). Paglia identifies qualities of performance and theatricality in Dickinson's work which can be seen in her sadomasochistic expressions – part of what Paglia calls the 'art of sexual personae'.[9] Paglia's discussion of Dickinson's 'sadomasochism' is useful here as it highlights the dramatized embodied and disembodied selves in Dickinson's poetic palette along with a lengthy list of theatrical props. Paglia catalogues Dickinson's sadomasochistic uses of the body, where brains are split, splinters are dangled, lungs are perforated and hearts have arteries without their bungs ready to gush out blood. Her painterly depictions of sunsets using blood as a metaphor are lingered over and a Civil War–era poem, 'The name – of it – is "Autumn"' (Fr 465 / M 233), is examined for its use of blood, which Paglia puts down to Dickinson's experience, not of the Civil War and its effects, but of the kitchen and 'probably the decapitation and evisceration of chickens!' Paglia states that 'A mass murder seems to have been committed in Amherst' without reference to the Civil War, but to 'Jehovah's rape-murder of pagan mother nature' where 'Sadean reality triumphs over Wordworth's illusions'. Dickinson's 'Wordsworthian' mode of representation encompasses poems which are not mawkish and sentimental but are part of a 'closed system of sexual reference' where they are 'designed to dovetail with those of violence and suffering'.[10] Paglia's reading of Dickinson's poetic personae sees the drama of the poems isolated from their historical moments, where the central concern is the performance of identities which escape or are defined in relation to gendered theories of literary production.

If the notion of performance is crucial to an understanding of how Dickinson's poetry is constructed and how we as readers perform and imagine those alternative possibilities for our identities, for gender and beyond, then the range of multiple voices and the poem's ability to shift our perspectives as we read it are perhaps also a clue to her lasting popularity within our own culture. The multiplicity of voices in Dickinson is something considered by Paul Crumbley. He argues in his essay 'Dickinson's Dialogic Voice' (1998) that the reason Dickinson has been so difficult to place within a literary tradition is partly because of her commitment to dialogism; that her poems possess multiple speakers who are also 'capable of possessing more than one voice'.[11] Therefore, on the one hand, Dickinson's commitment to dialogism has meant that she does not fit easily within a particular literary tradition, but on the other hand this has in turn led to an ever-increasing and -expanding level of popularity, appeal and critical approaches throughout the many years and shifting cultural landscapes since her death in 1886. If her poetry allows us as readers to engage with and imaginatively perform the various possibilities it suggests for us, then it is no surprise that her work has been enthusiastically taken up and interpreted in various media formats.

6.2 Dickinson and popular culture

Dickinson's sense of what was popular within her own culture is now a thriving area of critical interest. However, for many of the early critics of her work, and indeed up until relatively recent times, Dickinson's tendency to stay indoors in her mid-to-later years was evidence of her disconnection from the world around her. David S. Reynolds's work on Dickinson and popular culture did much to dispel this myth.[12] His essay 'Emily Dickinson and Popular Culture' (2002) considers the ways in which Dickinson was engaged with popular literature, music, news items and what was happening politically. He concludes his essay with the statement that Dickinson was a 'private-public poet':

> It is fair to generalize from these and other letters that Dickinson was unique among American women of her day in the breadth of her awareness of the most experimental tendencies in contemporary American culture. Her excitement over press reports of tragedies, her attraction to the new religious style, and her interest in women's writing all reveal a sensibility that was absorbing various kinds of popular images. Dickinson recognized the need for an artistic form that would serve to control and fuse these often contradictory elements. She appropriated the iambic rhythms and simple verse patterns of English hymnody, which had been famously utilized in the Isaac Watts hymns she knew from childhood, as controlling devices to lend structure and resonance to these disparate themes. In her poetry, therefore, Dickinson was both inscribing her culture and personalizing it. She was that rare oxymoronic being, a private-public poet.[13]

Reynolds's argument that Dickinson's popularity in our own culture stems from the sheer amount of popular culture her own work absorbs and conveys is compelling:

> A major reason for her enduring popularity is that she was extraordinarily receptive to the popular literature and culture of her own time. She was thoroughly familiar not only with classic literary sources – especially the Bible, Shakespeare, Keats, the Brontë sisters, Elizabeth Barrett Browning, Emerson, and Thoreau – but also with many popular contemporaries that have since fallen from view. Her poems and letters reveal that she was a highly receptive witness of many phenomena in nineteenth-century popular culture, including imaginative sermons, reform movements, penny newspapers, best-selling novels, and women's literature. She was unique among American women of her day in the breadth of her awareness of the most experimental tendencies

in contemporary American culture. Much of her poetry can be viewed as an individualistic adaptation of popular literary strategies.[14]

Much of what makes Dickinson new to us is the collision between old and new styles that her poetry incorporates and makes explicit. Reynolds gives the example of the tension between old and new sermon styles which is evident within the poems.[15]

Popular literature of the time, as well as the notion of literary celebrity, is something which touched Dickinson's life, inevitably infiltrating her work. Elizabeth Petrino considers Dickinson's position as literary fan of figures such as Elizabeth Barrett Browning and George Eliot in '"I went to thank Her –": Dickinson's Tributes to Literary Celebrities' (2017), and reads her responses to their work through the nineteenth-century cult of transatlantic literary celebrity. This essay is part of a special issue of *The Emily Dickinson Journal* on the topic of 'Dickinson and Celebrity', edited by Paul Crumbley.[16] Petrino analyses Dickinson's memorializing of one of her literary heroines, Elizabeth Barrett Browning, in the form of letters and three elegies: 'Her – last – Poems' (Fr 600 / M 274), 'I think I was enchanted' (Fr 627 / M 308) and 'I went to thank Her' (Fr 637 / M 322). She argues that Dickinson's reading of Barrett Browning's life and work suggests that the cult of celebrity and the highly romanticized version of the poet had superseded her literary output:

> Dickinson's elegies and letters respond to the saintly image of a literary celebrity perpetuated by editors and readers in the period, but they also questioned the degree to which readers might be able to access a personal knowledge of the writer.[17]

Interestingly, Petrino sees Dickinson's letters about Barrett Browning and George Eliot as emphasizing her own 'status as a literary celebrity in the making', where she appears to speak from a vantage point shared with those writers she elevates, signing her letter with just 'Dickinson'.[18] Petrino concludes her essay by asking readers to consider how Dickinson might have viewed the posthumous distribution of the daguerreotype of her, something which contributed to her own posthumous literary fame.

Sandra Runzo's book *'Theatricals of Day': Emily Dickinson and Nineteenth-Century American Popular Culture* (2019) has shown the extent and scope of Dickinson's engagement with popular forms, trends and interests:

> Dickinson was an enthusiast of the traveling circus, a performer of popular musical numbers on her piano, a collector of sheet music of popular songs, and […] an occasional audience member of performances by musicians such

as the Germania Serenade Band, the popular singer Jenny Lind, and, likely, the Hutchinson Family Singers, one of the most prominent of the family singing groups of the nineteenth century. [...] Dickinson experienced the popular culture that infused and shaped 'ordinary life.' The proliferating sites of popular amusement and mass culture in nineteenth-century America – such as circuses, traveling shows, dime museums, minstrelsy, literary fiction, and early photography – provided abundant opportunities to contemplate the host of troubles, struggles, and anxieties that pervaded the nation. America obsessively examined forms of freedom and captivity, categories of human identity, and definitions of normality and aberration, yet these persistent and pressing issues of the nineteenth century were more like puzzles than clear-cut questions [...]. Whatever her aspirations were or were not regarding participation in a public arena, the rich world of popular culture offered Dickinson access to public discussions regarding the key social and political struggles of her time.[19]

An important element of Runzo's argument is to illuminate the ways that Dickinson's poetry, like other formats available to her in the popular culture of her day, examines and reflects the contemporary concerns of her nation. We can see in Dickinson's poems the examination and dramatization of what were popular themes – 'forms of freedom and captivity, categories of human identity, and definitions of normality and aberration'. Runzo illustrates how popular culture provided Dickinson with access to the social and political debates of her time and how her work reflects them. In this, she joins scholars such as Jay Leyda, David S. Reynolds, Barton Levi St. Armand, Cristanne Miller, Shira Wolosky and others who have sought to show how Dickinson was far from being detached from the pressing political and social issues of her day. Although her study is on the nineteenth-century popular culture of Dickinson's day, Runzo's introduction includes a discussion of what a reader/viewer might see in the 'phenomena' of Emily Dickinson, and the 'many Emily Dickinsons' we see in our own popular culture, and the various interpretations of her life and work. Runzo uses the debate around daguerreotype images of Dickinson as well as the dramatic portrayal of Dickinson in William Luce's *The Belle of Amherst* (1976) to demonstrate the ways in which conjecture can quickly turn to revelation in our quest to know Dickinson, and ourselves:

This phenomenon whereby the person we think of as Emily Dickinson is accepted as a combination of fact and fiction is vividly demonstrated in stories regarding visual images of her. [...] The talismanic energy of these photographic images is so great that even photographs of a woman (or women) merely conjectured to be Emily Dickinson can be treated as revelatory of her. Many 'Emily Dickinson's have entered contemporary popular culture in the form of novels, plays, and a recent film, all extensions of this compulsion to ponder her life and writing from different angles and to consider new possibilities, however fantastical, to account for her. [...] *The Belle of Amherst* proposes that if Dickinson is regarded as the town oddity, the incomprehensible – if fascinating – 'Myth' that Mabel Loomis Todd and others surmised, it is a perception of Dickinson's own creation and perpetuated for her own amusement. [...] In Luce's version, Dickinson knowingly performs as the town 'curiosity,' concocting stories and playing roles for her own entertainment as much as for her neighbors.[20]

Runzo's study is useful as it shows how the 'obsessive' examination and questioning of mid-nineteenth-century society fed into the popular forms Dickinson was consuming and rehearsing in her own work. It also highlights the proximity between the representations of Dickinson within our own contemporary culture and the quest for meaning and social definition on a variety of issues, such as, in recent times, the expression of personal identity.

George Boziwick has recently produced a book-length study showing how intimately Dickinson was influenced by the popular music of her day. In *Emily Dickinson's Music Book and the Musical Life of an American Poet* (2022) Boziwick contributes to the historical turn in Dickinson studies to provide a fresh look at the popular music Dickinson knew, offering a new perspective on its centrality to her life and work as an accomplished musician. His book provides unparalleled discussion of Dickinson's 'Music Book' (her collection of sheet music) and offers in-depth background detail on the various composers, music sellers and publishers associated with the sheet music procured by the Dickinsons. Boziwick provides examples from letters and poems, biographical and other sources to point to Dickinson's involvement with the music he discusses. For example, citing the poem 'The Show is not the Show' (Fr 1270 / M 565) he discusses the way Dickinson associates herself with a 'menagerie of concertgoers' and suggests this, as well as a few of Dickinson's letters from 1872 to 1873, references the pianist Anton Rubinstein's (1829–94) performance in Springfield during this period.[21]

Boziwick takes us carefully through the back stories of the popular waltzes, quick-steps, polkas and jigs she acquired to show how Dickinson's music book belied an engagement with the social and cultural milieu of her day, crossing musical, literary, religious, as well as social and political boundaries. His discussion of the 'virtuosi' is also crucial to our understanding of Dickinson's accomplishments in both music and poetry. Importantly, Boziwick shows us how Dickinson's consumption of sheet music was above average and that her music book provides evidence of a person who was seriously engaged with music above and beyond the level of convention expected of a woman of her class. Dickinson was learned, not just amateurish in her approach to music, and her collection of sheet music – and the breadth of its scope to include various high and low forms – was crucial to her developing poetical sensibility. Moreover, Boziwick shows us how central music was in Dickinson's world and to her own positioning of herself within the world of her closest correspondents, delineating a cultural cache which permeates the discourse of their letters.

As Reynolds, Runzo and Boziwick have shown in their discussions of elements of nineteenth-century American popular culture in Dickinson's work, there is a connection to be made between the influence of those popular forms, themes and preoccupations and the readiness with which her work is taken up into our own popular culture through the various adaptations of her poems and the facts of her biography. The performativity of Dickinson's poetry lends itself to myriad creative interpretations of her life and work. The various guises, masks and voices that inhabit Dickinson's poems have been readily embodied and embellished for fictional purposes in novels, music, theatre, film and, more recently, in television. In turn, we can therefore also begin to talk about the 'performance' of Dickinson within popular culture – what she looks like within this space, and the various responses to it.

Jonnie Guerra's essay 'Dickinson Adaptations in the Arts and the Theatre' (1998) provides an excellent introduction to Dickinson adaptation and covers twentieth-century interpretations of her work in various forms of media. She states at the beginning of this essay that:

> Adaptations of Emily Dickinson's life and poetry in drama, dance, the visual arts and music have been widespread in the United States throughout the twentieth century and are becoming so abroad. They open an important new avenue to a full understanding of Dickinson's reception and influence – to date one most scholars have bypassed in their studies.[22]

With the increased presence of Dickinson in films and on television, this 'important new avenue' through which to fully understand the reception of Dickinson and the influence of her work within popular culture, which Guerra identified in 1998, has become ever broader in the twenty-first century. Dickinson's life has been re-imagined creatively many times within popular culture as well as television and cinema; it has been portrayed within novels, plays, music and the visual arts. Depictions of her life in novel format for popular consumption include *The Heart Has Many Doors* (2015) by Susan Snively and

Miss Emily (2015), a novel by Nuala O'Connor, and in *The Lovers of Amherst* (2015) by William Nicholson where the affair between Dickinson's brother Austin and Mabel Loomis Todd is re-imagined for the purposes of adult fiction. In this latter title, set in 2013 and the 1880s, a would-be screen writer Alice Dickinson goes to Amherst to research the lives of Dickinson's brother Austin and his mistress, Mabel Loomis Todd, encountering tales of secrets and romance along the way.²³ Dickinson scholar Joanne Dobson has used Dickinson as the subject of her work of fiction *Quieter than Sleep: A Modern Mystery of Emily Dickinson* (1997), where the central character, a Dickinson scholar herself, is thrown into a murder mystery scenario. Plays on Dickinson's life include *The Belle of Amherst* by William Luce (premiered and published in 1976) and *Emily Dickinson and I: The Journey of a Portrayal* by Jack Lynch and Edie Campbell (premiered 1999, published 2005).

Musical interpretations of Dickinson's work are numerous. Composer and conductor Oliver Knussen's requiem for his wife entitled *Requiem – Songs for Sue* sets a composite of four Dickinson poems, together with others by W. H. Auden, Rainer Maria Rilke and Antonio Machado, for soprano and a fifteen-piece ensemble. This piece premiered in 2006. As musical settings have been and continue to be numerous, there has also been a need to document and provide a critical explanation for them. Carlton Lowenberg's book *Musicians Wrestle Everywhere: Emily Dickinson and Music* (1992) lists in detail each of the 1,615 musical settings of Dickinson's poems by 276 composers from as early as 1896 up to 1991,²⁴ including notable American composers such as Aaron Copland (1951). In his essay on the earliest musical settings of Dickinson's poetry and the musicality of her poems, Gerard Holmes (2019) lists five features of Dickinson's poetry which he sees as being qualities which make them more readily adaptive to musical settings. He includes qualities of the poems such as 'they are easily scanned but not rhythmically predictable' and 'there is a governing metaphor or thematic progression across the stanzas' and, perhaps more interestingly, 'Though the feelings are easy to relate to, there is in places a hint of mystery: what is "almost loneliness?"' He suggests that it is these interesting features and her unorthodox understanding of metre – the aspects of her work which early critics of her verse took to be 'flaws' – which make Dickinson's work so attractive to composers:

> It may be that Dickinson's work was so readily set to music because the qualities that early critics, and Dickinson's own early editors found objectionable were heard not as flaws but as intriguing features by Parker, Blumenthal, and others not bound by the orthodox understanding of meter that persisted in 1890s literary criticism.²⁵

In other words, Holmes sees the spaces and 'irregularities' in Dickinson's work as precisely that which has lent itself to the creative interpretation of musical composers. This thesis could be applicable to the various other media which her work has been expressed through, for example, in the three-channel video art installation made by Polish artist Izabela Maciejewska entitled 'Emily Dickinson's Room' (2009/2020). Maciejewska explains the rationale of the installation as

> an attempt to recreate the place that triggered Emily Dickinson's creative potential. It is a space where, without any rules, and often defying logic, reality is mixed with fantasy, the world of art with life, the world outside with the world of the interior, the artist's world with the world of the viewer.[26]

Here Dickinson's room is described as a 'space' 'without any rules', where the 'creative potential' is enabled by the mixture of different perspectives. Crucially, Maciejewska references the intermingling between the artist's world and that of the viewer. Her work is a visual representation of the relationship between viewer and artist, between Dickinson and her readers rendered in a popular medium.

The 'performance' of Dickinson within popular culture is an interesting strand of research because it keeps on changing with such advancements in media – the various ways in which we 'consume' Dickinson the poet, and ways in which Dickinson's work itself keeps evolving. The way we receive and perceive popular culture keeps changing also, with social media playing an increasingly more significant role. Dickinson's visibility has grown in a wider sense; more people have access to sound bites and to short stanzas of her work here and there via social media and the internet. Almost inevitably, Dickinson's words are frequently wrenched from their contexts by the increasing online supply of 'Inspirational Quotes' from her poems, our modern-day commonplaces. Dickinson-related Twitter and Instagram accounts provide a networking space, and also often a source of humour, for Dickinson scholars, devotees and everyone else. On Twitter, The Emily Dickinson Museum (@DickinsonMuseum) has 15K followers, whilst the Emily Dickinson Bot (@emilydicknsnbot), which posts regular excerpts from Dickinson's poems and intimate letters to Susan Huntington Gilbert Dickinson, currently has a following of 42.4K. There are numerous online blogs in which readers inhabit the persona of Dickinson as well as discuss the merits of her work. Therefore, the way we read Dickinson the poet as a public figure who is being represented to the world, and the way we read her work, have merged even more so now than it had during those early years of her initial publication and the production of the 'myth of Amherst' persona.

Late-nineteenth-century and early-twentieth-century popular conceptions of the poet were based upon the 'myth of Amherst' proliferated by early biographers and critics. In recent times, popular perception of Dickinson has shifted to encompass both a caricatured view of those early portraits and the inflections of the critical interventions which have been made describing the scope of her connectedness, both to those around her and to the culture and politics of her day. Exhibitions such as the one held at the Morgan Library and Museum in New York in 2017, entitled *'I'm Nobody! Who Are You? The Life and Poetry of Emily Dickinson'*, and the ensuing companion publication by Mike Kelly et al., *The Networked Recluse: The Connected World of Emily Dickinson* (2017), have done much to generate this more rounded public perception of Dickinson. The exhibition brought together 100 items including rarely seen letters and manuscripts as well as visual material such as daguerreotypes, hand-cut silhouettes, photographs and contemporary illustrations to show how Dickinson was deeply connected within her own network of correspondents as well as within the cultural and intellectual environment in which she produced her poetry. The authors of the exhibition's companion publication underscored the need to challenge the 'iconic' and therefore widely held public view of Dickinson as a sequestered recluse, thus also attending to the need to produce clear evidence for a new 'iconic' (public) view of her as 'networked' and 'connected' to replace it.[27] The shape of the public perception of Dickinson is much more fluid now than it has ever been, and it is constantly evolving. The iconic, culturally enshrined versions of Dickinson – the 'recluse', the 'Myth of Amherst', America's quintessential (and quaint) nature poet – now compete on platforms alongside a 'networked' Dickinson, and Dickinson as a re-envisioned LGBTQ+ icon. The bite-size snapshots of Dickinson's life and work which are now increasingly visible through social media and the internet more generally mean the margin for interpretation has become much wider. Creative engagement with her work across a variety of media has also increased, as a result.

When considering Dickinson's position within our own popular culture the poet's own thoughts about the route to this are interesting to consider. As we have seen, Paul Crumbley's edited special issue of *The Emily Dickinson Journal* 'Dickinson and Celebrity' (2017) includes essays which focus on Dickinson's complex relationship to publication, the idea of fame and celebrity, as well as the issue of literary tourism and of creating a literary museum at the Dickinsons' Homestead as a focal point for the ever-increasing numbers of Dickinson fans.[28]

In the twenty-first century, there has also been a turn towards filmic and televisual representations of Dickinson's life and work, which has in turn generated more interest in Dickinson across social media platforms. *A Quiet Passion* (2016) written and directed by British film director Terence Davies, starring Cynthia Nixon as Dickinson, successfully put into picture an inner life as well as the scenes of her day-to-day encounters. The biopic was called both unconventional and sensitive by reviewers and was praised for its poetical portrayal of the poet.[29] The Liverpool-based production company Hurricane Films produced a companion piece, a documentary about the poet's life entitled *My Letter to the World* (2018) which featured academic opinion as well as an interview with director Terence Davies. *Wild Nights with Emily* (2018) is an American romantic comedy film written and directed by Madeleine Olnek which stars Molly Shannon as Emily Dickinson and focuses largely upon the Emily–Sue relationship. Apple TV's comedy-drama series *Dickinson* fuses historical fact with blatant, self-conscious historical anachronisms which invite the audience-viewer and would-be blogger to relate to the experiences being portrayed. The recent American production available to Apple TV subscribers, which ran for three seasons from 1 November 2019 to 24 December 2021, presents an image of Dickinson which is surprising to those who know little of her work but also to those who take her work seriously. Set in the mid-nineteenth century with a few modern twists, each episode of the series takes one of Dickinson's poems as its title. For example, the episode 'Because I could not stop for death' sees an updated version of death as the gentleman caller. Dickinson (played by Hailee Steinfeld) is seen boarding a carriage dressed in red to greet her muse – a joint-smoking, dreadlocked personification of 'Death' – who is portrayed brilliantly by US rapper Wiz Khalifa. In this televisual interpretation, Steinfeld's Dickinson oozes the sexual, social and intellectual liberation that the poem suggests. The luscious visual exposition of the central idea of the gentleman caller as a muse with whom to consort offers the viewer an immediacy which illuminates one of her most famous poems. In the 'Wild Nights!' episode we see the Dickinson siblings hosting a house party in which Dickinson hallucinates, seeing a giant Bee, after much opium sipping and irreverent merriment. Here the character Dickinson is seen openly sharing sexual experiences with her soon-to-be sister-in-law Sue, as well as putting up with gender-biased injustices dished out by her dour father. American audiences are perhaps more used to the story of Dickinson as the poet-recluse who dressed in white, communing with the birds and bees for company, thus throwing this comical, rebellious and ironically angsty Dickinson into sharper relief. Another episode sees her interviewing the poet Henry David Thoreau at Walden, hilariously observing his noble self-sufficiency as being somewhat augmented by the assistance of various nearby friends and family. The comedy of the series and the exaggerated representations of elements of Dickinson's life and of her personality have two main effects. The first is that we question what idea of Dickinson and what knowledge of Dickinson's work the average viewer has. Dickinson is an iconic, canonical American poet whose work features in many academic curricular in the United States. She, or a version of her, is known, familiar and culturally available to many American viewers in a way that she is perhaps not to European and global viewers and audiences. European viewers, and viewers in other countries around the world, perhaps have a rather different regard for Dickinson, whose work infrequently reaches their school curricular; audiences for whom Dickinson is not a (or perhaps even the) national poet. The series raises questions about whether enough is known of Dickinson's work itself to enable such satire to be effective, cross-culturally. Do viewers know enough about Dickinson to readily accept the modes of subversion of any given knowledge of her life and work at play in a series such as *Dickinson*? The second, related effect is that we consider the influence of such contemporary settings of Dickinson, and the representation of her as a poet, and how this might feed into our readings of the poems themselves. Is Dickinson's place within the literary canon secure enough to have fun with? Marianne Noble has commented upon the role of popular culture in twenty-first-century reception of Dickinson, and her discussion of why there has been a recent explosion in scholarly and popular-creative attention to her is instructive:

> Many of Dickinson's readers today value her feminism, queerness, and open-endedness. More than ever before, we notice and challenge racist and sexist discourses that flew under the radar in the past. We view pronouns as a choice not a fact and embrace or at least accept gay marriage. We are sceptical about concepts like sacredness, patriotism, and freedom, which can function as Trojan Horses swarming with systematic injustice, and we want those concepts dismantled, the oppression exposed and demystified, and the values reclaimed and made real. Dickinson's poetry speaks to this hunger. It obstructs conventionality in every syllable, refusing dismissible meanings. It explores interiority, revealing the harm that clichés impose on the lived experiences of normal human beings. Yet instead of being cynical, her poetry validates the other – or rather, the otherness of all people – imagining a life of meaning, dignity, possibility, and sacredness. Because it does so in language that is nondogmatic, honest, and arresting – full of surprises – it reclaims these values. The reader makes the meaning on their own terms, bathing in sensual images and effects. The result is

a surprising and – for me, anyway – unparalleled intimacy. I think this intimacy is particularly gratifying for female and queer readers, whose convictions are shaping popular culture today as never before. Three aspects of our society account, I think, for the current explosion of interest in Emily Dickinson: queer and feminist publics, the rise of networked selves, and changes in how we access and interpret Dickinson's work.[30]

Noble sees Dickinson's visibility within the zeitgeist as the result of our comparative openness and acceptance of LGBTQ+ identities, as well as the technological platforms which allow us to make our own interactions with, and interpretations of, Dickinson's work visible too. In her discussion of historical fiction, Stephanie Russo (2021) uses the phrase 'intentional anachronism' to describe the way that the conflict between periods and styles is directly confronted in Apple TV series *Dickinson*:

> Apple TV+'s comedy/drama *Dickinson*, in particular, entirely by-passes the question of accuracy by embracing intentional anachronism or what Thomas M. Greene labels 'creative' anachronism in his taxonomy of anachronisms (1986, 208). Creative anachronisms 'confront and us[e] the conflict of period styles self-consciously': with its soundtrack of contemporary music and a contemporary queer progressive sensibility, *Dickinson* uses anachronism to suggest a new way of thinking about one of the most mythologised and enigmatic of American literary icons (Greene 1986, 208). The show is both tethered to the 'facts' of Dickinson's life at the same time as it asks us to imagine an Emily Dickinson who sounds and acts like a contemporary millennial. *Dickinson*'s use of intentional or creative anachronism collapses past and present to emphasise history's familiarity, rather than its strangeness. The past in *Dickinson* is not a foreign country, to use L.P. Hartley's famous formulation, but instead, startlingly familiar.[31]

In its presentation to the viewer of what is familiar in *Dickinson*, Russo argues that what is produced by this intentional anachronism is an 'affective authenticity' which translates Dickinson's life and work into a common ground, making her life and work relatable to viewers:

> In its use of intentional anachronism, and its insistence on capturing a sense of emotional accuracy, *Dickinson* suggests a new way of thinking about the function and form of historical fiction in the twenty-first century. This new kind of historical fiction embraces what Thomas Greene calls creative anachronism in order to construct an affective authenticity that has the effect of drawing subject and audience closer together, bound by transhistorical emotions and experiences.[32]

In Russo's view, by bringing Dickinson into the twenty-first century in this way, screenwriter and producer Alena Smith and the team behind the series *Dickinson* suggest to us ways that Dickinson's poetry might be relevant to a twenty-first-century audience and present 'transhistorical emotions and experiences'. In this regard, it could be argued that Dickinson is finally returned to an old-school liberal humanism, whereby great literature transcends its historical moment by virtue of its ability to convey truth.

More recently, in his essay '"You'll Be the Only Dickinson They Talk about in Two Hundred Years": Queer Celebrity, Thomas Wentworth Higginson, *A Quiet Passion, Wild Nights with Emily*, and Apple TV+'s *Dickinson*' (2022) Páraic Finnerty connects Dickinson's negotiations with nineteenth-century celebrity culture with her contemporary celebrity status and her twenty-first-century position as a queer icon. Drawing upon work which has been done on Dickinson and celebrity, and the role of popular culture, such as Sandra Runzo's *'Theatricals of Day': Emily Dickinson and Nineteenth-Century American Popular Culture* (2019), it argues that Dickinson's self-fashioned identity as a rebellious, unconventional poet was enabled by her appropriation of nineteenth-century celebrity discourse. Her relationship with nineteenth-century literary celebrity culture is ambivalent – showing both defiance and indirectness in her approach to fame and publication, whilst also sending work out to friends, revising, organizing and presenting it in the form of fascicles, as discussed in Chapter 1. It is this relationship which aids an understanding of the way she has been presented in recent biopics which accentuate her queer iconicity.[33] He argues that Dickinson's self-curated representation of herself for Thomas Wentworth Higginson in letters and in their meeting, as well as Higginson's description of his meeting with her, sets her up as a literary celebrity despite the fact she eschews fame and celebrity in her poems and letters. Dickinson's self-styled evasiveness, both in her letters and in her poems, belies an ambivalent relationship with celebrity culture. Her engagement with it also enables her own queering of it:

> Borrowing and revising key characteristics of nineteenth-century celebrities, Dickinson defiantly queers them by fashioning herself as wholly private, uninterested in publication, and anxious about publicity.[34]

Her ambivalence about publication and fame also allows for social and poetic unconventionality. Finnerty argues that the screen adaptations of Dickinson: *A Quiet Passion, Wild Nights with Emily*, and *Dickinson* underscore this social and poetic unconventionality as part of their queer appropriation of the poet. He shows how these representations complicate views of Dickinson as a recluse by emphasizing the ways in which she was connected to the world around her and provide a counterpoint to views such as those promoted by Higginson. Importantly, these screen adaptations of Dickinson highlight her intellectual and erotic relationships with women, and the emerging scholarship and reviews they have generated have ultimately contributed to her status as a queer ally and twenty-first-century LGBTQ+ icon:

> The transference of scholarly and biographical insights about Dickinson's non-heteronormativity to recent popular cultural representations of the poet show the reach and scope of Dickinson's recalcitrant celebrity and the specific use to which it has been put to extend the visibility of LGBTQ+ identities. *A Quiet Passion*, *Wild Nights with Emily*, and *Dickinson* differently showcase Dickinson's defiance and provide their perspective on Dickinson's stylization of herself as a non-publishing, publicity-averse poet, and Higginson's subsequent publicization of this. Importantly, these works complicate Higginson's emphasis on her reclusive genius by showing her social connections, particularly her intellectual and erotic relationships with other women, in ways that realize potentials within feminist and LGBTQ+ scholarship. These recent screen adaptations present Dickinson as a queer ally whose defiant life and writings endorse non-heteronormative lives. The reviews and emerging scholarship of these biopics underscore Dickinson's growing visibility as a twenty-first-century LGBTQ+ icon.[35]

Therefore, we can see how Dickinson's place within our own popular culture keeps evolving, with new ways to experience and view her work. With this come further opportunities to interrogate contemporary issues by reading Dickinson, and to forge new critical directions within the field of Dickinson studies.

6.3 Digital Dickinson and international reception

We are now well into the new millennium, when new technology and new ways of viewing Dickinson's work are widely available. Most of Dickinson's corpus is readily accessible online, as well as hundreds of images of the poetic fragments she collected throughout her life. We can also view items from her home, enabling a worldwide audience to engage with the life and work of Emily Dickinson in different ways. In 2013 Harvard University launched the largest online archive of Dickinson manuscript images after Amherst College made their collection of Dickinson manuscripts available online (https://acdc.amherst.edu/browse/). The *Emily Dickinson Archive* (EDA) (www.edickinson.org) is an open-access online resource providing high-resolution images of manuscripts of Dickinson's poetry, as well as transcriptions and annotations from selected historical and scholarly editions. The site brings together Dickinson manuscripts from each of the institutions which currently hold them, including Amherst College.

This is a vital resource to Dickinson scholars and students, and the aim is to provide a single site for access to images of all surviving Dickinson autograph manuscripts. The *Dickinson Electronic Archives* (DEA) (www.emilydickinson.org) was launched in 1994 and now has another branch to it, which is the *Dickinson Electronic Archives 2* with Martha Nell Smith as Executive Editor and Co-Ordinator. DEA2 is a creative-critical collaboratory featuring new critical and theoretical work on Dickinson. It also provides a space for a network of Dickinson scholars, students and readers to explore the possibilities for interdisciplinary and collaborative research. The DEA is also home to a blog on Dickinson and a Forum where readers can contribute their own discussion about the blog (www.emilydickinson.org/blog). *The Emily Dickinson Lexicon* (https://edl.byu.edu/index.php) was set up in 1991 at Brigham Young University and provides open access to a database of words used by Dickinson in her poems, as well as to Noah Webster's *An American Dictionary of the English Language* (1844), Volumes One and Two, which she most probably used for reference. The lexicon is a dictionary of alphabetized headword entries for all the words in Emily Dickinson's collected poems (Johnson 1955 and Franklin 1998 editions). The lexicon has been set up to assist scholars who are interested in the lexical intricacies of her poems and to aid the translation of Dickinson's work into other languages by supplying definitions of individual words. Exciting new digital humanities projects continue to emerge, such as the dickinsonsbirds.org project which has gathered over 300 Dickinson manuscripts which represent 237 poems which contain bird imagery or reference birds. It has also collected over 300 sound and sonogram files of the associated bird calls and songs. The curators state that *Dickinson's Birds* 'combines elements of the documentary archive, the scholarly edition, and the environmental installation to invite new questions at the intersection of poetics, ecology and ethics'.[36] Digital technology has enabled us to hear the bird sounds Emily heard and referenced in her poems and we can look around the house and bedroom she lived in. The Emily Dickinson Museum's website offers a virtual tour of the poet's house (www.emilydickinsonmuseum.org/homestead-parlors/), where it is possible to 'visit' the rooms in the homestead, including Dickinson's bedroom. Images from the Homestead are accompanied by information about the family, and excerpts from Dickinson's letters animate these spaces for the online visitor. We are now in a technological era where Dickinson critics are also, in many instances, the curators of Dickinson's work and life in different ways.

With the various new technologies which enable us to read Dickinson's work and to view aspects of her life, it is perhaps unsurprising that there has been recently more critical interest in these technologies and how they affect our readings and experience of Dickinson. Critics such as Seth Perlow have become interested in the imaging technologies that have presented Dickinson's manuscripts. In chapter one of his book *The Poem Electric: Technology and the American Lyric* (2018) entitled 'Affect: The Possessions of Emily Dickinson', he argues that the imaging technologies which present Dickinson's work to the reader such as the electroplating process which enabled the first volume of her *Poems* to be printed in 1890

> do not serve primarily analytic or informational ends but foster a rhetoric of lyric exemption that empowers affective reading practices to reshape Dickinson's legacy.[37]

Perlow's argument is that the technological processes themselves enable a paradoxical embracing of the opposite to the rational logic implied by technology, where 'affect', 'chance', 'anonymity' and 'improvisation' are all able to flourish. In his discussion of Dickinson's use of dashes, which were interpreted by editors as short en dashes or longer em dashes or hyphens, he asserts that 'the dash also refers us to the noninformational register of affect'.[38] Perlow's emphasis on affect being made available to Dickinson readers because of technology is particularly compelling when considering the twentieth- and twenty-first-century advancements in the Dickinson digital archive, arguing that Dickinson 'often figures powerful emotion as electrical, anticipating the affective responses today's electronics make possible'.[39] In his essay '"Textures Newly Visible": Seeing and Feeling the Online Dickinson Archives' (2019) Perlow identifies common traits in manuscript-oriented research and anticipates the strengths and limitations of the digital archives whilst also placing archives such as the EDA within a history of publishing Dickinson's work:

> These archives represent a new phase in the publication of Dickinson manuscripts: they are more comprehensive than earlier online collections and are visually richer than their book-bound counterparts. They enable anyone with Internet access to view Dickinson's manuscripts and to explore the complex textual apparatus that editors have developed. Ironically, even as these online archives support new ways to study Dickinson, they also perpetuate familiar assumptions about the value of seeing her handwriting, encouraging us to invest Dickinson's script with gnomic powers. The manuscript images do not necessarily make her poems easier to read. Instead, they endow her papers with an almost magical allure, holding out the promise of a close encounter with the poet's own lyrical passions. [...] Even when scholars directly consult the

manuscripts, rather than facsimiles, they respond to the development of new technologies for reproducing Dickinson's handwriting.[40]

In Perlow's view, the technologies used to reproduce Dickinson's handwriting play an important role, almost as much as the texts themselves, in critical responses to her work. Therefore, we can see that the digital age of Dickinson has produced new critical responses. The effects and features of the various technologies which presented Dickinson's work to the world can be traced from the earliest editing and printing of her work right through to the digital archive and the various other digitized methods of viewing her life and work which we now have available to us in the twenty-first century.

The international reception of Dickinson's work has naturally expanded in line with the digital archive's accessibility and the increasing online visibility of Dickinson's work and details of her life. A variety of perspectives on the work of Dickinson is available from around the globe, with more rapidly emerging. The subject of the international reception of Dickinson's work is such a rich area that it can only be explored briefly here, looking at a few of the new perspectives from around the world. However, as early as 1970 there was a need to document the many translations of Dickinson into other languages as well as the scholarship by non-English speakers. Willis J. Buckingham's edited *Emily Dickinson: An Annotated Bibliography: Writings, Scholarship, Criticism and Ana 1850–1968* (1970) includes a section on 'Foreign Language Materials' which lists translations of Dickinson's poetry and letters, as well as criticism and scholarship by non-English speakers. The largest entries are on European (Italian, French, German, Dutch, Spanish and Portuguese) editions of her work as well as criticism, followed by a smaller entry on Japanese publication and criticism. The final section, 'Other Languages', includes a list of translations and introductions, as well as criticism in (again, for the most part, European) languages such as Norwegian, Swedish, Finnish, Hungarian, Romanian, Polish, Czech, Croatian, Russian, Hebrew, Yiddish and Vietnamese.[41]

The collection of essays *The International Reception of Emily Dickinson* edited by Domhnall Mitchell and Maria Stuart in 2009 marked the first book-length study dedicated to the subject of the international reception of Dickinson's work outside of North America. In their Introduction the editors claim the book's contribution in its examination of the different stages of Dickinson's reception beyond North America and the impact her work has had on academics, teachers, artists, composers, dramatists, poets, readers, students, translators and writers. They also provide essays which analyse the interaction between Dickinson's language and the various languages into which her work has been translated. They see this work as a form of travel itself:

> 'To shut our eyes is Travel', wrote Dickinson in 1870 to her friend Elizabeth Holland (L354). If travel involves exposing ourselves to different cultures and languages, and thus learning more about them, about our own cultures and languages, and not least about ourselves, then reading what scholars and translators from outside the United States have to say about and on behalf of Dickinson is a form of travel. As, indeed, it is to read Emily Dickinson herself. The range and quality of the responses in languages other than English and in places outside North America – reviews and articles, translations, theses, monographs, dance, theatrical and musical performances, visual installations, paintings, and sculptures – reflect the complexities and obliquities of Dickinson's writings, and their ability constantly to generate new readings. In that sense they represent something more than postcards from abroad: they perform some of the work that Dickinson herself defined as 'Bulletins … from Immortality.'
>
> (Fr 820 / M 405)[42]

The collection of essays takes the reader on a journey across the globe to include places the Dickinson scholar has seen before (Europe), bringing together scholarship on the predominantly European-language reception of Dickinson, except for essays on Dickinson in Hebrew and Dickinson in Japan. It also ventures further afield to include an essay by Carlos Daghlian, 'Emily Dickinson in Brazil'. This charts the introduction of her work to Portuguese-language readers in Brazil by the poet Manuel Bandeira, amongst others, in the 1940s, through to twenty-first-century Brazilian scholarship such as the work of the poet and translator Jose Lira.[43]

We have travelled a bit further since their book was published. A special edition of *The Emily Dickinson Journal* 'International Dickinson: Scholarship in English Translation' (2020) provides translations of Dickinson criticism from countries such as China, France, Hungary, Italy, Mexico, Taiwan and Spain. The editors explain their rationale in the introduction to the special edition:

> because Dickinson is an American author, because the United States is historically a center for Dickinson scholarship, and because English is a dominant language globally, excellent scholarship in other languages does not gain the recognition or carry the impact and influence that it merits. […] interest in Dickinson's writing continues to grow in Europe, Asia, Latin America, and other parts of the world. Major translation projects have been undertaken recently, for example, in Brazil, China, Spain, Mexico, Japan, and Taiwan. Indeed, global interest in

Dickinson's work has surpassed scholarly communication networks, which tend to be restricted by national and linguistic boundaries. For that reason, this special issue of the *Emily Dickinson Journal*, 'International Dickinson: Scholarship in English Translation,' seeks to promote scholarly dialogue across languages and cultures. It indicates the international diversity of Dickinson studies by presenting scholarly work published in other languages now translated for the first time into English. We include abstracts as well as essay-length translations of peer-reviewed work published in China, France, Hungary, Italy, Mexico, Taiwan, and Spain.[44]

The dialogue which cuts across languages and cultures is crucial as it gives critical space to important questions about the relationship between translation and reception and about the setting up of critical expectations. Important questions surrounding the reception of Dickinson's work, as addressed by critics such as Zofia Burr (2002), have become perhaps more pertinent now than ever. Burr's argument that the limits of dominant critical reception could change to see poetry as communicative rather than as a form self-expression alone still holds. So too do the questions she asks, such as, 'What are the elements that shape the reception of Dickinson and what expectations do critical responses to her work set up?'[45] As the availability of Dickinson's work becomes more widespread throughout the world, it has therefore never been more important for the voices of international critics of her work to be heard. With these new critical responses to Dickinson also comes a new set of critical expectations as well as the replacement of outmoded ones.

In what can only be a brief sample, the last section of this chapter highlights some of the criticism which has given Dickinson studies an international voice in recent years, and which has gone some way to dispel the outmoded expectations of critics as well as creating newer, more contemporary ones within the field. The perception of Dickinson from Latino/a and Chicano/a perspectives can be explored in texts which describe her presence as a canonical American poet. In her essay 'Latino/a Literature in the Arab World' (2012), Dalia M. A. Gomaa discusses the appeal of Chicana literature and Chicana feminism and names Dickinson alongside Charlotte and Emily Brontë and other well-known British and American writers as representing an unfamiliar type of feminism:

> Chicanas' feminism sounded more contemporary to me than nineteenth-century and early twentieth-century American and British feminism by women writers such as Jane Austen, Charlotte and Emily Brontë, Virginia Woolf, Louisa May Alcott, Emily Dickinson, and Sylvia Plath.[46]

Dickinson is mentioned in this collection of essays as a canonical and 'fundamental' American writer, a benchmark of what is important in American culture – which the book aims to change by presenting another literary history with the contribution of Latino/a and Chicano/a literatures:

> Further, it is tantalizing to ponder what effect these materials will have on shaping contemporary Hispanic or American writing as this literary history becomes as well known and fundamental as any Hawthorne or Twain, or Dickinson or Bishop.[47]

The reception of Dickinson within Latino/a and Chicano/a perspectives can be heard in the critical voices, including those of translators, which shape this literary history. The translation of Dickinson into Spanish is discussed by the Mexican poet and translator Alberto Blanco in Frances Ann Day's book *Latina and Latino Voices in Literature: Lives and Works* (2003) and he comments on the difficulties this posed:

> One of his many fascinating projects is his translations of the poetry of Emily Dickinson. Her poems were difficult to translate because of the contradictions and sensitivity in her work. He notes, 'She's a master of rhymes and rhythms, so what I found was that not each and every poem of Emily Dickinson can be translated into Spanish, but I think I have succeeded in some.'[48]

The difficulties of translating Dickinson into Spanish are considered by Spanish critic María-Milagros Rivera Garretas. Crucially, she describes the act of translation as an act of intimacy between the living history of the poet and that of her translators.[49] Brazilian translations of Dickinson are compared by Brazilian translator and scholar Marcela Santos Brigida and Brazilian scholar Davi Ferreira de Pinho (2019). They offer comparative readings of translations of the poem 'I'm Nobody! Who are you?' (Fr 260 / M 128) by Aila de Oliveira Gomes and Augusto de Campos to analyse the relationship between reception and translation and question the legacy of the Dickinson myth of poetic isolation.[50]

The challenges and expectations that translators of Dickinson into Chinese come up against are considered by critics such as Cuihua Xu (2013). Xu's discussion of the process of translating Dickinson into Chinese is instructive. Xu examines Chinese translations of Dickinson during the years 1984–2011 by twelve translators whose work is in book form and by four other translators whose work appears in monographs and anthologies. It describes the problems encountered by the translators in aiming to capture the 'essence' of Dickinson and the concerns they have over themes and representing her words with their multivalency. Specific challenges such as those encountered whilst translating

Dickinson's various puns, her use of polysemy, homonyms and metaphors are also considered.[51] The reception of Dickinson in China has been addressed by scholars such as Baihua Wang, in 'Emily Dickinson's Reception in China: A Brief Overview, Part 1' (2012), which is an overview of the history of that reception. In this fascinating and illuminating essay, amongst other things, Wang identifies an article entitled 'Outline of American Literature' which was published in 1926 in one of China's most influential journals, *Fiction Monthly*, as being the first reference to her work in China.[52]

The Emily Dickinson Journal recently included the work of Yu Kwang-Chung (1928–2017), a Nanjing-born poet and literary translator of Dickinson who lived in Taiwan, to promote Dickinson studies on the global stage and for the voice of Taiwan to be heard in the English-speaking world. His influential essay 'Emily Dickinson: A Bee Gatecrashing Eternity', which was originally published as an introduction to his translation of thirteen of Dickinson's poems in *Anthology of American Poetry* (1961), examines the poetic features of Dickinson's work whilst critically comparing her to other English and American poets.

Masako Takeda's essay 'Emily Dickinson and Japanese Aesthetics' (2013) is a brilliant example of how cross-cultural understanding of Dickinson's work can provide fresh insights. Takeda's concern with the notion of 'brevity' and 'ma' (the aesthetics of absence) in Dickinson's work and within Japanese culture shows how both haiku and Dickinson's poems treat brevity as instantaneous understanding. In this way, Takeda draws parallels between Japanese culture's understanding of 'ma' and the way its meaning is central to art and culture and Dickinson's use of it, which appears in the rendering of the natural world into the imaginative world of poetry.[53] As we have seen in the previous chapter, the relationship between Japanese culture and Dickinson's poetics has also been examined in the work of Japanese bilingual poet and translator Miho Nonaka (2014).[54]

Iraqi poet and translator Naseer Hassan appears in Michelle Kohler's edited volume, *The New Emily Dickinson Studies* (2019). In his essay 'Emily Dickinson in Baghdad' Hassan explains his affinity with Dickinson, whom he translated into Arabic, and expresses his appreciation for the quality her poetry has in retaining hope.[55]

There has been a drive within Dickinson studies in recent years to promote a dialogue across languages and cultures, and to bring together international voices to expand the field. The presence of translated critical texts in key journals such as *The Emily Dickinson Journal* and their special issue on 'International Dickinson: Scholarship in English Translation' (2020) reflects this. The emergent and burgeoning array of new international voices and new perspectives highlighted here conveys the sheer scope and potential for that dialogue to continue to forge future directions and critical expectations within Dickinson studies. In examining the role of performance as an important element within Dickinson's poetry, and by focusing on how her adoption of personae, her use of dialogic voices and multivalency readily invite multiple readings and perspectives, the critics discussed in this chapter have each emphasized, in different ways, how expansive Dickinson's work is. The international reception of Dickinson shows that this reader-oriented experience is felt globally.

Notes

1. George Boziwick, '"My Business Is to Sing": Emily Dickinson's Musical Borrowings', *Journal of the Society for American Music*, 8.2 (2014), 130–66; and 'Emily Dickinson's Music Book: A Performative Exploration', *The Emily Dickinson Journal*, 25.1 (2016), 83–107.
2. For example, see Thomas H. Johnson, ed., *Emily Dickinson: Selected Letters*, eleventh printing (Cambridge, MA: Belknap Press, 2002), pp. 94–5.
3. Johnson, ed., *Selected Letters*, p. 167 (Letter 248).
4. Jessica L. Jessee, 'An Orator of Feather unto an Audience of Fuzz': Performance as Subject and Setting in Emily Dickinson's Poems', *The Emily Dickinson Journal*, 23.2 (2014), 1–23.
5. Gilbert and Gubar, p. 587.
6. Gilbert and Gubar, p. 583.
7. For discussion of Gilbert and Gubar's approach to Dickinson, see Lucia Aiello, 'Mimesis and Poiesis: Reflections on Gilbert and Gubar's reading of Emily Dickinson' in *Gilbert and Gubar's The Madwoman in the Attic after Thirty Years*, ed. by Annette R. Federico (Columbia: University of Missouri Press, 2009), pp. 237–56. Aiello takes issue with the lack of differentiation in their analysis of writers such as Dickinson, in that they do not consider the different literary forms writers use to negotiate gender.
8. Elizabeth Phillips, *Emily Dickinson: Personae and Performance* (University Park: Pennsylvania State University Press, 1988).
9. Camille Paglia, *Sexual Personae: Art and Decadence from Nerfertiti to Emily Dickinson* (London and New Haven: Yale University Press, 1990), p. 648.
10. Paglia, *Sexual Personae*, pp. 635–8.
11. Paul Crumbley, 'Dickinson's Dialogic Voice' in *The Emily Dickinson Handbook*, ed. by Gudrun Grabher, Roland Hagenbuchle and Cristanne Miller, pp. 93–109 (p. 99).
12. David. S. Reynolds, 'Emily Dickinson and Popular Culture' in Martin, ed., *The Cambridge Companion to Emily Dickinson*, pp. 167–90. See also: David S. Reynolds,

'"Vesuvius at Home": Emily Dickinson, Amherst, and Nineteenth-Century Popular Culture', in *Amherst in the World*, ed. by Martha Saxton (Amherst: Amherst College Press, 2020), pp. 201–16.
13 Reynolds, 'Emily Dickinson and Popular Culture', p. 189.
14 Reynolds, p. 168.
15 Reynolds, p. 168.
16 Elizabeth Petrino, '"I went to thank Her—": Dickinson's Tributes to Literary Celebrities', *The Emily Dickinson Journal*, 26.2 (2017), 6–24. 'Special Issue: Dickinson and Celebrity' ed. by Paul Crumbley.
17 Petrino, 'I went to thank Her—', p. 10.
18 Petrino, p. 11.
19 Sandra Runzo, *'Theatricals of Day': Emily Dickinson and Nineteenth-Century American Popular Culture* (Boston and Amherst: University of Massachusetts Press, 2019), pp. 1–2.
20 Runzo, *'Theatricals of Day'*, pp. 9–10.
21 George Boziwick, *Emily Dickinson's Music Book and the Musical Life of an American Poet* (Boston and Amherst: The University of Massachusetts Press, 2022), pp. 150–3.
22 Jonnie Guerra, 'Dickinson Adaptations in the Arts and the Theatre', in *The Emily Dickinson Handbook*, ed. by Grabher, Hagenbuchle and Miller, pp. 385–407 (p. 385).
23 William Nicholson, *The Lovers of Amherst* (London: Quercus, 2015).
24 Carlton Lowenberg, *Musicians Wrestle Everywhere: Emily Dickinson and Music* (Berkeley: Fallen Leaf, 1992).
25 Gerard Holmes, 'Invisible, as Music -': What the Earliest Musical Settings of Emily Dickinson's Poems, including Two Previously Unknown, Tell Us about Dickinson's Musicality', *The Emily Dickinson Journal*, 28.2 (2019), 73–105 (p. 102).
26 Izabela Maciejewska is quoted by Alicja Cichowicz from The City Art Gallery in Lodz, 2016. See: https://www.lab.malamegi.com/art_contest_lab19/contestpreview.php?id=6295
27 Mike Kelly, Marta L. Werner, Carolyn Vega, Susan Howe and Richard Wilbur, *The Networked Recluse: The Connected World of Emily Dickinson* (Amherst College, 2017).
28 See Paul Crumbley, ed., 'Special Issue: Dickinson and Celebrity' *The Emily Dickinson Journal*, 26.2 (2017). Páraic Finnerty, '"If Fame Belonged to Me, I Could Not Escape Her": Dickinson and the Poetics of Celebrity', *The Emily Dickinson Journal*, 26.2 (2017), 25–50, and Jane Wald, 'The "Poet Hunters": Transforming Emily Dickinson's Home into a Literary Destination', *The Emily Dickinson Journal*, 26.2 (2017), 71–98.
29 See: A. O. Scott, 'Review: "A Quiet Passion" Poetically Captures Emily Dickinson' in *The New York Times*, April 13, 2017.
30 Marianne Noble, 'Emily Dickinson in the Twenty-First Century', *American Literature*, 93.2 (2021), 283–305.

31 Stephanie Russo, 'You Are, like, So Woke': Dickinson and the Anachronistic Turn in Historical Drama', *Rethinking History*, 25:4 (2021), 534–54 (p. 535).
32 Russo, 'You Are, like, So Woke', p. 551.
33 Páraic Finnerty, '"You'll Be the Only Dickinson They Talk about in Two Hundred Years": Queer Celebrity, Thomas Wentworth Higginson, *A Quiet Passion*, *Wild Nights with Emily*, and Apple TV+'s *Dickinson*', *The Emily Dickinson Journal*, 31.1 (2022), 1–30.
34 Finnerty, 'You'll Be the Only Dickinson They Talk about in Two Hundred Years', pp. 10–11.
35 Finnerty, p. 14.
36 https://dickinsonsbirds.org/project/about/overview
37 Seth Perlow, *The Poem Electric: Technology and the American Lyric* (Minneapolis: University of Minnesota Press, 2018), p. 37.
38 Perlow, *The Poem Electric*, p. 71.
39 Perlow, p. 33.
40 Seth Perlow, 'Textures Newly Visible: Seeing and Feeling the Online Dickinson Archives', in Kohler, ed., *The New Emily Dickinson Studies*, pp. 239–57 (p. 239).
41 Buckingham, ed., *Emily Dickinson: An Annotated Bibliography*, pp. 165–201.
42 *The International Reception of Emily Dickinson*, ed. by Domhnall Mitchell and Maria Stuart (London: Continuum, 2009), p. 5.
43 Mitchell and Stuart, eds., pp. 137–51.
44 Adeline Chevrier-Bosseau, Li Hsin-Hsu and Eliza Richards, 'Editorial Introduction: Testing our Horizons', *The Emily Dickinson Journal*, 29.2 (2020), pp. ix–xiv (p. ix). It is worth including the lengthy footnote from p. ix here to indicate the new developments the editors list: 'Dickinson translation in the Spanish-speaking and Lusophone world is equally exciting. In Spain, the complete poems of Dickinson were translated recently by Enrique Goicolea (*Obra poética completa*, Ediciones Amargord, 2012), José Luis Rey (*Poesías completas*, Visor libros, 2013), and Ana Mañeru Méndez and María-Milagros Rivera Garretas, in three volumes (Sabina, 2012, 2013 and 2015). In Latin America, recently published selections of Dickinson's poems include *Carta al mundo: poemas de Emily Dickinson*, translated by Hernán Bravo Varela (Tierra Adentro, 2016) in Mexico; *Emily Dickinson: Zumbido*, translated by Rodrigo Olavarría, Enrique Winter, and Verónica Zondek (Universidad de Valparaíso, 2018) in Chile; *Purple Traffic*, translated by Rafael Ramírez (2015) in Cuba; and Argentinian poet María Negroni's rewriting of Dickinson in *Archivo Dickinson* (Vaso Roto Ediciones, 2020). Recently, Adalberto Müller in Brazil relied on Cristanne Miller's edition of *Emily Dickinson's Poems as She Preserved Them* (Harvard, 2016) for his translation of Dickinson's fascicles in the first volume of *Emily Dickinson. Poesia Completa, v. 1. Os Fascículos* (Editora Universidade de Brasília, 2020). In Mexico, Juan Carlos Calvillo, who has an

essay included in this special issue, recently published a collection of Dickinson's envelope poems, scraps, and other fragments in a facsimile edition entitled *Las Ruedas de las Aves* (*The Wheels of Birds*) (Aquelarre Ediciones and Los Otros Libros, 2021). Calvillo is currently working on a book-length research project entitled *Emily Dickinson en nuestra lengua. Retratos de traductores* (*Emily Dickinson in Our Tongue. Portraits of Translators*), a historical survey of all the poets and translators who have rendered Dickinson into Spanish' (p. ix).

45 Zofia Burr, *Of Women, Poetry and Power: Strategies of Address in Dickinson, Miles, Brooks, Lorede, and Angelou* (Champaign-Urbana: University of Illinois Press, 2002).

46 Dalia M. A. Gomaa, 'Latino/a Literature in the Arab World' in *The Routledge Companion to Latino/a Literature*, ed. by Frances R. Aparicio and Suzanne Bost (London: Routledge, 2012), pp. 124–30 (p. 127).

47 Jose F. Aranda Jr., 'Recovering the US Hispanic Literary Heritage', in Aparicio and Bost, eds., pp. 476–84 (p. 483).

48 Frances Ann Day, *Latina and Latino Voices in Literature: Lives and Works, Updated and Expanded* (Connecticut: The Greenwood Press, 2003), p. 111.

49 María-Milagros Rivera Garretas, 'Traducir como Intimar' ('Translating as Becoming Intimate'), *DUODA: Estudios de la Diferencia Sexual*, 46 (2014), 58–69, María-Milagros Rivera Garretas, trans. by Caroline Wilson, Review of 'Translating as Becoming Intimate', by María-Milagros Rivera Garretas, *The Emily Dickinson Journal*, 29.2 (2020), 138.

50 Marcela Santos Brigida, and Davi Ferreira de Pinho, 'To Be or Not to Be Nobody: Emily Dickinson in Two Brazilian Translations', *Gragoatá*, 24.49 (2019), 368–89.

51 Cuihua Xu, 'A Scrutiny into Chinese Translations of Emily Dickinson's Poetry (1984–2011)', *The Emily Dickinson Journal*, 22 (2013), 107–27.

52 Baihua Wang, 'Emily Dickinson's Reception in China: A Brief Overview, Part I', *The Emily Dickinson Journal*, 21 (2012), 110–16.

53 Masako Takeda, 'Emily Dickinson and Japanese Aesthetics', *The Emily Dickinson Journal*, 22.2 (2013), 26–45.

54 Miho Nonaka, 'Season of Eternity: The Resonance of Dickinson's Poems in Japanese', *Religion and Literature*, 46.1 (2014), 187–95.

55 Naseem Hassan, 'Emily Dickinson in Baghdad', in Kohler, ed., *The New Emily Dickinson Studies*, pp. 299–307(p. 306).

Conclusion

Reading Dickinson in the twenty-first century, and reading the essential critical texts engaged with the issues her work raises, remains as exciting a prospect as ever. Looking back over the decades of criticism this book has covered, it bears repeating that Dickinson's work stimulates an extremely creatively engaged brand of criticism, regardless of its perspective and related themes. Perhaps like Spenser, or Robert Browning, Dickinson should be viewed as 'the poet's poet', and this could also be extended to 'the critic's poet' – in reference to some of the critical texts this guide has discussed, which merge creative and critical responses to the poems.[1] It is evident in essays from Adrienne Rich's 'Vesuvius at Home' (1976) to Camille Paglia's 'Amherst's Madame de Sade' (1990) that there was a moment in the twentieth century when critical reception of Dickinson occupied a space where the creative and critical were deeply enmeshed. As has been shown in this guide, Dickinson's work has inspired many singularly creative responses including those in novel form, from Dickinson's critics themselves, such as Joanne Dobson's novel *Quieter than Sleep: A Modern Mystery of Emily Dickinson* (1997) and Judith Farr's *I Never Came to You in White* (1996). Even in the twenty-first century, Dickinson's readers wish to inhabit her world, and for Dickinson's work to illuminate their own. Critics, and creative artists alike, engage with the various Dickinson myths and wish to shape them to fit their particular place and time. As was shown, Vivian R. Pollak crafted a theoretical framework to describe this sphere of influence in *Our Emily Dickinsons: American Women Poets and the Intimacies of Difference* (2017). From blog posts to poetry collections, many Dickinson readers wish, metaphorically and sometimes literally, to put on (or take off) Dickinson's clothes in popular cultural imaginings of her.[2]

We have also seen the way historicist approaches have engendered a move away from the privileging of identity, and from the concomitant merging of the poet-reader experience. The late-twentieth-century critical drive to impart historical information about Dickinson's particular moment, and her social status, has occupied much critical space. Betsy Erkkila's excellent work in this area, and particularly her essay 'Emily Dickinson and Class' (1992), are a case in point.[3] The critical attention which has been given to re-locating Dickinson within her socio-historical context has been covered thematically in this guide, for example, in the chapters on Dickinson and the Civil War, and on Dickinson and Religion. Essential research on race and developments within the areas of hymnody and devotional forms have been examined in relation to these themes to show how critics reposition Dickinson within specific historical and social contexts.

This guide has taken the reader through the essential key areas in criticism, spanning from the earliest late-nineteenth-century reviews of her work to the key current critical interventions of the twenty-first century. We have seen how biographies of Dickinson occupy a somewhat contested space, tracing what we know about Dickinson from those very first descriptions offered by Susan Huntington Gilbert Dickinson ('Sue'), in her obituary of Dickinson (1886), to the biographies which make new headway in colouring the details of Dickinson's life, such as the familial relationships and feuds examined by Lyndall Gordon in *Lives like Loaded Guns: Emily Dickinson and Her Family's Feuds* (2010). Critical interest in Dickinson's self-generated conception of herself as poet and the issue of her self-publication have been explored with reference to twentieth-century feminist critics as well as to the more recent critical interventions which have been made on the materiality of the manuscripts. The way the 'fascicles' were used by critics as a framework to make claims about Dickinson's life, as well as any poetic intentions, has been charted with reference to critics such as Miller (1968), Shurr (1983), Oberhaus (1995), Cameron (1998) and White (2008).

By focusing on 'Style' and 'Meaning' in Chapter 2, the guide has shown the ways in which her reception has been affected by perceptions about her poetic style. Citing early reviews, the chapter shows how her compressed style, unconventional syntax and grammar, and overall 'lack' of punctuation were perceived negatively by critics. It has then shown how this unconventional style was reappraised by twentieth-century critics such as Porter (1981), who illustrated how her style anticipated modernism, and Miller (1987), who describes Dickinson's alternative 'grammar'. Critics who have staked various claims on Dickinson's particular style and how it relates to meaning occupy a large area of critical debate within the field. Various critical foci have been explored, such as Farr's (1992) deft consideration of the influence of nineteenth-century visual art on Dickinson's poetic style. Ecocritical readings such as Marrs (2017) were explored to show how Dickinson's representation and organization of the non-human, for example, is another way in which her meanings are dependent upon style. Marrs's notion of Dickinson's 'negative ecology'[4] was discussed as a style of representation which codifies meaning in a specific way. The work of critics such as Weisbuch (1998) and Vendler (2004) was examined in terms of its concern with the complex connection between Dickinson's style and the ways of thinking her poems actively reproduce in the reader.

In its consideration of gender, sexuality and the female tradition the guide has walked the reader through the twentieth-century feminist debates about Dickinson's positioning of gender and the body. The influence of psychoanalytic theory and feminist theory was discussed in relation to critics such as Sielke (1997) and Shoobridge (2000) who apply central tenets of both theoretical approaches to formulate theories about intertextual networking and to examine Dickinson's negotiations of gender. The role of queer theory in Dickinson criticism was examined in relation to the work of critics such as Bennett (1990), Galvin (1999), Smith (1992), Juhasz (2005) and Snediker (2010). LGBTQ+ readings of Dickinson and gender non-binary identity were considered in the work of Glover (2017), Ladin (2013), Henneberg (1995) and Noble (2021). The issues surrounding placing Dickinson within a female tradition were highlighted with key examples from critics such as Walker (1982), Petrino (1998) and Pollak (2017).

The later-twentieth-century critical drive to historicize Dickinson was explored in relation to critics who are concerned with Dickinson's engagement with the American Civil War as well as those who scrutinize debates about representations of race in her work. Eberwein (1998) was referred to as an introduction to Dickinson's multiple perspectives and the issues surrounding the act of locating her historically. Key examples of the various ways Dickinson can be contextualized historically were given from Leyda (1960), Pollak (2004), Erkkila (2004) and Walker (2004). For example, Erkkila's analysis of class and Walker's discussion of Dickinson's contemporaries show how her work can be located within specific political and cultural nineteenth-century contexts respectively. Critical interventions on Dickinson and the Civil War were examined, spanning from Dandurand (1984) through to Wolosky (1984; 2004; 2015), Marcellin (2000), Barrett (2013) and Richards (2019). This section described a critical arc which begins with twentieth-century critics having to defend their view of Dickinson's engagement with the Civil War per se, to Richards's confident location of Dickinson within the genre of Civil War poetry. Dickinson's treatments of abolition as laid out by Sanchez-Eppler (1993) and Wardrop (1999) formed part of the discussion about her representations of race as considered by critics such as Pollak (2000), Bennett (2002), Finnerty

(2002), Erkkila (2004) and Fretwell (2020). Debates about the representations of ethnicity in Dickinson (Mitchell, 2000) as well as the racial other Uno (2008) and Hsu (2013) were also explored.

In Chapter 5, Dickinson's relation to religion and hymn culture was framed within three thematic sections which considered critical texts concerned with the notion of Dickinson's rejection of orthodoxy, the relationship between religion and aesthetics in Dickinson's poetry, and, finally, by examining the work of critics who take Dickinson and hymnody as their focus. Using Molson (1978) as a starting point, the first part of the chapter described the ways in which critics set up a polarized view of Dickinson's relation to religion, citing Habegger (1997), and then Eberwein (2004), to show how others view Dickinson's religious oscillations as being reflective of her culture. Martin's (2007) work on Dickinson's unorthodox uses of the Bible was examined. The shifting nature of Dickinson's relation to religion which is taken as a given by critics such as McIntosh (2004) and Lundin (1998) was explored. McIntosh considers the dualistic nature of Dickinson's relation to orthodoxy, and Lundin explores the positive impact religion had on Dickinson's poetry in biographical work on Dickinson. Drawing from these debates the chapter moved on to discuss the works of critics who consider the shape of Dickinson's religious imagination and the role of aesthetics within this such as Oberhaus (1986; 1987) and Freedman (2011), as well as feminist readings of Dickinson's use of religious aesthetics in the work of Harde (2004), Ramirez (1998; 2002) and Phillips (2005). Readings of Dickinson which are emerging from theological perspectives rooted within religious practices such as Murphy (2019) were explored. A history of the critical discussion of Dickinson's engagement with hymnody was provided, citing key critical texts by England (1966), Miller (1987), Wolosky (1988), Small (1990) and Ross (2001). The chapter then considered the introduction of a broader study by Morgan (2010), which expanded the arguments on the influence of Watts made by critics such as Wolosky and England, who also see Dickinson's style of poetics as directly related to her critical engagement with orthodox religion, to take in other key elements of Dickinson's experience of hymn culture. Morgan's examination uncovered the work of Antebellum female hymnists familiar to Dickinson through the matrilineal heritage of the Praying Circles and described their influence on Dickinson's alternative metaphors for the divine, re-envisioned versions of hymn address, and theological perspective. The work of Duncan (2021) and the method of defamiliarization in Dickinson's treatment of faith were then considered. The chapter concluded with a discussion of the special Forum on Dickinson in *Religion and Literature* edited by Roger Lundin in 2014 which suggests new possibilities for reading Dickinson and religion in a pluralist or post-secular world alongside developments in contemporary theology.

The guide's final chapter considered the role of performance within Dickinson studies and the ways that critics have utilized notions of performance in their analyses of gender and the various personae being presented in Dickinson's work. The work of Gilbert and Gubar (1979), Phillips (1988), Paglia (1990) and Juhasz and Miller (2002) were discussed in relation to this, as well as Jessee (2014), who sees performance as a topic in its own right within Dickinson's work. Leading on from Juhasz and Milller's (2002) argument that the performance of gender in Dickinson's poetry is crucial to our understanding of its construction, the chapter then considers the popularity of Dickinson within our own culture and the critical view that Dickinson's poetry often responds to the popular culture of her own era. The work of Reynolds (2006) and Runzo (2019) was examined to show how Dickinson's poetry reflects the themes and political concerns of her day via her own engagement with nineteenth-century popular culture. Boziwick (2022) was cited as an important new study which considers the influence of nineteenth-century popular music on Dickinson's work. Boziwick's arguments about the centrality of music within her poetic development were also considered. Runzo's (2019) contention that our own popular conception of Dickinson is characterized by an acceptance of a mixture of fact and fiction was used to lead into a discussion about contemporary popular representations of the poet. Guerra's (1998) introduction to this area was employed before many artistic interpretations were described, such as adult fiction which draws upon the myths of the poet as much as the biographical details, musical settings of Dickinson's poetry, including discussion of Lowenberg's (1992) study on the subject as well as critical reflection upon the musicality of Dickinson in Holmes (2019), filmic as well as televisual interpretations and critical responses such as Russo (2021) as well as art installations and museum exhibitions. The work of Finnerty (2022) which considers the *Dickinson* series and Dickinson's status as an LGBTQ+ icon was also examined. Discussion of the digital age of Dickinson studies explored the new ways of accessing Dickinson in the twenty-first century, not least because of the *Emily Dickinson Archive* (EDA) but also because of the increased visibility of Dickinson online in the form of social media posts and blogs. The variety of ways we now approach and consume Dickinson, and how this has been shaped by technology, was considered in discussion of the work of Perlow (2018; 2019). Perlow shows how the technologies which present Dickinson's work to the world have played a part in shaping our responses to it, from the earliest electroplating of her *Poems* (1890) with the selective editorial incisions, deletions and inclusion of 'correct' punctuation and titles to the digital world of the EDA. Discussion about the availability of Dickinson's work online fed into a survey of the international reception of Dickinson's work and the current relationship between the international reception and translation of Dickinson's poetry.

Bringing together essential critical texts, including those by poets and translators, the guide's final section brought the international reception of Dickinson into focus. Key critical texts on the subject from Buckingham (1970) to Mitchell and Stuart (2009) were examined to foreground debates about reception generally and the notion of expectation and formation of literary cannons posed by Burr (2002) as well as critics writing about Latino/a and Chicano/a literary history such as Gomaa (2012) and Aranda (2012). The special issue of *The Emily Dickinson Journal*, entitled 'International Dickinson: Scholarship in English Translation', was considered, and particular attention was given to the editors' introduction to the special issue with its important footnote outlining the recent major translation projects, as well as studies on translation, which are currently underway.[5]

The specific challenges of translating Dickinson into other languages such as Spanish and Chinese were considered in the work of critics such as Rivera Garretas (2014; 2020) and Xu (2013). Reception of Dickinson in China was considered in Wang (2012) as well as the republication by *The Emily Dickinson Journal* in 2020 of a key critical Chinese text by Kwang-Chung (1961). Japanese reception of Dickinson was considered by detailing the work of Takeda (2013) and Nonaka (2014). The scope of international reception was broadened to encompass discussion of the reception of Dickinson in Iraq in the work of poet and poetry translator Hassan (2019) as well as a comparative analysis of Brazilian translations of Dickinson by Santos Brigida and Ferreira de Pinho (2019). The relatively recent inclusion of translated works of criticism within primary journals such as *The Emily Dickinson Journal* was explained as a commitment to bringing together international voices within the field.

In conclusion, it is a stimulating time for Dickinson's readers. Future directions in Dickinson studies are ever emergent, with much more to be done on translations of Dickinson from other languages, on Dickinson's reading, her understanding of philosophy, geology and art, and on the place of Dickinson's poetry within the areas of intersectionality theory, LGBTQ+ and gender non-binary readings of Dickinson, on her place within race studies, queer theory, disability studies, ecocriticism and globalism, to name just a few areas of potential study. In one sense, Dickinson's poetry is also repeatedly 'new' to the tenacious reader, and critics often recount their critical steps to modify and extend earlier arguments along the path to understanding the fullness of her work. The variety of critical texts examined in this guide illustrates how critiquing Dickinson is, in many ways, an 'endless quest', as noted by Robert Weisbuch (1998), where 'any thought is open to revision or extension':

> 'The soul should always stand ajar' is something of a motto for Dickinson's endless quest, where any thought is open to revision or extension, and it needs to become her reader's motto as well. [...] You will let go, spreading your fingers to gather her plural paradises. You will forswear selfish ownership to gain far greater bounty as a medium. Prisming, you will allow her her bronzes and blazes, all her colors.[6]

It is hoped that this guide has provided a way into the historical, vast and fascinating corpus of Dickinson criticism, to equip readers to find their own way to Dickinson's 'plural paradises', and 'all her colors'. Augmented by its bibliography, and items for suggested further reading, it has highlighted some of the key moments in the past, current and future critical directions for Dickinson studies. In this, the guide offers readers of Dickinson, and current and future critics of her work, a platform from which to explore, 'stand ajar' and expand upon these essential and engaging critical debates.

Notes

1 See: William Alfred Quayle, *The Poet's Poet and Other Essays*, 3rd edn (New York: Eaton and Mains, 1897), pp. 7–38.
2 Former American Poet Laureate Billy Collins entitled one of his poetry collections *Taking Off Emily Dickinson's Clothes* (London: Picador, 2000).
3 Betsy Erkkila, 'Emily Dickinson and Class', *American Literary History*, 4.1 (1992), 1–27. See also: Erkkila, 'Emily Dickinson and the Art of Politics', in Pollak, ed., *A Historical Guide to Emily Dickinson,* pp. 133–74.
4 Marrs, 'Dickinson in the Anthropocene', p. 203.
5 Adeline Chevrier-Bosseau, Li Hsin-Hsu and Eliza Richards, 'Editorial Introduction: Testing Our Horizons', *The Emily Dickinson Journal*, 29.2 (2020), pp. ix–xiv.
6 Robert Weisbuch, 'Prisming Dickinson; or, Gathering Paradise by Letting Go', in *The Emily Dickinson Handbook*, ed. by Gudrun Grabher, Roland Hagenbuchle and Cristanne Miller, pp. 222–3.

Bibliography

I. Books

Aparicio, Frances R., and Suzanne Bost, eds., *The Routledge Companion to Latino/a Literature* (London: Routledge, 2012).

Baldick, Chris, *The Concise Oxford Dictionary of Literary Terms* (Oxford: Oxford University Press, 1990).

Barrett, Faith, *To Fight Aloud Is Very Brave: American Poetry and the Civil War* (Amherst: University of Massachusetts Press, 2012).

Barrett, Faith, and Cristanne Miller, eds., *'Words for the Hour': A New Anthology of American Civil War Poetry* (Amherst: University of Massachusetts Press, 2005).

Bennett, Paula, *Emily Dickinson: Woman Poet* (New York and London: Harvester Wheatsheaf, 1990).

Bervin, Jen, Marta Werner, and Susan Howe, *The Gorgeous Nothings: Emily Dickinson's Envelope Poems* (New York: New Directions, 2013).

Bianchi, Martha Dickinson, *Emily Dickinson Face to Face; Unpublished Letters with Notes and Reminiscences* (Boston: Houghton Mifflin, 1932) (Hamden, CN: Archon, 1970).

Bianchi, Martha Dickinson, ed., *The Life and Letters of Emily Dickinson* (Boston: Houghton Mifflin, 1924).

Bianchi, Martha Dickinson, ed., *The Single Hound: Poems of a Lifetime, with an Introduction by Martha Dickinson Bianchi* (Boston: Little, Brown and Co., 1914).

Bingham, Millicent Todd, *Emily Dickinson's Home: Letters of Edward Dickinson and His Family* (New York: Harper, 1955).

Bingham, Millicent Todd, *Ancestors' Brocades: The Literary Debut of Emily Dickinson* (New York: Harper, 1945).

Blake, Caesar R., and Carlton F. Wells, eds., *The Recognition of Emily Dickinson: Selected Criticism Since 1890* (Ann Arbor: The University of Michigan Press, 1964).

Blasing, Mutlu Konuk, *American Poetry: The Rhetoric of Its Forms* (New Haven and London: Yale University Press, 1987).

Boswell, Jeanetta, *Emily Dickinson: A Bibliography of Secondary Sources, with Selective Annotations, 1890 through 1987* (Jefferson, NC: McFarland, 1989).

Boziwick, George, *Emily Dickinson's Music Book and the Musical Life of an American Poet* (Boston and Amherst: The University of Massachusetts Press, 2022).

Buckingham, Willis J., *Emily Dickinson's Reception in the 1890s: A Documentary History* (Pittsburgh: University of Pittsburgh Press, 1989).

Buckingham, Willis J., ed., *Emily Dickinson: An Annotated Bibliography: Writings, Scholarship, Criticism and Ana 1850–1968* (Bloomington: Indiana University Press, 1970).
Burr, Zofia, *Of Women, Poetry and Power: Strategies of Address in Dickinson, Miles, Brooks, Lorede, and Angelou* (Champaign-Urbana: University of Illinois Press, 2002).
Bushnell, Horace, *God in Christ* (Hartford: Brown and Parsons, 1849).
Cavillo, Juan Carlos, *Las Ruedas de las Aves (The Wheels of Birds)* (Veracruz: Aquelarre Ediciones and Guanajuato: Los Otros Libros, 2021).
Charyn, Jerome, *A Loaded Gun: Emily Dickinson for the Twenty-First Century* (New York: Bellevue Literary Press, 2016).
Cody, John, *After Great Pain: The Inner Life of Emily Dickinson* (Cambridge, MA: Harvard University Press, 1971).
Day, Frances Ann, *Latina and Latino Voices in Literature: Lives and Works, Updated and Expanded* (Connecticut: The Greenwood Press, 2003).
Diehl, Joanne Feit, *Dickinson and the Romantic Imagination* (Princeton: Princeton University Press, 1981).
Deppman, Jed, Marianne Noble, and Gary Lee Stonum, eds., *Dickinson and Philosophy* (Cambridge: Cambridge University Press, 2013).
Deppman, Jed, *Trying to Think with Emily Dickinson* (Amherst: University of Massachusetts Press, 2008).
Dobson, Joanne, *Dickinson and the Strategies of Reticence* (Bloomington: Indiana University Press, 1989).
Dyer Lucas, Dolores, *Emily Dickinson and Riddle* (DeKalb: Northern Illinois University Press, 1969).
England, Martha Winburn, and John Sparrow, *Hymns Unbidden: Donne, Herbert, Blake, Emily Dickinson and the Hymnographers* (New York: New York Public Library, 1966).
Farr, Judith, with Louise Carter, *The Gardens of Emily Dickinson* (Cambridge, MA: Harvard University Press, 2004).
Farr, Judith, *The Passion of Emily Dickinson* (Cambridge, MA: Harvard University Press, 1992).
Federico, Annette R., ed., *Gilbert and Gubar's the Madwoman in the Attic after Thirty Years* (Columbia: University of Missouri Press, 2009).
Ferlazzo, Paul J., ed., *Critical Essays on Emily Dickinson* (Boston, MA: G. K. Hall, 1984).
Finnerty, Páraic, *Emily Dickinson's Shakespeare* (Amherst: University of Massachusetts Press, 2006).
Franklin, R. W., ed., *The Poems of Emily Dickinson: Variorum Edition* (Cambridge, MA: The Belknap Press of Harvard University Press, 1998).
Franklin, R. W., *The Manuscript Books of Emily Dickinson: A Facsimile Edition*, ed. R. W. Franklin (Cambridge, MA: The Belknap Press of Harvard University Press, 1981).

Freedman, Linda, *Emily Dickinson's Religious Imagination* (Cambridge: Cambridge University Press, 2011).

Fretwell, Erica, *Sensory Experiments: Psychophysics, Race, and the Aesthetics of Feeling* (Durham, NC: Duke University Press, 2020).

Galvin, Mary E., *Queer Poetics: Five Modernist Women Writers* (Connecticut and London: Greenwood Press, 1999).

Gilbert, Sandra M., and Susan Gubar, *The Madwoman in the Attic: The Woman Writer and the Nineteenth-Century Literary Imagination* (1979), rev. edn (New Haven: Yale University Press, 2000).

Gilpin, W. Clark, *Religion around Emily Dickinson* (Pennsylvania: Pennsylvania State University Press, 2014).

Goldensohn, Lorrie, ed., *American War Poetry* (New York: Columbia University Press, 2006).

Gordon, Lyndall, *Lives like Loaded Guns: Emily Dickinson and Her Family's Feuds* (London: Virago, 2010).

Grabher, Gudrun, Roland Hagenbuchle, and Cristanne Miller, eds., *The Emily Dickinson Handbook* (Amherst: University of Massachusetts Press, 1998).

Griffith, Clark, *The Long Shadow: Emily Dickinson's Tragic Poetry* (New Jersey: Princeton University Press, 1964).

Habegger, Alfred, *My Wars Are Laid Away in Books: The Life of Emily Dickinson* (New York: Random House, 2001).

Hart, Ellen Louise, and Martha Nell Smith, eds., *'Open Me Carefully': Emily Dickinson's Intimate Letters to Susan Huntington Dickinson* (Ashfield, MA: Paris Press, 1998).

Homans, Margaret, *Women Writers and Poetic Identity: Dorothy Wordsworth, Emily Bronte and Emily Dickinson* (Princeton: Princeton University Press, 1980).

Howe, Susan, *The Birth-Mark: Unsettling the Wilderness in American Literary History* (Hanover: Wesleyan University Press, 1993).

Humm, Maggie, *A Reader's Guide to Contemporary Feminist Literary Criticism* (Oxford: Routledge, 2013).

Jackson, Virginia, *Dickinson's Misery: A Theory of Lyric Reading* (Princeton: Princeton University Press, 2005).

Johnson, Thomas H., ed., *Emily Dickinson: Selected Letters*, eleventh printing (Cambridge, MA: The Belknap Press of Harvard University Press, 2002).

Johnson, Thomas H., *The Complete Poems of Emily Dickinson*, 2nd edn (London: Faber and Faber, 1975).

Johnson, Thomas H., ed., *The Complete Poems of Emily Dickinson* (Boston: Little, Brown, 1960).

Johnson, Thomas H., and Theodora Ward, eds., *The Letters of Emily Dickinson, 3 Vols* (Cambridge, MA: Harvard University Press, 1958).

Johnson, Thomas H., ed., *Emily Dickinson: An Interpretive Biography* (Cambridge, MA: Harvard University Press, 1955).

Johnson, Thomas H., ed., *The Poems of Emily Dickinson, 3 Vols* (Cambridge, MA: Harvard University Press, 1955).
Johnson, Thomas H., ed., *The Poems of Emily Dickinson, 1 Vol* (Cambridge, MA: Harvard University Press, 1951).
Juhasz, Susan, ed., *Feminist Critics Read Emily Dickinson* (Bloomington: Indiana University Press, 1983).
Juhasz, Susan, *Naked and Fiery Forms: Modern American Poetry by Women, A New Tradition* (New York: Harper and Row, 1976).
Kame, Lord, and Henry Home, *Elements of Criticism* (Boston, MA: S. Etheridge for J. White, 1796).
Kohler, Michelle, ed., *The New Emily Dickinson Studies* (Cambridge: Cambridge University Press, 2019).
Ladin, Joy, *Soldering the Abyss: Emily Dickinson and Modern American Poetry* (Saarbrücken: VDM Verlag, Dr Muller, 2010).
Lease, Benjamin, *Emily Dickinson's Readings of Men and Books: Sacred Soundings* (Houndmills: Macmillan, 1990).
Leder, Sharon, and Andrea Abbott, *The Language of Exclusion: The Poetry of Emily Dickinson and Christina Rossetti* (New York: Greenwood Press, 1987).
Leyda, Jay, *The Years and Hours of Emily Dickinson, 2 vols* (New Haven: Yale University Press, 1960).
Lindberg-Seyersted, Brita, *The Voice of the Poet: Aspects of Style in the Poetry of Emily Dickinson* (Cambridge: Harvard University Press, 1968).
Loeffelholz, Mary, *Dickinson and the Boundaries of Feminist Theory* (Urbana and Chicago: University of Illinois Press, 1991).
Longsworth, Polly, *Austin and Mabel: The Amherst Affair and Love Letters of Austin Dickinson and Mabel Loomis Todd* (New York: Farrar, Straus and Giroux, 1984).
Lowenberg, Carlton, *Musicians Wrestle Everywhere: Emily Dickinson and Music* (Berkeley: Fallen Leaf, 1992).
Lowenberg, Carlton, *Emily Dickinson's Textbooks* (Lafayette, California: C. Lowenberg, 1986).
Lundin, Roger, *Emily Dickinson and the Art of Belief*, 2nd edn (Michigan: William B. Eerdmans Publishing Co., 1998; 2004).
Martin, Wendy, *The Cambridge Introduction to Emily Dickinson* (Cambridge: Cambridge University Press, 2007).
Martin, Wendy, ed., *The Cambridge Companion to Emily Dickinson* (Cambridge: Cambridge University Press, 2002).
Martin, Wendy, *An American Triptych: Anne Bradstreet, Emily Dickinson, Adrienne Rich* (Chapel Hill: University of North Carolina Press, 1984).
McClatchy, J. D., ed., *Poets of the Civil War* (New York: American Poets Project; Library of America, 2005).
McGann, Jerome, *Black Riders: The Visible Language of Modernism* (Princeton, NJ: Princeton University Press, 1993).

McIntosh, James, *Nimble Believing: Dickinson and the Unknown* (Ann Arbor: The University of Michigan Press, 2004).

Messmer, Marietta, *A Vice for Voices: Reading Emily Dickinson's Correspondence* (Amherst: University of Massachusetts Press, 2001).

Miller, Cristanne, and Karen Sanchez-Eppler, eds., *The Oxford Handbook of Emily Dickinson* (Oxford: Oxford University Press, 2022).

Miller, Cristanne, *Emily Dickinson's Poems: As She Preserved Them* (Cambridge, MA: Harvard University Press, 2016).

Miller, Cristanne, *Reading in Time: Emily Dickinson in the Nineteenth Century* (Massachusetts: University of Massachusetts Press, 2012).

Miller, Cristanne, *Emily Dickinson: A Poet's Grammar* (Cambridge, MA: Harvard University Press, 1987).

Miller, Ruth, *The Poetry of Emily Dickinson* (Middletown, CT: Wesleyan University Press, 1968).

Mitchell, Domhnall, and Maria Stuart, eds., *The International Reception of Emily Dickinson* (London: Continuum, 2009).

Mitchell, Domhnall, *Measures of Possibility: Emily Dickinson's Manuscripts* (Amherst: University of Massachusetts Press, 2005).

Mitchell, Domhnall, *Emily Dickinson: Monarch of Perception* (Amherst: University of Massachusetts Press, 2000).

Morgan, Victoria N., *Emily Dickinson and Hymn Culture: Tradition and Experience* (Burlington: Ashgate, 2010; repr., London: Routledge, 2016).

Murphy, Charles M., *Mystical Prayer: The Poetic Example of Emily Dickinson* (Collegeville, MN: Liturgical Press, 2019).

Murray, Aife, *Maid As Muse: How Emily Dickinson's Servants Changed Her Life and Language* (Hanover and London: University Press of New England, 2009).

Negroni, Maria, *Archivo Dickinson* (Madrid: Vaso Roto Ediciones, 2020).

Newman, Samuel Philips, *A Practical System of Rhetoric, or, the Principles and Rules of Style, Inferred from Examples of Writing, to Which Is Added a Historical Dissertation on English Style* (New York: Dayton and Newman, 1842).

Nicholson, William, *The Lovers of Amherst* (London: Quercus, 2015).

Olavarría, Rodrigo, Enrique Winter, and Verónica Zondek, trans., *Emily Dickinson: Zumbido* (Valparaiso: Universidad de Valparaíso, 2018).

Oberhaus, Dorothy Huff, *Emily Dickinson's Fascicles: Method and Meaning* (University Park: Pennsylvania State University Press, 1995).

Paglia, Camille, *Sexual Personae: Art and Decadence from Nerfertiti to Emily Dickinson* (London and New Haven: Yale University Press, 1990).

Patterson, Rebecca, *Emily Dickinson's Imagery* (Amherst: University of Massachusetts Press, 1979).

Perlow, Seth, *The Poem Electric: Technology and the American Lyric* (Minneapolis: University of Minnesota Press, 2018).

Petrino, Elizabeth, *Emily Dickinson and Her Contemporaries: Women's Verse in America 1820–1855* (Lebanon, NH: University Press of New England, 1998).
Phillips, Elizabeth, *Emily Dickinson: Personae and Performance* (University Park: Pennsylvania State University Press, 1988).
Pollak, Vivian R., *Our Emily Dickinsons: American Women Poets and the Intimacies of Difference* (Philadelphia: University of Pennsylvania Press, 2017).
Pollak, Vivian R., ed., *A Historical Guide to Emily Dickinson* (Oxford: Oxford University Press, 2004).
Pollak, Vivian R., *Dickinson: The Anxiety of Gender* (Ithaca: Cornell University Press, 1984).
Porter, David, *Dickinson: The Modern Idiom* (Cambridge, MA: Harvard University Press, 1981).
Porter, Ebenezer, *The Rhetorical Reader, Etc.* (1831; Andover, New York: Flagg & Gould, 1841).
Quayle, William Alfred, *The Poet's Poet and Other Essays*, 3rd edn (New York: Eaton and Mains, 1897).
Richards, Eliza, *Battle Lines: Poetry and Mass Media in the U.S Civil War* (Philadelphia: University of Pennsylvania Press, 2019).
Richards, Eliza, ed., *Emily Dickinson in Context* (Cambridge: Cambridge University Press, 2013).
Richardson, Mark, ed., *The Cambridge Companion to American Poets* (Cambridge: Cambridge University Press, 2015).
Runzo, Sandra, *'Theatricals of Day' : Emily Dickinson and Nineteenth-Century American Popular Culture* (Boston and Amherst: University of Massachusetts Press, 2019).
Sanchez-Eppler, Karen, *Touching Liberty: Abolition, Feminism and the Politics of the Body* (Berkeley: University of California Press, 1993).
Saxton, Martha, ed., *Amherst in the World* (Amherst: Amherst College Press, 2020).
Sedgwick, Eve Kosofsky, *Epistemology of the Closet* (Berkeley: University of California Press, 1990).
Sewall, Richard B., *The Life of Emily Dickinson, 2 Vols* (New York: Farrar, Straus and Giroux, 1974).
Shurr, William H., *The Marriage of Emily Dickinson: A Study of the Fascicles* (Lexington: University of Kentucky Press, 1983).
Sielke, Sabine, *Fashioning the Female Subject: The Intertextual Networking of Dickinson, Moore and Rich* (Ann Arbor: The University of Michigan Press, 1997).
Small, Judy Jo, *Positive as Sound: Emily Dickinson's Rhyme* (Georgia: University of Georgia Press, 1990).
Smith, Martha Nell, and Mary Loeffelholz, eds., *A Companion to Emily Dickinson* (Malden, MA: Blackwell Publishing, 2008).
Smith, Martha Nell, *Rowing in Eden: Rereading Emily Dickinson* (Austin: University of Texas Press, 1992).

Snediker, Michael D., *Queer Optimism: Lyric Personhood and Other Felicitous Persuasions* (Minnesota: University of Minnesota Press, 2008).
St. Armand, Barton Levi, *Emily Dickinson and Her Culture: The Soul's Society* (Cambridge: Cambridge University Press, 1984).
Stonum, Gary Lee, *The Dickinson Sublime* (Madison: The University of Wisconsin Press, 1990).
Sullivan, Nikki, *A Critical Introduction to Queer Theory* (Edinburgh: Edinburgh University Press, 2003).
Swift, Rebecca, *Poetic Lives: Dickinson* (London: Hesperus Press, 2011).
Taggard, Genevieve, *The Life and Mind of Emily Dickinson* (New York: Knopf, 1930).
Todd, Mabel Loomis, and Thomas Wentworth Higginson, eds., *Poems by Emily Dickinson* (Boston: Roberts Brothers, 1890).
Varela, Hernan Bravo, trans., *Carta al mundo: poemas de Emily Dickinson* (Mexico: Tierra Adentro, 2016).
Vendler, Helen, *Dickinson: Selected Poems and Commentaries* (Cambridge, MA: Harvard University Press, 2010).
Vendler, Helen, *Poets Thinking: Pope, Whitman, Dickinson, Yeats* (Cambridge, MA: Harvard University Press, 2004).
Walker, Cheryl, *The Nightingale's Burden: Women Poets and American Culture before 1900* (Bloomington: Indiana University Press, 1982).
Watts, Isaac, *The Poetical Works of Isaac Watts, with a Memoir* (Boston: Little, Brown and Company, 1866).
Watts, Isaac, *Psalms, Hymns, and Spiritual Songs*, 3 bks. in 1 vol. (Boston: James Loring and Lincoln & Edmunds, 1832).
Whicher, George Frisbie, *This Was a Poet: A Critical Biography of Emily Dickinson* (New York: Scribner's, 1938).
White, Fred D., *Approaching Emily Dickinson: Critical Currents and Crosscurrents since 1960* (New York: Camden House, 2008).
Wineapple, Brenda, *White Heat: The Friendship of Emily Dickinson and Thomas Wentworth Higginson* (New York: Anchor Books, 2008).
Wolff, Cynthia Griffin, *Emily Dickinson* (New York: Knopf, 1986).
Wolosky, Shira, *Emily Dickinson: A Voice of War* (New Haven: Yale University Press, 1984).

II. Book chapters

Ackmann, Martha, 'Biographical Studies of Dickinson' in Grabher, Gudrun, Roland Hagenbuchle, and Cristanne Miller, eds., *The Emily Dickinson Handbook* (Amherst: University of Massachusetts Press, 1998), pp. 11–23.
Aiello, Lucia, 'Mimesis and Poiesis: Reflections on Gilbert and Gubar's reading of Emily Dickinson' in Federico, Annette R., ed., *Gilbert and Gubar's the Madwoman in the Attic after Thirty Years* (Columbia: University of Missouri Press, 2009), pp. 237–56.

Aranda, Jose F., Jr., 'Recovering the US Hispanic Literary Heritage' in Aparicio, Frances R., and Suzanne Bost, eds., *The Routledge Companion to Latino/a Literature* (London: Routledge, 2012), pp. 476–84.

Barrett, Faith, 'Slavery and the Civil War' in Richards, Eliza, ed., *Emily Dickinson in Context* (Cambridge: Cambridge University Press, 2013), pp. 206–15.

Bennett, Paula Bernat, 'Emily Dickinson and Her American Women Poet Peers' in Martin, Wendy, ed., *The Cambridge Companion to Emily Dickinson* (Cambridge: Cambridge University Press, 2002), pp. 215–35.

Cameron, Sharon, 'Dickinson's Fascicles' in Grabher, Gudrun, Roland Hagenbuchle, and Cristanne Miller, eds., *The Emily Dickinson Handbook* (Amherst: University of Massachusetts Press, 1998), pp. 138–80.

Crumbley, Paul, 'Dickinson's Dialogic Voice' in Grabher, Gudrun, Roland Hagenbuchle, and Cristanne Miller, eds., *The Emily Dickinson Handbook* (Amherst: University of Massachusetts Press, 1998), pp. 93–109.

Eberwein, Jane Donahue, '"Is Immortality True?" Salvaging Faith in an Age of Upheavals' in Pollak, Vivian R., ed., *A Historical Guide to Emily Dickinson* (Oxford: Oxford University Press, 2004), pp. 67–102.

Eberwein, Jane Donahue, 'Dickinson's Local, Global, and Cosmic Perspectives' in Grabher, Gudrun, Roland Hagenbuchle, and Cristanne Miller, eds., *The Emily Dickinson Handbook* (Amherst: University of Massachusetts Press, 1998), pp. 27–43.

England, Martha Winburn, 'Emily Dickinson and Isaac Watts' in England, Martha Winburn, and John Sparrow, eds., *Hymns Unbidden: Donne, Herbert, Blake, Emily Dickinson and the Hymnographers* (New York: New York Public Library, 1966), pp. 113–47.

Erkkila, Betsy, 'Emily Dickinson and the Art of Politics' in Pollak, Vivian, ed., *A Historical Guide to Emily Dickinson* (Oxford: Oxford University Press, 2004), pp. 133–74.

Finnerty, Páraic, 'Global Dickinson' in Kohler, Michelle, ed., *The New Emily Dickinson Studies* (Cambridge: Cambridge University Press, 2019), pp. 187–203.

Gilbert, Sandra M., and Susan Gubar, 'A Woman-White: Emily Dickinson's Yarn of Pearl' in Gilbert, Sandra M., and Susan Gubar, eds., *The Madwoman in the Attic: The Woman Writer and the Nineteenth-Century Literary Imagination* (1979), rev. edn (New Haven: Yale University Press, 2000), pp. 581–650.

Gomaa, Dalia M. A., 'Latino/a Literature in the Arab World' in Aparicio, Frances R., and Suzanne Bost, eds., *The Routledge Companion to Latino/a Literature* (London: Routledge, 2012), pp. 124–30.

Guerra, Jonnie, 'Dickinson Adaptations in the Arts and the Theatre' in Grabher, Gudrun, Roland Hagenbuchle, and Cristanne Miller, eds., *The Emily Dickinson Handbook* (Amherst: University of Massachusetts Press, 1998), pp. 385–407.

Hassan, Naseem, 'Emily Dickinson in Baghdad' in Kohler, Michelle, ed., *The New Emily Dickinson Studies* (Cambridge: Cambridge University Press, 2019), pp. 299–307.

Juhasz, Suzanne, and Cristanne Miller, 'Performances of Gender in Dickinson's Poetry' in Martin, Wendy, ed., *The Cambridge Companion to Emily Dickinson* (Cambridge: Cambridge University Press, 2002), pp. 107–28.

Juhasz, Suzanne, 'Materiality and the Poet' in Grabher, Gudrun, Roland Hagenbuchle, and Cristanne Miller, eds., *The Emily Dickinson Handbook* (Amherst: University of Massachusetts Press, 1998), pp. 427–39.

Kohler, Michelle, 'Introduction: Dickinson Dispersed' in Kohler, Michelle, ed., *The New Emily Dickinson Studies* (Cambridge: Cambridge University Press, 2019), pp. 1–14.

Messmer, Marietta, 'Dickinson's Critical Reception' in Grabher, Gudrun, Roland Hagenbuchle, and Cristanne Miller, eds., *The Emily Dickinson Handbook* (Amherst: University of Massachusetts Press, 1998), pp. 299–322.

Mitchell, Domhnall, 'Dickinson and Class' in Martin, Wendy, ed., *The Cambridge Companion to Emily Dickinson* (Cambridge: Cambridge University Press, 2002), pp. 191–214.

Paglia, Camille, 'Amherst's Madame de Sade: Emily Dickinson' in Paglia, Camille, ed., *Sexual Personae: Art and Decadence from Nerfertiti to Emily Dickinson* (London and New Haven: Yale University Press, 1990), pp. 623–73.

Perlow, Seth, 'Textures Newly Visible: Seeing and Feeling the Online Dickinson Archives' in Kohler, Michelle, ed., *The New Emily Dickinson Studies* (Cambridge: Cambridge University Press, 2019), pp. 239–57.

Porter, David, 'Searching for Dickinson's Themes' in Grabher, Gudrun, Roland Hagenbuchle, and Cristanne Miller, eds., *The Emily Dickinson Handbook* (Amherst: University of Massachusetts Press, 1998), pp. 183–96.

Reynolds, David S., 'Emily Dickinson and Popular Culture' in Martin, Wendy, ed., *The Cambridge Companion to Emily Dickinson* (Cambridge: Cambridge University Press, 2002), pp. 167–90.

Reynolds, David S., '"Vesuvius at Home": Emily Dickinson, Amherst, and Nineteenth-Century Popular Culture' in Saxton, Martha, ed., *Amherst in the World* (Amherst: Amherst College Press, 2020), pp. 201–16.

Smith, Martha Nell, 'Forever Young: Rereading Emily Dickinson in the Twenty-First Century' in Richardson, Mark, ed., *The Cambridge Companion to American Poets* (Cambridge: Cambridge University Press, 2015), pp. 119–35.

Walker, Cheryl, 'Dickinson In Context: Nineteenth-Century American Women Poets' in Pollak, Vivian, ed., *A Historical Guide to Emily Dickinson* (Oxford: Oxford University Press, 2004), pp. 175–200.

Weisbuch, Robert, 'Prisming Dickinson; or, Gathering Paradise by Letting Go' in Grabher, Gudrun, Roland Hagenbuchle, and Cristanne Miller, eds., *The Emily Dickinson Handbook* (Amherst: University of Massachusetts Press, 1998), pp. 197–223.

Wolosky, Shira, 'War and the Art of Writing: Emily Dickinson's Relational Aesthetics' in Hutchison, Coleman, ed., *A History of American Civil War Literature* (Cambridge: Cambridge University Press, 2015), pp. 195–210.

Wolosky, Shira, 'Public and Private in Dickinson's War Poetry' in Pollak, Vivian, ed., *A Historical Guide to Emily Dickinson* (Oxford: Oxford University Press, 2004), pp. 103–31.
Wolosky, Shira, 'Emily Dickinson: Being In the Body' in Martin, Wendy, ed., *The Cambridge Companion to Emily Dickinson* (Cambridge: Cambridge University Press, 2002), pp. 129–41.
Zapedowska, Magdalena, 'Critical History II: 1955 to the Present' in Richards, Eliza, ed., *Emily Dickinson in Context* (Cambridge: Cambridge University Press, 2013), pp. 321–31.

III. Journal articles and special issues

Ackmann, Martha, review of *'Open Me Carefully'*, *The Emily Dickinson Journal*, 8.2 (1999), 111–13.
Barrett, Faith, 'Public Selves and Private Spheres: Studies of Emily Dickinson and the Civil War, 1984–2007', *The Emily Dickinson Journal*, 16.1 (2007), 92–104.
Bennett, Paula, '"The Negro Never Knew": Emily Dickinson and Racial Typology in the Post-Bellum Period', *Legacy: A Journal of American Women Writers*, 19.1 (2002), 53–61.
Boziwick, George, 'Emily Dickinson's Music Book: A Performative Exploration', *The Emily Dickinson Journal*, 25.1 (2016), 83–107.
Boziwick, George, '"My Business Is to Sing": Emily Dickinson's Musical Borrowings', *Journal of the Society for American Music*, 8.2 (2014), 130–66.
Chaudron, Patricia, 'From Local Colour to Modernist Poet: Revisiting Emily Dickinson's Critics in the 1890s', *The Emily Dickinson Journal*, 25.1 (2016), 1–28.
Chevrier-Bosseau, Adeline, Li-Hsin Hsu, and Eliza Richards, 'Editorial Introduction: Testing our Horizons', *The Emily Dickinson Journal*, 29.2 (2020), ix–xiv.
Crumbley, Paul, ed., 'Dickinson's Environments: Special Issue', *ESQ: A Journal of Nineteenth-Century American Literature and Culture*, 63.2 (2017), 198–358.
Crumbley, Paul, ed., 'Dickinson and Celebrity', *The Emily Dickinson Journal*, 26.2 (2017), 1–106.
Crumbley, Paul, 'Introduction to a Special Issue of the Emily Dickinson Journal: Dickinson and Celebrity', *The Emily Dickinson Journal*, 26.2 (2017), 1–5.
Dandurand, Karen, 'New Dickinson Civil War Publications', *American Literature*, 56.1 (1984), 17–27.
Duncan, Emma M., 'Defamiliarizing Faith: Emily Dickinson's Use of Hymns, Scripture, and Prayer', *Women's Studies*, 50.2 (2021), 157–74.
Erkkila, Betsy, 'Emily Dickinson and Class', *American Literary History*, 4.1 (1992), 1–27.
Finnerty, Páraic, '"You'll Be the Only Dickinson They Talk about in Two Hundred Years": Queer Celebrity, Thomas Wentworth Higginson, *A Quiet Passion*, *Wild*

Nights with Emily, and Apple TV+'s *Dickinson*', *The Emily Dickinson Journal*, 31.1 (2022), 1–30.

Finnerty, Páraic, '"If Fame Belonged to Me, I Could Not Escape Her": Dickinson and the Poetics of Celebrity', *The Emily Dickinson Journal*, 26.2 (2017), 25–50.

Finnerty, Páraic, '"We Think of Others Possessing You with the Throes of Othello": Dickinson Playing Othello, Race and Tommaso Salvini', *The Emily Dickinson Journal*, 11.1 (2002), 81–90.

Fretwell, Erica, 'Emily Dickinson in Domingo', *J19: The Journal of Nineteenth-Century Americanists*, 1.1 (2013), 71–96.

Friedlander, Benjamin, 'Emily Dickinson and the Battle of Ball's Bluff', *PMLA*, 124.5 (2009), 1582–99.

Garretas, María-Milagros Rivera, 'Traducir como Intimar' ('Translating as Becoming Intimate'), *DUODA: Estudios de la Diferencia Sexual*, 46 (2014), 58–69.

Garretas, María-Milagros Rivera, and Caroline Wilson, Review of 'Translating as Becoming Intimate' by María-Milagros Rivera Garretas, *The Emily Dickinson Journal*, 29.2 (2020), 138.

Glover, Maggie, 'I'm Ceded: Sexual, Social and Gender Role Rebellion in the Poems of Emily Dickinson', *Articulāte*, 10.2 (2017), 11–12.

Goluboff, Benjamin, '"If Madonna Be": Emily Dickinson and Roman Catholicism', *The New England Quarterly*, 73.3 (2000), 355–85.

Habegger, Alfred, 'Evangelicalism and Its Discontents: Hannah Porter versus Emily Dickinson', *The New England Quarterly*, 70.3 (1997), 386–414.

Harde, Roxanne, '"Some—Are like My Own—": Emily Dickinson's Christology of Embodiment', *Christianity and Literature*, 53.3 (2004), 315–36.

Henneberg, Sylvia, 'Neither Lesbian Nor Straight: Multiple Eroticisms in Emily Dickinson's Love Poetry', *The Emily Dickinson Journal*, 4.2 (2009), 1–19.

Holmes, Gerard, '"Invisible, as Music -": What the Earliest Musical Settings of Emily Dickinson's Poems, including Two Previously Unknown, Tell Us about Dickinson's Musicality', *The Emily Dickinson Journal*, 28.2 (2019), 73–105.

Hubbard, Melanie, review of *Trying to Think with Emily Dickinson* by Jed Deppman, *The Emily Dickinson Journal*, 18.1 (2009), 108–10.

Hsu, Li-Hsin, 'Emily Dickinson's Asian Consumption', *The Emily Dickinson Journal*, 22.2 (2013), 1–25.

Jessee, Jessica L. '"An Orator of Feather unto an Audience of Fuzz": Performance as Subject and Setting in Emily Dickinson's Poems', *The Emily Dickinson Journal*, 23.2 (2014), 1–23.

Juhasz, Suzanne, 'Amplitude of Queer Desire in Dickinson's Erotic Language', *The Emily Dickinson Journal*, 14.2 (2005), 24–33.

Kasraie, Mary Rose, review of Camille Paglia's *Sexual Personae: Art and Decadence from Nerfertiti to Emily Dickinson*, *South Atlantic Review*, 58.4 (1993), 132–5.

Kern, Robert, 'Birds of a Feather: Emily Dickinson, Alberto Manguel, and the Nature Poet's Dilemma', *Interdisciplinary Studies in Literature and Environment*, 16.2 (2009), 327–42.

Koski, Lena, 'Sexual Metaphors in Emily Dickinson's Letters to Susan Gilbert', *The Emily Dickinson Journal*, 5.2 (1996), 26–31.

Ladin, Joy, 'Supposed Persons: Emily Dickinson and "I"', *The Emily Dickinson International Society Bulletin*, 25.1 (2013), 15–24.

Landry, H. Jordan, 'Animal/Insectual/Lesbian Sex: Dickinson's Queer Version of the Birds and the Bees', *The Emily Dickinson Journal*, 9.2 (2000), 42–54.

Lundin, Roger, ed., 'Dickinson and Religion – a Forum', *Religion and Literature*, 46.1 (2014), 138–203.

Lundin, Roger, Introduction to 'Dickinson and Religion – A Forum', *Religion and Literature*, 46.1 (2014), 138–43.

Lundin, Roger, 'The Tender Pioneer in the Prairies of the Air: Dickinson and the Differences of God', *Religion and Literature*, 46.1 (2014), 149–56.

Macdonald, Joyce Green, 'Acting Black: Othello, Othello Burlesques and the Performance of Blackness', *Theatre Survey*, 46 (1994), 233–46.

Marcellin, Leigh-Anne Urbanowicz, '"Singing off the Charnel Steps": Soldiers and Mourners in Emily Dickinson's War Poetry', *The Emily Dickinson Journal*, 9.2 (2000), 64–74.

Marrs, Cody, 'Dickinson in the Anthropocene', *ESQ: A Journal of Nineteenth-Century American Literature and Culture*, 63.2 (2017), 201–25.

Messmer, Marietta, 'Reviewer's Despair: The Politics of Dickinson's Critical Reception during the 1890s', *Amerikastudien/American Studies*, 45.3 (2000), 373–86.

Mitchell, Domhnall, 'Northern Lights: Class, Color, Culture and Emily Dickinson', *The Emily Dickinson Journal*, 9.2 (2000), 75–83.

Molson, Francis J., 'Emily Dickinson's Rejection of the Heavenly Father', *The New England Quarterly*, 47.3 (1974), 404–26.

Morgan, Victoria N., '"When Bells Stop Ringing": Tracing Dickinson's "Circumference" through the Tradition of the Praying Circle', *Religion and Literature*, 46.1 (2014), 172–9.

Noble, Marianne, 'Emily Dickinson in the Twenty-First Century', *American Literature*, 93.2 (2021), 283–305.

Nonaka, Miho, 'Season of Eternity: The Resonance of Dickinson's Poems in Japanese', *Religion and Literature*, 46.1 (2014), 187–95.

Oberhaus, Dorothy Huff, '"Tender Pioneer": Emily Dickinson's Poems on the Life of Christ', *American Literature*, 59 (1987), 341–58.

Oberhaus, Dorothy Huff, '"Engine against th'Almightie": Emily Dickinson and Prayer', *ESQ: A Journal of Nineteenth-Century American Literature and Culture*, 32.3 (1986), 153–72.

Petrino, Elizabeth, '"I Went to Thank Her—": Dickinson's Tributes to Literary Celebrities', *The Emily Dickinson Journal*, 26.2 (2017), 6–24.

Phillips, Siobhan, '"Loved Philology": Emily Dickinson's Trinitarian Word', *ESQ: A Journal of the American Renaissance*, 51.4 (2005), 250–75.

Pollak, Vivian, 'Dickinson and the Poetics of Whiteness', *The Emily Dickinson Journal*, 9.2 (2000), 84–95.

Pugh, Christina, 'Ghosts of Meter: Dickinson, after Long Silence', *The Emily Dickinson Journal*, 16.2 (2007), 1–24.

Ramirez, Anne West, 'Harriet Beecher Stowe's Christian Feminism in "The Minister's Wooing": A Precedent for Emily Dickinson', *Christianity and Literature*, 51.3 (2002), 407–24.

Ramirez, Anne West, 'The Art to Save: Emily Dickinson's Vocation as Female Prophet', *Christianity and Literature*, 47.4 (1998), 387–401.

Rich, Adrienne, 'Compulsory Heterosexuality and Lesbian Existence', *Signs: Journal of Women, Culture and Society*, 5.4 (1980), 631–60.

Rich, Adrienne. '"Vesuvius at Home": The Power of Emily Dickinson', *Parnassus: Poetry in Review*, 5.1 (1976), 49–74.

Ross, Christine, 'Uncommon Measures: Emily Dickinson's Subversive Prosody', *The Emily Dickinson Journal*, 10.1 (2001), 70–98.

Russo, Stephanie, '"You Are, like, So Woke": Dickinson and the Anachronistic Turn in Historical Drama', *Rethinking History*, 25.4 (2021), 534–54.

Santos Brigida, Marcela, and Davi Ferreira de Pinho, 'To Be or Not to Be Nobody: Emily Dickinson in Two Brazilian Translations', *Gragoatá*, 24.49 (2019), 368–89.

Shackelford, Aaron, 'Dickinson's Animals and Anthropomorphism', *The Emily Dickinson Journal*, 19.2 (2010), 47–66.

Shoobridge, Helen, '"Reverence for Each Other Being the Sweet Aim": Dickinson Face to Face with the Masculine', *The Emily Dickinson Journal*, 9.1 (2000), 87–111.

Short, Bryan C., 'Emily Dickinson and the Scottish New Rhetoric', *The Emily Dickinson Journal*, 5.2 (1996), 261–6.

Takeda, Masako, 'Emily Dickinson and Japanese Aesthetics', *The Emily Dickinson Journal*, 22.2 (2013), 26–45.

Uno, Hiroko, 'Emily Dickinson's Encounter with the East: Chinese Museum in Boston', *The Emily Dickinson Journal*, 17.1 (2008), 43–67.

Wald, Jane, 'The "Poet Hunters": Transforming Emily Dickinson's Home into a Literary Destination', *The Emily Dickinson Journal*, 26.2 (2017), 71–98.

Wang, Baihua, 'Emily Dickinson's Reception in China: A Brief Overview, Part I', *The Emily Dickinson Journal*, 21 (2012), 110–16.

Wardrop, Daneen, '"That Minute Domingo": Emily Dickinson's Co-optation of Abolitionist Diction and Franklin's Variorum Edition', *The Emily Dickinson Journal*, 8.2 (1999), 72–86.

Wells, Anna Mary, 'Early Criticism of Emily Dickinson', *American Literature*, 1.3 (1929), 243–59.

Wolff, Cynthia Griffin, '[Im]pertinent Constructions of Body and Self: Dickinson's Use of the Romantic Grotesque', *The Emily Dickinson Journal*, 2.2 (1993), 109–23.

Wolosky, Shira, 'Rhetoric or Not: Hymnal Tropes in Emily Dickinson and Isaac Watts', *The New England Quarterly*, 61 (1988), 214–32.

Wu, Colleen Shu-Ching, 'Overcoming Oneself as Subject in Dickinson's Poetry: Adorno and Heidegger', *Style*, 49.3 (2015), 334–53.

Xu, Cuihua, 'A Scrutiny into Chinese Translations of Emily Dickinson's Poetry (1984–2011)', *The Emily Dickinson Journal*, 22 (2013), 107–27.

IV. Online resources and articles

Blog on Emily Dickinson: www.emilydickinson.org/blog.
Cichowicz, Alicja, 'Emily Dickinson's Room by Izabela Maciejewska', The City Art Gallery, Lodz, trans. Elżbieta Rodzeń – Leśnikowska, 2016: https://www.lab.malamegi.com/art_contest_lab19/contestpreview.php?id=6295.
Dickinson's Birds: https://dickinsonsbirds.org/project/about/overview.
Dickinson Electronic Archives (DEA): http://www.emilydickinson.org.
Emily Dickinson Archive (EDA): https://www.edickinson.org.
The Emily Dickinson Lexicon: https://edl.byu.edu/index.php.
Friedersdorf, Conor, 'Camille Paglia Can't Say That', *The Atlantic*, May 1, 2019: https://www.theatlantic.com/ideas/archive/2019/05/camille-paglia-uarts-left-deplatform/587125/.
Scott, A. O., '"A Quiet Passion" Poetically Captures Emily Dickinson' (review), *The New York Times*, April 13, 2017: https://www.nytimes.com/2017/04/13/movies/review-a-quiet-passion-poetically-captures-emily-dickinson.html.
Susan Dickinson's obituary for Emily Dickinson can be accessed via the DEA: http://www.emilydickinson.org/writings-by-susan-dickinson/reviews-essays-and-other-criticism/obituary-for-emily-dickinson.

V. Selected adaptations and exhibition material

Charyn, Jerome, *The Secret Life of Emily Dickinson* (London: W. W. Norton and Co., 2010).
Davies, Terence, dir., *A Quiet Passion* (Chicago, IL: Music Box Films, 2016).
Dobson, Joanne, *Quieter than Sleep: A Modern Mystery of Emily Dickinson* (New York: Bantam Books, 1997).
Farr, Judith, *I Never Came to You in White* (Boston: Houghton Mifflin Harcourt, 1996).
Hurricane Films, *My Letter to the World* (film; 2018).
Kelly, Mike, Marta L. Werner, Carolyn Vega, Susan Howe, and Richard Wilbur, *The Networked Recluse: The Connected World of Emily Dickinson* (Amherst: Amherst College, 2017). Companion publication from the exhibition '*I'm Nobody! Who Are You? The Life and Poetry of Emily Dickinson*' held at The Morgan Library and Museum, New York, in 2017.
Knussen, Oliver, *Requiem – Songs for Sue* (music; premiered in 2006).

Lynch, Jack, and Edie Campbell, *Emily Dickinson and I: The Journey of a Portrayal* (play; premiered 1999, published 2005).
Maciejewska, Izabela, 'Emily Dickinson's Room: A Three-Channel Video Installation', 2009/2020: http://kreator.interoptyka.nazwa.pl/emily-dickinsons-room-3eec.html.
O'Connor, Nuala, *Miss Emily* (Inverness: Sandstone Press, 2015).
Olnek, Madeleine, dir., *Wild Nights with Emily* (Universal City, CA: Universal, 2018).
Smith, Alena, creator., *Dickinson* (Apple TV+ television series, aired 1/11/19-24/12/21).
Snively, Susan, *The Heart Has Many Doors* (Amherst: White River Press, 2015).

VI. Suggested further reading

I Biographies and publication

Benfey, Christopher, *Emily Dickinson: Lives of a Poet* (New York: Braziller, 1986).
Crumbley, P., and E. E. Heginbotham, eds., *Dickinson's Fascicles: A Spectrum of Possibilities* (Columbus, OH: Ohio State University Press, 2014).
Franklin, R. W., *The Editing of Emily Dickinson: A Reconsideration* (Madison: University of Wisconsin Press, 1967).
Garbowsky, Maryanne M., *The House without the Door: A Study of Emily Dickinson and the Illness of Agoraphobia* (London: Associated University Presses, 1989).
Heginbotham, Eleanor Elson, *Reading the Fascicles of Emily Dickinson: Dwelling in Possibilities* (Columbus: Ohio State University Press, 2003).
Miller, Cristanne, 'Emily Dickinson's Letters: A Preview', *The Emily Dickinson Journal*, 30.1 (2021), 27–44.
Myerson, Joel, *Emily Dickinson: A Descriptive Biography* (Pittsburgh: University of Pittsburgh Press, 1984).

II Style and meaning

Cameron, Sharon, *Lyric Time: Dickinson and the Limits of Genre* (Baltimore: The Johns Hopkins University Press, 1979).
Carper, Thomas, and Derek Attridge, *Meter and Meaning: An Introduction to Rhythm in Poetry* (London: Routledge, 2003).
Kilcup, Karen L., 'Scarlet Experiments: Dickinson's New English and the Critics', *The Emily Dickinson Journal*, 24.1 (2015), 22–51.
Rogoff, Jay, 'Certain Slants: Learning from Dickinson's Oblique Precision', *The Emily Dickinson Journal*, 17.2 (2008), 39–54.
Sevik, Greg, 'Protomodernism and Rhyme: Dickinson and Hopkins 1876–1886', *Style: A Quarterly Journal of Aesthetics, Poetics, Stylistics, and Literary Criticism*, 54.2 (2021), 223–40.

Sielke, Sabine, '"The Brain – Is Wider than the Sky –" or: Re-Cognizing Emily Dickinson', *The Emily Dickinson Journal*, 17.1 (2008), 68–85.

Simons, Jefferey, 'Dickinson's Prosodic Music and the Songs on Death in Hamlet', *The Emily Dickinson Journal*, 30.2 (2021), 134–60.

Werner, Marta, 'Sparrow Data: Dickinson's Birds in the Skies of the Anthropocene', *The Emily Dickinson Journal*, 30.1 (2021), 45–84.

III The female tradition, gender and sexuality

Bennett, Paula, *My Life a Loaded Gun: Female Creativity and Feminist Poetics* (Boston: Beacon, 1986).

Douglas, Ann, *The Feminization of American Culture* (New York: Alfred A. Knopf, 1977).

Erkkila, Betsy, *The Wicked Sisters: Women Poets, Literary History, and Discord* (New York: Oxford University Press, 1992).

Kaplan, Cora, *Sea Changes: Essays on Culture and Feminism* (London: Verso, 1986).

Kilcup, Karen A., ed., *Soft Canons: American Women Writers and Masculine Tradition* (Iowa City, IA: University of Iowa Press, 1999).

McNeil, Helen, *Emily Dickinson* (London: Virago Press, 1986).

Meiners, Benjamin, 'Lavender Latin Americanism: Queer Sovereignties in Emily Dickinson's Southern Eden', *The Emily Dickinson Journal*, 27.1 (2018), 24–44.

Showalter, Elaine, ed., *The New Feminist Criticism: Essays on Women, Literature and Theory*, 4th edn (London: Virago, 1993).

Snediker, Michael D., *Contingent Figure: Chronic Pain and Queer Embodiment* (Minneapolis: University of Minnesota Press, 2021).

Wang, Baihua, trans. Xiaohong, '"Will You Ignore My Sex?": Emily Dickinson's 1862 Letters to T. W. Higginson Revisited', *The Emily Dickinson Journal*, 29.2 (2020), 91–122.

IV History, Civil War and race

Bergland, Renée, 'The Eagle's Eye: Dickinson's View of Battle' in Smith, Martha Nell, and Mary Loeffelholz, eds., *A Companion to Emily Dickinson* (Oxford: Blackwell, 2008).

Friedlander, Benjamin, 'Auctions of the Mind: Emily Dickinson and Abolition', *Arizona Quarterly*, 54.1 (1998), 1–25.

Holland, J. G., and Vivian Pollak, 'Three Weeks on a Cotton Plantation', *The Emily Dickinson Journal*, 24.1 (2015), 72–95.

Hsu, Li-Hsin, '"To Make a Prairie It Takes a Clover and One Bee": Dickinson's Manufacturing of the Wild West', *The Emily Dickinson Journal*, 30.2 (2021), 97–115.

Hutchinson, Coleman, '"Eastern Exiles": Dickinson, Whiggery and War', *The Emily Dickinson Journal*, 13.2 (2004), 1–26.

Richards, Eliza, '"How News Must Feel When Travelling": Dickinson and Civil War Media' in Smith, Martha Nell, and Mary Loeffelholz, eds., *A Companion to Emily Dickinson* (Oxford: Blackwell, 2008), 157–79.

Wolosky, Shira, *Poetry and Public Discourse in Nineteenth-Century America* (New York: Palgrave Macmillan, 2010).

V Religion and hymn culture

Bercovitch, Sacvan, ed., *The American Puritan Imagination* (Cambridge: Cambridge University Press, 1974).

Bush, Harold K., and Brian Yothers, *Above the American Renaissance : David S. Reynolds and the Spiritual Imagination in American Literary Studies* (Amherst and Boston: University of Massachusetts Press, 2018).

Cook, Carol, 'Emily Dickinson: Poet as Pastoral Theologian', *Pastoral Psychology*, 60.3 (2011), 421–35.

Hobbs, June Hadden, *'I Sing for I Cannot Be Silent': The Feminization of American Hymnody, 1870–1920* (Pittsburgh: University of Pittsburgh Press, 1997).

Keane, Patrick J., *Emily Dickinson's Approving God: Divine Design and the Problem of Suffering* (Columbus: University of Missouri Press, 2008).

Morgan, Victoria, and Clare Williams, eds., *Shaping Belief: Culture, Politics and Religion in Nineteenth-Century Writing* (Liverpool: Liverpool University Press, 2008).

Wadsworth, Sarah, '"Lifted Moments": Emily Dickinson, Hymn Revision, and the Revival Music Meme-Plex', *The Emily Dickinson Journal*, 23.1 (2014), 46–74.

VI Performance and reception

Bartram, R., J. Brown-Saracino, and H. Donovan, 'Uncertain Sexualities and the Unusual Woman: Depictions of Jane Addams and Emily Dickinson', *Social Problems*, 68.1 (2021), 168–84.

Behnke, Kerstin, 'Dickinson's Poetry in Translation: The Example of Paul Celan' in Grabher, Gudrun, Roland Hagenbuchle, and Cristanne Miller, eds., *The Emily Dickinson Handbook* (Amherst: University of Massachusetts Press, 1998), pp. 408–24.

Biederman, Lucy, 'Unauthorized Editions: New American Poets Remediating Dickinson', *The Emily Dickinson Journal*, 27.1 (2018), 1–23.

Calvillo, Juan Carlos, 'Untranslatability and Interpretive Resemblance in Emily Dickinson's Renderings into Spanish', *The Emily Dickinson Journal*, 29.2 (2020), 57–72.

Collins, Billy, *Taking Off Emily Dickinson's Clothes* (London: Picador, 2000).

Freeman, Margaret H., Gudrun Grabher, and Roland Hagenbuchle, eds., 'Translating Dickinson (Special Issue)', *The Emily Dickinson Journal*, 6.2 (1997), 1–188.

Furui, Yoshiaki, *Modernizing Solitude: The Networked Individual in Nineteenth-Century American Literature* (Tuscaloosa, AL: University of Alabama Press, 2019).
Gelpi, Albert, 'Emily Dickinson's Long Shadow', *The Emily Dickinson Journal*, 17.2 (2008), 100–12.
Inge, M. Thomas, ed., *Handbook of American Popular Culture, Vols. I–II* (Connecticut: Greenwood Press, 1980).
Landau, Samantha, '"Invisible, as Music-": Sheet Music and Communication in the Dickinson Family', *Women's Studies*, 50.2 (2021), 140–56.
Raza-Sheikh, 'Dickinson's Lasting Queer Legacy', *Gay Times*, November 24, 2021: www.gaytimes.co.uk/culture/ella-hunt-and-alena-smith-on-dickinsons-lasting-queer-legacy/.

Index

abolitionism 77, 97–8, 111, 114
Ackmann, Martha 14–18
aesthetics 1, 6, 37, 48, 52, 77, 109–10,
    118–20, 134–9, 147–8, 155, 179,
    188, *see also* religion
  racialized 118–20
  of relation 37, 48, 77, 147–8
  Victorian 52
Aiello, Lucia 180
American Civil War (1861–5) 1, 5, 23, 28,
    55–6, 97–101, 108–19, 128, 159,
    186–7, *see also* abolitionism,
    slavery
  Battle of Ball's Bluff, the 116
  battlefield imagery 109–12
  canon of American Civil War Poets
    116, 124
  Dickinson's Civil War poetry 5, 98,
    110–16
  Dickinson's 'inner Civil War' 108, 111–12
Anthropocene 54–5
Aranda Jr., Jose F 178, 190
Atlantic Monthly 24, 41, 121

Barrett, Faith 111–12, 124 n. 28, 187
Bennett, Paula Bernat 6, 24–5, 67, 74–5,
    82–5, 98, 107, 117–18, 187
Bianchi, Martha Dickinson 13, 16–17, 44
Bingham, Millicent Todd 14, 27–8
biographies 11–24, 74, 99, 186, 206
  biographical approaches 15–24
  early biographical sketches 12–14
Blake, Caesar R., and Carlton F. Wells
  The Recognition of Emily Dickinson,
    Selected Criticism Since 1890 39,
    42–5
Blanco, Alberto 178
Boziwick, George 7, 163–4, 189
Brontë, Emily 40, 71, 158, 177
Brown, Phoebe Hinsdale 132, 147–8
Browning, Elizabeth Barrett 83, 160–1
Buckingham, Willis J. 39–41, 61 n. 10, 190

Burr, Zofia 177
Bushnell, Horace 136

Cameron, Sharon 26, 186
Charyn, Jerome 12, 22
Chaudron, Patricia 44
Chevrier-Bosseau, Adeline 182 n. 44
Civil War, *see* American Civil War
Cixous, Hélène 72, 74
class 5, 12, 97, 101–4, 112, 117–21, 164,
    186–7
Cody, John 18–19, 74
Crumbley, Paul 54, 155, 159, 161

Dandurand, Karen 108, 116, 187
Day, Frances Ann 8, 178
Deppman, Jed 59, 123 n. 19
Dickinson (TV series) 156, 168–72
Dickinson, Emily Elizabeth (poet)
  correspondence 4, 12–24, 35, 40, 46–7,
    53–4, 67–9, 76–7, 84–7, 91,
    104–5, 109, 117–32, 146, 157,
    160–7, 171–5
  daguerreotype 91, 162
  as LGBTQ+ icon 68, 91, 156, 167–72,
    189
  as nature poet 54–6, 167
  obituary 12–15, 23, 30, 32 n. 4, 186
    (*see also* Dickinson, Susan
    Huntington Gilbert)
  reading 100, 105, 113, 129, 135–8, 161,
    190
  as reclusive 12, 14, 22, 70, 105–6, 158,
    172
  religious faith 127–34
  as religious thinker 133–4, 138
  servants, cultural exchange with 6, 98,
    121–2
  working processes of 31–2
  works:
    'A dying tiger moaned for drink'
      114–15

'After great pain, a formal feeling comes –' 58
'All the letters I can write' 84
'A Pit – but Heaven over it –' 142
'Before I got my eye put out' 59
'Civilization spurns the leopard!' 114
'Color – Caste – Denomination –' 112, 117–18
'Come slowly – Eden!' 84
'Go slow, my soul to feed thyself' 142
'He gave away his Life' 110
'He scanned it – Staggered' 110
'Her – last Poems –' 161
'How News must feel when travelling' 112–13
'I felt a Funeral, in my Brain' 57–8
'I think I was enchanted' 161
'I went to thank Her –' 161
'I would not paint a picture' 53
'I'm Nobody! Who are you?' 89–90, 157–8, 178
'It feels a shame to be Alive –' 111
'Just so – Christ – Raps' 52
'Mine – by the Right of the White Election!' 117
'My Life had stood – a Loaded Gun' 22, 25, 79, 89
'My Portion is Defeat – today –' 110–11
'One anguish in a crowd' 115
'One of the ones that Midas touched' 114–15
'Ourselves – we do inter – with sweet derision' 128
'Publication – is the Auction' 111
'Renunciation – is a piercing Virtue' 59
'Some keep the Sabbath going to Church –' 146–7
'Tell all the Truth but tell it slant' 86
'The first Day's Night had come –' 58
'The Grass so little has to do' 37, 48
'The Heart asks Pleasure – first –' 57
'The Malay – took the Pearl' 117–18
'The name – of it – is "Autumn" –' 55–6, 111, 113, 159
'The only news I know' 176
'The Show is not the Show' 163
'The Soul selects her own society' 99
'They shut me up in Prose' 86
'Those – dying then' 47, 128
'When I was small, a Woman died' 116
'Why – do they shut me out of Heaven?' 38
Dickinson, Emily Norcross (mother) 15, 128
Dickinson studies 1–2, 8, 18, 65–8, 82, 90, 97–108, 179–80, 190–1
  future directions 1–2, 8, 9 n. 1, 179–80, 190–1
  historical turn 99, 106
  material turn 97, 103
Dickinson, Susan Huntington Gilbert 4, 12–15, 19, 22–3, 26, 30, 54, 67–9, 86–8, 166, 186
  author of obituary 12–15
  as influence 30, 67–9, 86, 23, 30, 32 n. 4, 186
  relationship with Dickinson 4, 30, 54, 67–9, 86–8, 166
digital Dickinson 156, 172–5, 189–90
  Dickinson Electronic Archives (DEA) 8, 12, 23, 173
  Emily Dickinson Archive (EDA) 8, 23, 172–4, 189–90
Dobson, Joanne 67, 71, 165, 185
domesticity 77, 104
Douglass, Frederick 115
Duncan, Emma M. 149, 188
Dyer Lucas, Dolores 46

early criticism 39–45
early publication 11, 24, 30–2
early reviews 39–45, 186, *see also* style
Eberwein, Jane Donahue 99–100, 128–9, 187–8
ecocriticism 54–6, 186, 190
Edwards, Jonathan 136–7
Eliot, George 83, 158, 161
Emerson, Ralph Waldo 45, 68, 78, 109, 133, 137, 160
England, Martha Winburn 6, 47, 130, 140–1, 148–9, 188
envelope poems 28–9, 35, 106
Erkkila, Betsy 5, 97, 103–4, 117, 186–8
ethnicity 5, 97–8, 111, 116–22, 188, *see also* race

fascicles 3, 21, 26–31, 122, 137, 171, 186
  organization of 26–30, 171 (*see also* self-publication)
  thematic structure in 27–30, 137
Farr, Judith 5, 52–4, 97, 105, 185–6
female poet contemporaries 5, 24, 67–73
female tradition, the 65, 68–73, 135, 187
  and exceptionalism 1, 73
  intertextual networking 75–6, 187
  of reformulating religious aesthetics 135
  as set of stereotypes 70–1
  speaking across periods 71–2
feminism 5, 77, 98, 114, 135, 169, 177
feminist criticism 4, 24, 65–85, 102, 148
Ferreira de Pinho, Davi 178, 190
Finnerty, Páraic 100, 120–1, 156, 171–2, 187, 189
Follen, Eliza Lee 147–8
Franklin, Ralph W 10 n. 3, 28, 31, 35, 173
Freedman, Linda 6, 135, 188
Fretwell, Erica 6, 118–20, 188
Friedlander, Benjamin 116

Galvin, Mary E 4, 85–6, 187
gender 1–4, 15–16, 24, 65–92, 101–3, 114, 131, 157–9, 168, 187–90, *see also* performance, LGBTQ+
  gender-fluid identity 67–8, 79, 82
  gendering of nature 71, 78, 80–1
  non-binary identity 4, 67–8, 79–83, 88–9, 187
  non-gendered identity 82, 89–90
  trans perspectives 4, 67–8, 82, 88–9, 187
Gilbert, Sandra M., and Susan Gubar
  The Madwoman in the Attic 24, 78, 90, 157–8, 189
Gilpin, W. Clark 127
Glover, Maggie 89–90, 187
Goluboff, Benjamin 129–30
Gomaa, Dalia M. A 177–8, 190
Gordon, Lyndall 13, 19, 21–22, 186
Guerra, Jonnie 7, 156, 164

Habegger, Alfred 6, 14, 20–1, 127–8, 131–2, 136, 188
Harde, Roxanne 135, 188
Hart, Ellen Louise 67, 87
Hassan, Naseem 179, 190
Henneberg, Sylvia 91, 187

Higginson, Thomas Wentworth 3, 22–31, 36, 106, 119, 129, 156–7, 171
historicizing Dickinson 97–107
Holmes, Gerard 165–6
Homans, Margaret 71
Howe, Susan 51
Hsu, Li-Hsin 122, 188
hymnody 6–7, 47–50, 69, 116, 129, 140–9, 160
  devotional purpose of 130, 143
  Dickinson's knowledge and experience of 146–9
  female hymnists 132, 147–8 (*see also* Phoebe Hinsdale Brown and Eliza Lee Follen)
  hymn culture 1, 3, 6–7, 116, 129, 146–8, 188
  hymn form 37–8, 50, 86, 140, 144 (*see also* metre)
  hymnal tropes 6, 39, 47, 141–3
  hymnic space 147
  'I-Thou' model of address in 147
imagery 6, 22, 48, 52, 74–6, 81, 83–5, 102, 109–12, 115, 127–39, 141, 146–50, 173, 188
international reception 172, 175–80, 190, *see also* translation
  beyond North America 175
  Brazil 176, 178
  China 6, 122, 176–9, 190
  Europe 175
  Iraq 179
  Japanese aesthetics and reception 150, 175, 179, 190
  Latino/a Chicano/a perspectives 177–8
  Taiwan 179
  translations in the Spanish-speaking and Lusophone world 182 n. 44, 190
Irigaray, Luce 72–6, 81, 85

Jackson, Helen Hunt 70, 72–3, 83
Jackson, Virginia 50, 107
Jacobs, Harriet 77, 114–15
Jessee, Jessica L. 157, 189
Johnson, Thomas H 17–19, 31, 115, 142, 173
Juhasz, Suzanne 28, 80, 90, 103, 187, 189

Keller, Karl 87, 109
Kohler, Michelle 73
Koski, Lena 87
Kristeva, Julia 72, 74–5
Kwang-Chung, Yu 179, 190

Ladin, Joy 4, 88, 187
Landry, H. Jordan 81
Lease, Benjamin 67, 69, 129
Leder, Sharon and Andrea Abbott 5, 67, 71
Leyda, Jay 15–17, 101–2, 162, 187
LGBTQ+ 156, 167, 170–2, *see also* gender, sexuality, queering Dickinson
Lind, Jenny 162
Lindberg-Seyersted, Brita 46
Loeffelholz, Mary 68–9
Lowenberg, Carlton 47, 165
Lundin, Roger 20, 133–5, 149–50, 188
lyric poetry 45, 50, 80, 82, 107, 110, 114, 145, 174

Maciejewska, Izabela 166
Marcellin, Leigh-Anne Urbanowicz 110–11, 187
Marrs, Cody 55–6, 186–7
Martin, Wendy 71, 132–3
materiality 2, 28, 35, 103, 119, 186
matrilineal inheritance 7, 147–50, 188
McIntosh, James 133–5, 150, 188
Messmer, Marietta 29, 41, 46–7
Metaphysical poets 19, 137–8
metre 3, 37–8, 42, 46–51, 75, 140–1, 165, *see also* style
  abuses of 46, 86
  ballad stanza 5, 37, 50, 75, 98, 144
  common hymnic 37–8, 75, 86
  common particular 37
  metrical experiments 140–3, 145
  short and long 37
  tetrameter and trimeter 37
Miller, Cristanne 3, 9, 31–2, 49–51, 80, 90, 131, 143–4, 162, 186, 188–9
Miller, Ruth 29
Mitchell, Domhnall 51, 104–5, 175–6, 188, 190
Molson, Francis J 127, 188
Morgan, Victoria N 6–7, 130, 146–50, 188
Murphy, Charles M 138–9, 188
Murray, Aífe 6, 98, 121–2

music 7, 8, 41, 50, 65, 140–6, 156, 160–6, 176, 189, *see also* hymnody
  Dickinson's piano playing 106, 144, 161–4
  music book 7, 156, 161–4, 189
  musical settings to poems 8, 164–6, 176, 189
mysticism 42, 44, 138–9
  St. Teresa of Ávila 138–9

nature 28, 43, 49, 52–6, 71, 74–8, 81–5, 110, 132, 139, 148, 150, 157–9, 167, 173, 179
  divine in 49, 52
New Criticism 42–3, 45, 51, 101
Nicholson, William 8, 165
Noble, Marianne 7, 91, 169–70, 187
Nonaka, Miho 150, 179, 190
Norcross, Betsy (née Fay) 132, 147

Oberhaus, Dorothy Huff 3, 29–30, 137–8, 186, 188

Paglia, Camille 78–81, 88–9, 158–9, 189
pastoral genre 113
performance 1, 7, 24, 30, 46, 77–81, 120–1, 155–9, 180, *see also* popular culture
  of Dickinson's life 24, 156, 164–72
  of gender 78–81
  readers as performers 80
  within poems 46, 77–81, 155–64
Perlow, Seth 174–5, 189
Petrino, Elizabeth 70, 161, 187
Phillips, Elizabeth 158, 189
Phillips, Siobhan 136–7, 188
Plath, Sylvia 73, 103, 177
politics 3, 5, 41–4, 66, 71–2, 77, 82–92, 103–5, 114–22, *see also* class, gender, race, LGBTQ+
  Whig 20, 103, 150
Pollak, Vivian R 6, 16, 24, 72–3, 98, 108–9, 118, 185, 187
popular culture 1, 7, 8, 24, 52, 68, 70, 155–6, 160–172, 189
  Apple TV series *Dickinson* 156, 168–9
  exhibitions 8, 167
  films 156, 168, 171–2
  musical interpretations 8, 165–6

nineteenth-century 1, 7, 52, 70, 156, 160–4
novels 8, 164–5
plays 7, 156, 164
social media, role of 166–7
Porter, David 36, 39, 44, 109, 186
psychoanalysis 4, 65, 68, 74–7, 79
public *vs* private 103–4, 109, 114, 116–17, 60, 171
Pugh, Christina 51

queering Dickinson 82–92, 156, 170–2, *see also* sexuality, gender, LGBTQ+
queer theory 4, 67–8, 82–3, 90–1, 187, 190

race 1, 5, 6, 97–100, 111–22, 169, 186–8, 190, *see also* ethnicity
  racial other 122, 188
  racial stereotyping 117–18
  racism in Dickinson 107, 117–18, 122, 169
Ramirez, Anne West 135, 188
reader-response theories 80
reception, *see* international reception
relational theory 109–10
religion 1, 6–7, 20, 47, 59, 83, 85–6, 99, 127–50, 186, 188–9, *see also* hymnody, mysticism
  and aesthetics 1, 134–9, 188
  biblical imagery 52, 127, 132–6
  biblical texts 29, 76, 141
  Christian feminism 135
  and 'circumference' 149–50
  devotional texts 129–32, 137–8, 143, 147–8, 186
  Dissenting tradition 140–1, 146–8
  Evangelicalism 6, 127–8, 131–2
  feminist theology 147–8
  new devotional paradigm 138
  polarized thinking on 1, 6, 127–30, 134, 188
  prayer 137–9, 149
  praying circles 132, 147–8, 150
  Protestantism 79, 133, 148–9
  Puritanism 20, 45, 127, 130–1, 139–41, 150
  re-envisioned divine 6, 147, 188
  rejecting orthodoxy 131–4

religious imagery 129–30, 134–9, 146–50, 188
religious imagination 6, 134–5, 149, 188
Roman Catholicism 129–30, 138
second Great Awakening 6, 127, 131
Trinitarian theology 134–6
Reynolds, David S 7, 160–4, 189
rhetoric 6, 39, 45–9, 72, 77, 109, 111, 114, 130, 141–5, 174, *see also* abolitionism, style
Rich, Adrienne 5, 24–5, 66, 71–2
Richards, Eliza 100, 112–14, 131, 187
Rivera Garretas, María-Milagros 178, 182 n. 44, 190
Romanticism 71, 78, 80–1, 128
Ross, Christine 49, 145–6, 188
Runzo, Sandra 161–4, 171, 189
Ruskin, John 52–4
Russo, Stephanie 170–1, 189

St. Armand, Barton Levi 52, 162
Sanchez-Eppler, Karen 5, 77, 98, 114, 187
Santos Brigida, Marcela 178, 190
Scott, A.O 168
Sedgwick, Eve Kosofsky 83
self-publication 11, 21, 24–31, 186, *see also* fascicles
Sewall, Richard B 14–15, 18–21, 30
sexuality 65, 74, 77, 82–92, *see also* gender, LGBTQ+, queering Dickinson
  eroticism 78–91
  homoeroticism 67, 75, 82–5
  lesbian identity 67, 87–8
  sexual all-inclusiveness 80
Shakespeare, William 19, 98, 120–1, 160
Shoobridge, Helen 76–7, 187
Shurr, William H 27, 186
Sielke, Sabine 4, 67–8, 72, 74–6, 187
slavery 5, 98, 103, 111–12, 115, 117, 119, *see also* abolitionism
  anti-slavery fiction 114–15
  San Domingo slave revolts 115
  slave narratives 114–5
Small, Judy Jo 144, 188
Smith, Martha Nell 12, 30, 86–8, 91, 102, 105–6, 173, 187

Snediker, Michael D 68, 90–1, 187
Springfield Republican 19, 117
Stonum, Gary Lee 46, 59
Stowe, Harriet Beecher 115, 135
style 35–60, *see also* imagery, metre, rhetoric
   anti-teleological poetics 147, 150
   dashes 36–8, 174
   grammar 30, 36, 40–51, 56, 65, 75, 141–5, 186
   later revaluations of 45–60
   and meaning 35–9, 45, 186–7
   non-linearity 75, 147
   as precursor to modernism 36, 44–5, 52, 88, 103, 186
   as problematic 40–4 (*see also* early reviews)
   as rebellion 86, 119–20
   synecdoche 36–7, 48, 60 n. 5, 141
   of thinking 56–60 (*see also* Vendler, Helen)
Swift, Rebecca 22–3

Taggard, Genevieve 17–18
Takeda, Masako 179, 190
Todd, Mabel Loomis 12–16, 19, 21–2, 27–9, 31, 36, 91, 163, 165
translation 175, 178–9, 190, *see also* international reception

Uno, Hiroko 6, 98, 122, 188

Vendler, Helen 37, 51, 56–9, 187, *see also* style; of thinking
visual arts, the 5, 52–4, 164
   Luminists and Hudson River Painters 52
   Pre-Raphaelite movement 52–4
visual *vs* aural (debate) 39, 51–3, 144, 174

Wald, Jane 181 n. 28
Walker, Cheryl 4, 24, 66, 67, 69–70, 102–3, 187
Wang, Baihua 179, 190
Wardrop, Daneen 98, 114–15, 187
Watts, Isaac 6, 39, 47–9, 129–30, 140–8, 160, 188
Weisbuch, Robert 36, 187, 191
Werner, Marta and Jen Bervin
   Emily Dickinson: The Gorgeous Nothings 28–9, 35
Whicher, George Frisbie 17, 18
White, Fred D 27, 46–8, 186
Whitman, Walt 37, 44, 56, 80, 85, 113, 114, 144
Wolff, Cynthia Griffin 15, 47, 80–1
Wolosky, Shira 3, 39, 46, 48–9, 108–10, 141–3, 149, 162, 187, 188
writing the body 73–81
   and psychoanalysis 73–4
Wu, Colleen Shu-Ching 106–7

Xu, Cuihua 178–9, 190

Zapedowska, Magdalena 100–1

www.ingramcontent.com/pod-product-compliance
Lightning Source LLC
Chambersburg PA
CBHW052110300426
44116CB00010B/1603